Schnozz

ALSO BY DAVID L. FLEITZ
AND FROM McFARLAND

*Eddie Cicotte: The Life and Career
of the Banned Black Sox Pitcher* (2020)

*Rowdy Patsy Tebeau and the Cleveland Spiders: Fighting
to the Bottom of Baseball, 1887–1899* (2017)

Napoleon Lajoie: King of Ballplayers (2013)

Jack Chesbro: A Chapter from Ghosts in the Gallery at Cooperstown (2013)

Kid Nichols: A Chapter from Ghosts in the Gallery at Cooperstown (2013)

John Clarkson: A Chapter from Ghosts in the Gallery at Cooperstown (2013)

*Silver Bats and Automobiles: The Hotly Competitive, Sometimes
Ignoble Pursuit of the Major League Batting Championship* (2011)

The Irish in Baseball: An Early History (2009)

*More Ghosts in the Gallery: Another Sixteen
Little-Known Greats at Cooperstown* (2007)

Cap Anson: The Grand Old Man of Baseball (2005)

*Ghosts in the Gallery at Cooperstown: Sixteen
Little-Known Members of the Hall of Fame* (2004)

Louis Sockalexis: The First Cleveland Indian (2002)

Shoeless: The Life and Times of Joe Jackson (2001; paperback 2008)

Schnozz
The Baseball Life of Ernie Lombardi

DAVID L. FLEITZ

McFarland & Company, Inc., Publishers
Jefferson, North Carolina

LIBRARY OF CONGRESS CATALOGUING-IN-PUBLICATION DATA

Names: Fleitz, David L., 1955– author.
Title: Schnozz : the baseball life of Ernie Lombardi / David L. Fleitz.
Description: Jefferson, North Carolina : McFarland & Company, Inc., Publishers, 2023 | Includes bibliographical references and index.
Identifiers: LCCN 2023034499 | ISBN 9781476689210 (paperback : acid free paper) ∞
ISBN 9781476650500 (ebook)
Subjects: LCSH: Lombardi, Ernie, 1908–. | Catchers (Baseball)—United States—Biography. | Baseball players—United States—History—20th century—Biography. | Cincinnati Reds (Baseball team)—History—20th century.
Classification: LCC GV865.L65 E76 2023 | DDC 796.357092 [B]—dc23/eng/20230803
LC record available at https://lccn.loc.gov/2023034499

BRITISH LIBRARY CATALOGUING DATA ARE AVAILABLE

ISBN (print) 978-1-4766-8921-0
ISBN (ebook) 978-1-4766-5050-0

© 2023 David L. Fleitz. All rights reserved

No part of this book may be reproduced or transmitted in any form or by any means, electronic or mechanical, including photocopying or recording, or by any information storage and retrieval system, without permission in writing from the publisher.

Front cover: Catcher Ernie Lombardi waiting on a pop fly (National Baseball Hall of Fame Library, Cooperstown, New York)

Printed in the United States of America

McFarland & Company, Inc., Publishers
Box 611, Jefferson, North Carolina 28640
www.mcfarlandpub.com

Table of Contents

Acknowledgments   vii
Introduction   1

1. The Early Years   3
2. Brooklyn   13
3. Cincinnati   23
4. "The Giant Italian Catcher"   33
5. The Crosley Era   40
6. Night Baseball   49
7. An All-Star Year   57
8. Back to Last Place   66
9. MVP   77
10. Pennant   89
11. Tragedy and Triumph   101
12. Letdown   115
13. Boston   124
14. New York   135
15. The War Years   143
16. Backup   152

17. Back to the Minors	162
18. Aftermath	170
19. Later Years	176
20. The Hall of Fame	188
Appendix: Ernie Lombardi's Statistics	197
Chapter Notes	199
Bibliography	207
Index	209

Acknowledgments

I would like to thank a few people and organizations that helped make this book possible.

The Eugene C. Murdock and Charles W. Mears collections of baseball books and materials at the Cleveland Public Library were, as always, invaluable. The library in downtown Cleveland has opened a center for baseball research, called the Sports Research Center, which is a welcome development to anyone who loves baseball. As usual, I received fine assistance from the knowledgeable staff members at the National Baseball Hall of Fame Library in Cooperstown, New York. I also conducted research at the Troy Public Library in Troy, Michigan, where I live, and at Bowling Green State University in Ohio.

I would especially like to thank Gabriel Schechter, a baseball researcher and member of the Society for American Baseball Research (SABR), who provided me with a detailed analysis of the most famous play of Ernie Lombardi's life, his "snooze" at home plate in the fourth game of the 1939 World Series. Also, Chris Eckes, at the Cincinnati Reds Hall of Fame, was a great source for photos.

The availability of information on the Internet has boomed in recent years, and a terrific web site called Baseball Reference (http://www.baseball-reference.com) provides player game logs, box scores, and play-by-play descriptions. Sean Forman and his team deserve a great deal of credit for developing this constantly expanding resource, and this book would have been much more difficult to write without it.

Project Retrosheet is a web site founded in 1989 for the purpose of providing computerized play-by-play data for as many games as possible. It has blossomed into a site filled with useful information and is highly recommended as well. The statistics in this book come from Project Retrosheet, which in return asks only that the user includes this statement: *The information used here was obtained free of charge from and is copyrighted by Retrosheet. Interested parties may contact Retrosheet at www.retrosheet.org.*

Other helpful web sites include Newspapers.com, with digitized and searchable images of long-ago newspapers, and Paper of Record, which features images of *The Sporting News* beginning with its inaugural issue in 1886. The Brooklyn Public Library has digitized the *Brooklyn Eagle* from the years 1841 to 1902, and the LA84 Foundation, endowed with funds left over from the 1984 Olympic Games in Los Angeles, maintains a digital archive as well.

Another good source of information is Google Books (http://www.google.com). This archive is free and extremely useful to any sports researcher. SABR maintains a site called BioProject (http://bioproj.sabr.org), to which I have contributed several articles. BioProject has posted several thousand biographies of major league players of the past and the present, and the information found there has been highly useful.

And, last but not least, thanks to my wife Sally for her support and her patience.

Introduction

The 1940 Cincinnati Reds were one of the most underrated teams that ever won a World Series.

The Reds employed many outstanding players in that championship year. Pitchers Bucky Walters and Paul Derringer both won 20 games, first baseman Frank McCormick won the Most Valuable Player award, and catcher Ernie Lombardi batted .319, the second-best average in the league. Manager Bill McKechnie also built, in the words of historian Bill James, "perhaps the best defensive infield in major league history up to that point." The Cincinnati club won 100 games and coasted to the pennant, then defeated the Detroit Tigers in an exciting seven-game World Series. Not until 1975 would the Cincinnati Reds win their next world title.

But aside from manager McKechnie, and unlike almost every other world champion, only one of the 1940 Cincinnati Reds has been enshrined in the Baseball Hall of Fame as of 2022.

That player was Ernie Lombardi.

Ernie Lombardi, an eight-time All-Star catcher who played major league ball from 1931 to 1947, was a very big man, with huge hands, a large nose that gave him the nickname "Schnozz," and a cannon for an arm. He held his 46-ounce bat, the heaviest of his time, with an interlocking grip that golfers use (though Lombardi did not play golf). He was famous for his lack of speed; James called him "surely the slowest player ever to play major league baseball well." Infielders, especially later in his career, played Ernie back in the outfield grass because they could still throw him out from there. As Ernie once told Brooklyn Dodgers shortstop Pee Wee Reese, "You were in the league for three years before I realized you weren't an outfielder."

Despite all that, Ernie Lombardi won two National League batting titles and a Most Valuable Player award and compiled a career batting average of .306. He had huge arms and strong wrists that enabled him to smash the hardest line drives in baseball. He almost always made contact at the plate; in 1935 he played in 120 games and struck out only six times.

His throwing arm was legendary. He would fire the ball to second base while still in his crouch, and he was exceptionally good at picking runners off first base with a snap throw. When Johnny Vander Meer pitched his two consecutive no-hitters in 1938, Ernie Lombardi was the catcher who called all the pitches.

And Ernie was a fun player to watch. A friendly, gentle giant of a man, Ernie would sometimes drop a bunt down the third base line and beat the throw to first, just to show that he could do it. He stole only eight bases during his career, usually because the opposition was too shocked to react. And if his pitcher was not throwing hard enough, Ernie would reach out, catch the fastball with his bare hand, and fire it back to the mound. His nose was so big that it stuck out from behind his mask and sometimes got cut and scraped. Ernie was a shy man, uncomfortable with public attention and taciturn with the sportswriters, but the fans loved him for his human qualities. He became the most popular Cincinnati Red in team history until Pete Rose came along three decades later.

However, Ernie's life was not all sweetness and light. He had no idea what to do with himself after he left baseball, fell into a deep depression, and made an unsuccessful suicide attempt. He recovered, with the help of family and friends, and returned to baseball as a press box attendant for the San Francisco Giants. In later years, he longed to be elected to the Baseball Hall of Fame, a yearning that bordered on obsession. He was finally enshrined in the Cooperstown pantheon in 1986 but was not around to enjoy it. One of his sisters accepted the plaque in his stead, because Ernie had passed away seven years before.

The long history of baseball is filled with interesting, legendary, larger-than-life characters, and Ernie Lombardi was certainly one of them. His life, both inside and outside of baseball, was filled with the highest of highs and the lowest of lows.

1

The Early Years

"He loved baseball ever since he was so high. [...A]ll he ever thought about was playing ball."[1]
—Rena (Lombardi) Lenhardt, Ernie's sister, 1986

Italy was a tough place to live during the latter part of the 19th century.

The Italian peninsula had historically consisted of separate kingdoms (Savoy, Lombardy, Venetia, Sardinia, and the Two Sicilies), duchies such as Tuscany and Modegna, and the Papal States, ruled by the pope. But the *Risorgimento*, a decades-long effort to unite these states and kingdoms into a new nation, swept the peninsula, and in 1870 the movement conquered Rome. Italy was now united under a single ruler, King Vittorio Emmanuele II of the House of Savoy.

However, every new nation faces difficult hurdles, and Italy struggled to combine its many formerly independent states into one unit. Organized crime and brigandage flourished, and decades of war and revolution had left a legacy of violence and social chaos. Natural disasters and epidemics swept the peninsula, and widespread poverty led to riots and demonstrations against the new, inexperienced government and its fledgling institutions. The people of the new nation spoke in local dialects but had no common language, and only after decades had passed did *toscano*, the language of Tuscany, become the tongue we now know as Italian. Political violence raged in the larger cities, a disastrous war in Africa led to increasing unrest, and bread riots in Milan led to a massacre by government troops in 1898. In 1900 Umberto I, the second King of Italy, was assassinated by an anarchist.

Faced with these difficulties, many Italians decided to make new lives in America. During the 1880s, about 300,000 people left Italy and settled in the United States. That number increased to 600,000 during the 1890s, and during the first decade of the 20th century, more than 2,000,000 Italians left their native country and cast their lot with the growing, bustling nation across the Atlantic.

One of those immigrants was a 29-year-old laborer from Piedmont in northwestern Italy named Domenico Lombardi. In 1906 Domenico, his 26-year-old wife Marianna (called Maria), and their infant daughter Rena boarded a ship and set sail for a new life in America. They landed in New York, were processed through Ellis Island, and then traveled by train in a week-long cross-country journey to their final destination. They arrived in Oakland, California, the growing city that had already welcomed thousands of their countrymen.

The San Francisco Bay area was a haven for Italian immigrants. New arrivals from Italy created their own "Little Italy" enclaves, with stores and businesses that catered to their people. Most of the Italians in Oakland, like the Lombardi family, came from the northern provinces of Piedmont, Lombardy, and Liguria. Others moved to Oakland from San Francisco after losing their homes and businesses in the devastating earthquake in April of 1906. By 1910 Oakland owned one of the largest Italian populations in California.

Domenico Lombardi found work as a laborer in a railroad yard. The job was a physically taxing one, but Domenico proved himself as a steady and reliable worker. With a stable source of income, he and his wife Maria began to expand their family. Their only son, Ernesto Natali Lombardi, was born in Oakland on April 6, 1908, and was followed in 1911 by his sister Rose and in 1914 by another sister named Stella. Before long, Domenico Lombardi decided to Americanize his first name, if only slightly. He began to refer to himself, and to sign his name, as Dominic. The head of the Lombardi family saved his money and, after only a few years in America, was able to buy a house in West Oakland, at 1411 13th Street. The Lombardis would live in this house for more than four decades.

Ernesto, called Ernie, had brown eyes and black hair, and was a shy child who grew quickly. By his teenage years Ernie had acquired the big, ungainly-looking body that baseball fans would find instantly recognizable in the future. He was tall for his age, with huge hands, a very prominent nose, and a heavyset gait that interfered with his attempts to run. He was incredibly strong, perhaps the strongest teenager in his neighborhood. Ernie dutifully attended school, but was an indifferent student, because he, like so many sons of immigrants, fell in love with a uniquely American sport. That sport was baseball.

Ernie Lombardi was crazy about baseball from his early boyhood. His parents could not understand why young Ernie would rather be playing ball than attending to chores or studying, but baseball was the only thing that Ernie was interested in. The Lombardi house stood only a few blocks from Bay View Park[2] at 18th and Wood streets, and Ernie and the neighborhood kids spent their days on the baseball fields there. He would play ball all day if his parents allowed it, and sometimes when they did not.

Lombardi family lore states that Ernie, at the age of 10 or 11, went out to play ball one morning and did not return till late at night, missing a family wedding.

In her old age, Ernie's sister Rena recalled how much Ernie loved baseball. When Ernie was ten years old, Dominic Lombardi gave his son a small accordion as a present. "My father said, 'When you learn to play, I'll buy you a big one,'" said Rena. "You know what he did? He traded in the accordion for a baseball glove."

Ernie Lombardi was not alone. Baseball was hugely popular among Italian kids in the Bay Area, and all over Oakland, San Francisco, San Jose, and other growing communities, young men of Italian descent played baseball. Often, their immigrant parents could not understand the attraction. Dominic Lombardi was as mystified by his son's baseball mania as was Giuseppe DiMaggio, a Sicilian fisherman in San Francisco who wanted his five sons to follow him into the family trade. Like Ernie Lombardi, the youngest three DiMaggio sons—Vince, Dominic, and Joe—preferred to play ball instead.

Dominic Lombardi was not afraid of hard work, but he did not want to do backbreaking labor all his life. During the late 1910s, at the time of World War I, Dominic worked as a laborer in a shipyard, but he had bigger plans. With the money he saved during his years in his new country, Dominic opened a grocery store in his West Oakland neighborhood. Ernie, who was not interested in school anyway, dropped out at age 11 to work in the grocery store with his father. The store was now Ernie's main responsibility, but after much pleading, Dominic allowed his son to play for a baseball team sponsored by Ravoli's Meat Market.

Ernie, who both threw and batted right-handed, excelled on the baseball fields at Bay View Park, and his services were highly coveted by the organized leagues that played there under the supervision of Oakland's parks and recreation department. At first, his coaches put him in the outfield to take advantage of his incredibly strong and accurate arm, but he did not cover much ground. Ernie showed no interest in pitching, because he hit so well and so consistently that he knew he could play every day. He had to find a position, and there was one position on the field well suited to his talents. It didn't take long for Ernie to become a catcher.

Tragedy befell the family in 1921, when Maria Lombardi died at age 41. Now widowed, Dominic focused all his energies on his business, fully expecting his only son to do the same. But the lure of baseball was too powerful, and the strong-armed young catcher made a name for himself on the local baseball scene. During his teenage years, Ernie juggled his responsibilities at the grocery store with his love of baseball, not always successfully. Still, his reputation in Oakland semi-pro circles grew, and the name Ernest Lombardi began to appear in the sports sections of the Oakland newspapers.

He also gained a nickname on the playing fields of Bay View Park. To his friends and teammates, he was "Botch," from the lawn bowling game bocce, so popular with Italian immigrants in the Bay Area. Ernie most likely played bocce in the neighborhood, but only when there was not a baseball game in progress.

In November of 1925, the 17-year-old Ernie signed to play for the Flint Motors team in the Oakland Winter League. This was a fast six-team league that played through the winter months at Oaks Park, where the Oakland Oaks of the Pacific Coast League performed from spring to fall. Ernie, though one of the youngest players in the league, drew attention with his bat and his throwing arm, and caught the eye of Babe Pinelli, a San Francisco native who played shortstop for the Cincinnati Reds of the National League. Pinelli, whose real last name was Paolinelli, was part of the first wave of Italian American baseball stars from the Bay Area, and he was impressed by this tall, solidly-built teenager with the powerful arm. Because professional teams, major and minor, were always on the lookout for catching prospects, Pinelli recommended Lombardi to the Oakland Oaks. In late 1925 or early 1926, the Oaks offered Ernie a contract.

Initially, Ernie turned it down. He told the Oaks that he could not leave the grocery store because his father was ill, but that was only part of the story. Ernie, at age 18, did not want to leave his home and his close-knit family. The Oaks would no doubt send an unproven player like Ernie to one of its lower-level farm teams, and Ernie was not ready to leave Oakland. Instead, Ernie joined a semi-pro team sponsored by the Piggly Wiggly grocery chain during the spring of 1926. That team's manager, Bob Carter, also gave the Oaks a positive report on the young catcher.

A turning point came one day when Dominic was called out of town and left Ernie in charge of the store for a few days. Ernie's short tenure at the helm convinced him that baseball, not the grocery business, was his future. Dominic was not happy with his son's career choice. Ernie was his only son, and the sons of Italian families were supposed to defer to their fathers' wishes. But after a while, Dominic relented. He found other local kids to work in the grocery store and reluctantly allowed Ernie to pursue his passion. So Ernie contacted the Oaks and asked if they were still interested in him. Fortunately, they were, and on May 14, 1926, Ernie signed his first professional contract with the Oaks.

The Pacific Coast League was one of the three leagues on the highest level, then labeled AA, of the minors (the others were the International League and the American Association). Because of the mild West Coast weather, Oakland and the other seven league teams played between

180 and 200 games per season, usually in week-long series to cut down on travel expenses. The Oaks played at Oaks Park in Emeryville, an enclave just north of West Oakland and south of Berkeley, not far from the Lombardi family home. The ballpark, built in 1913, seated about 11,000 people and was easily accessible by streetcar.

In 1925 the Oaks, with Ivan Howard as manager, finished in sixth place with a losing record, but the league leaders from San Francisco and Salt Lake City lost some of their key players during the off-season. Paul Waner, the league batting champion from San Francisco, was sold to the Pittsburgh Pirates, while Salt Lake City slugger Tony Lazzeri, who hit an incredible 60 home runs,[3] was promoted to the New York Yankees. Minor league teams were constantly rebuilding after selling their best players to the majors, so the Oakland Oaks, who kept most of their best hitters and pitchers, hoped to move up the standings in 1926.

Oakland's biggest star, and perhaps the biggest star in the circuit, was a man Bill James called "the Babe Ruth of the minor leagues." Russell (Buzz) Arlett, 27 years old, was a dominating spitball pitcher who turned to the outfield when arm injuries drove him from the mound. Arlett became a slugging switch-hitting outfielder who belted more than 400 home runs in the minor leagues, setting a career record that lasted until 2015,[4] and once hit 54 in a season. Arlett was so popular with the Oakland fans that the Oaks resisted selling him to the majors.

Other Oaks of note were Harry Krause, who won 18 games for Connie Mack's Philadelphia A's in 1909, catcher Del Baker, a future major league manager, and Hub Pruett, who gained fame with the St. Louis Browns for his ability to strike out Babe Ruth. The Oaks had a few young guys like Ernie, but many of Ernie's new teammates were in their 30s, on their way down from the majors. Krause, at 38, was twice Ernie's age. But some older players actually preferred the Pacific Coast League to the American and National, especially those who grew up in the western states. The climate was pleasant, the level of competition was high, and the pay was often just as good.

The season was already 33 games old when Ernie joined the Oaks, but manager Howard had no intention of plugging a teenaged rookie into fast company. Ernie hit well in batting practice and impressed everyone with his throwing, but his overall defense was not yet passable. Also, the spitball was still legal in the Pacific Coast League, and the youngster would need a lot of development to be able to handle the wet deliveries of Krause and others.

Ernie remained with the Oaks for the rest of the 1926 season. He got into four games and batted only six times, with a double and single to show for it. Mostly, the teenaged catcher learned the professional game from the bench. Ernie warmed up pitchers, took batting practice, and worked on his catching skills, which were extremely raw. He had a lot to learn about calling pitches, chasing pop-ups, and fielding bunts. Despite his limited playing time, the Oaks saw potential in Ernie and chose to be patient. They were willing to carry Ernie on the roster and wait for him to develop.

In 1927, Oakland's top two catchers, Del Baker and Al Bool, figured to see almost all of the playing time, and manager Howard decided that the raw rookie needed some experience. So Howard sent Ernie to Oakland's farm team, the Ogden Gunners of the Utah-Idaho League in Class C, three levels below the Pacific Coast circuit.

The Utah-Idaho League was exactly what its name said it was. It consisted of three teams in Idaho (Pocatello, Twin Falls, and Idaho Falls) and three in Utah (Ogden, Salt Lake City, and Logan), each of which played about 100 games per season. It existed for only three years before it folded in 1928, but the league boasted a few prospects such as future major league stars Dolph Camilli of Logan and Wally Berger of Pocatello. The Ogden club was managed by Art Murphy, a minor league veteran who also played first base for the Gunners.

The Ogden Gunners held their spring training in early May at Myrtledale Hot Springs in Calistoga, California. There were 28 players on hand, fighting for a mere 14 roster spots, but Ernie Lombardi was never in danger of being cut. He was sent by the Oaks to Ogden to improve his defensive skills, so he was penciled in as the starting catcher from the beginning.

On Sunday, May 15, the Gunners played their final exhibition game before 1,000 fans against a local semi-pro aggregation sponsored by the Upstairs Clothes Shop. The opposing pitcher, Gordon Rhodes, was a star athlete at the University of Utah and was hailed as "peer of the semi-pro pitchers of the Rockies." He held the Gunners at bay for one inning, but the Ogden club exploded for six runs in the second and four in the third on the way to a 13–4 win. The hitting star of the day was Ernie Lombardi, who belted three hits and scored three runs.

The sports reporter for the local newspaper liked what he saw:

> Ernest Lombardi, 19-year-old receiver, should rank with the best catchers in the league. Lombardi has the game at heart and is up and at 'em from the first ball. The new receiver made a splendid impression Sunday. He performed in major league style back of the plate and contributed some timely sticking.[5]

He did, however, have a problem. Ogden, Utah, sits more than 5,700 feet above sea level, and many players from lower elevations had trouble adjusting to the thin, dry mountain air. Ernie grew up in the Bay Area much closer to sea level, and the blood vessels in his nose could not adapt to the Utah climate. He suffered from daily nosebleeds and began to lose weight.

Despite the nosebleeds, Ernie dominated the Utah-Idaho League. By now, Lombardi stood six feet two inches tall and weighed about 190 solidly-packed pounds, and his strong arm and solid hitting drew notice from the Ogden fans. "Lombardi is one of the most popular members of the Gunner squad," said the local newspaper in June. "His all-around playing has been a contributing factor in the showing of the locals in the pennant race.... He is polished and finished and deserves to be ranked as the best prospect in the catching department in the league."

In addition, "the new receiver has conquered the feat of picking up seven official baseballs in one hand at one time."[6]

After 50 games, despite his problem with nosebleeds, Ernie's batting average stood at .398, and the Oaks called him back to Oakland. Ernie was happy to leave Ogden. "I don't know whether they [the Oaks] brought me back to save my life or because I was hitting so good," Lombardi said. "But I'm sure glad they did."[7]

Back in Oakland, Ernie spent most of his time on the bench. He got into only 16 games in 1927, mostly as a pinch-hitter, with three hits in 20 times at bat. One of those hits was a home run. But the Oaks did not need him, winning the Pacific Coast League pennant by 14 and a half games over the San Francisco Seals.

By 1928, Ernie was ready for more action. Now 20 years old, he beat out Al Bool for the second-string catching job for the Oaks and shared the starting position with veteran Addison (Pete) Read. Though the defending league champions struggled in April and May, Lombardi and Buzz Arlett became the new slugging tandem for the Oaks. On June 10 at Los Angeles, the Angels swept the Oaks in a doubleheader, but both Arlett and Lombardi belted home runs. As the Oakland paper enthused, "This Lombardi boy is some slugger. He got three hits in the first game and when he was sent to bat for Read in the seventh inning of the second game he connected for a triple, only to die on the third bag."[8]

The Pacific Coast League teams played lots of doubleheaders, so Lombardi and Read split the catching duties, usually with each man catching one game and pinch-hitting in the other. But Read batted only .225 in 1928. Ernie Lombardi, not yet old enough to vote, raked the opposing pitchers for a .377 average, tops on the team. The Oaks did not defend their championship, finishing in fifth place with 91 wins and 100 losses, but Ernie Lombardi emerged as a star.

He took another step forward in 1929. Now 21 years old, Ernie took on the starting catching job full time, often catching both games of a twin bill and proving himself as a workhorse. His .365 average in 1929 included a power surge, with 24 home runs and 36 doubles. He was not named as the league's All-Star catcher—that honor went to the veteran Hank Severeid of the Hollywood Stars—but major league scouts had Ernie on their radar. In May of 1929, Oakland co-owner Del Howard declared that he would demand $100,000 for Lombardi's services. This sum would be the highest ever for a minor league catcher by far.

Though the Oaks had a disappointing season, Lombardi virtually knocked the Portland Ducks[9] out of the race for the second-half league title. In a doubleheader in Portland on September 29, Ernie belted a homer in the first game and three more in the second as Oakland posted two wins, both by the score of 8 to 2. In the second game he drove in six runs and scored four, for the "best exhibition of hitting ever witnessed at Vaughn street park."[10] Ernie's hitting put Portland five games behind with seven left to play as the Hollywood Stars won the second-half title and defeated the first-half winners from Mission in a playoff.

It was in Oakland that Ernie started to use an unusual grip on the bat. Because he wanted to protect a blister on the pinkie of his right hand, he decided to partially interlock his fingers on the bat, with the right pinkie sitting between, and on top of, the index and middle fingers of his left hand. People called it a golf grip, though Ernie did not play golf, and it gave the big catcher a firmer grip and more control of his massive bat. With this grip, and the 42-ounce bat he swung, he held his hands low and made

1, Brooks; 2, Boehler; 3, Lary; 4, Daglia; 5, Arlett; 6, Dumovich; 7, Reese; 8, McEvoy; 9, Lindquist; 10, Lombardi; 11, Craghead; 12, Kasich; 13, LaVeque; 14, Uhalt; 15, Dean; 16, Anton; 17, Fenton; 18, Ivan C. Howard, Mgr.; 19, Guisto; 20, McShane; 21, Young; 22, Vergez; 23, Read; 24, Frazier; 25, Baker; 26, Governor; 27, Mascot; 28, Brubaker; 29, Cooper; 30, Sparks.   Cohen, Photo.

OAKLAND CLUB—PACIFIC COAST LEAGUE.

The 1929 Oakland Oaks (Library of Congress).

a quick stroke at the ball. His strength made him a dangerous line drive hitter.

Ernie hit so well in 1929 that he held out for a higher salary for 1930. Despite the recent stock market crash and its effects on all businesses nationwide, Ernie and Buzz Arlett refused to report to the Oaks' spring camp in Fresno. Arlett soon capitulated, but Ernie never made it to Fresno. He worked out in Bay View Park, not far from the Lombardi family home in Oakland where he still lived with his father and his three sisters. Not until March 27, close to the start of the season, did he finally sign a contract and join the team.

The Oaks changed managers in 1930, after a new ownership group took control of the Oakland franchise. Carl Zamloch, a minor partner in the group, pitched briefly for the Detroit Tigers in 1913 and then spent 13 seasons as head baseball coach at the University of California at Berkeley. Zamloch, whose father was a famous magician, plied the same trade, performing as "The Great Zam" whenever he had the chance. Zamloch was an industrious sort; during the late 1920s he worked as a stockbroker in the mornings, coached baseball in the afternoons, and did his magic act in the evenings.

Under their new manager the Oaks started slowly in 1930, as did the man the papers called the "big Italian catcher." Ernie might have profited from spring training, as he struggled at the bat in the early going. A large cut in his knee, suffered in a close play at home plate in late April, put Lombardi out of action for more than two weeks. By May 27 he was hitting only .288.

It took a while, but he finally found his stroke. Ernie went on a tear, hitting at a .400 clip for the next eight weeks and climbing the batting average tables. On July 27 in San Francisco, Ernie walloped two long, high shots to left that would have been out of the park on any other day, but a strong wind kept them aloft long enough for the Seals outfielders to catch them against the fence. So Ernie adopted a new strategy. He drove two line drives over the right field wall for home runs and added a single too. The *Oakland Tribune* called his power display "the greatest exhibition of hitting [the fans] had ever witnessed in San Francisco and that includes the ones given by Babe Ruth."[11]

He also drew attention with his throwing arm, producing an incredible 95 assists in 1929 and 105 in 1930, leading the Pacific Coast League in putouts and assists in both seasons. He perfected the art of picking a runner off first with a snap throw from his crouch, and if a left-handed batter was at the plate, Ernie, with his long arms, simply threw the ball around him. Ernie's defense still needed work, but his cannon arm controlled the running game.

Now the major league teams renewed their interest in Ernie. Three years earlier, New York Yankees scout Bill Essick had brokered a deal that paid the Oaks $125,000 for infielders Lyn Lary and Jimmy Reese, and Essick was watching Lombardi closely. Other clubs, including the Boston Red Sox and Brooklyn Robins, had Ernie in their sights as well. Despite his defensive deficiencies—"his catching isn't on a par with his hitting," said a Sacramento newspaper—he would be sure to fetch a good price from some major league club. "If Lombardi ever learns what it's all about back of the bat," said a United Press report, "he'll certainly go up, for the boy can hit in any league."[12]

Ernie was one of the most popular players in the Pacific Coast League. When the Oaks played a string of exhibition games in smaller California towns like Taft and Bakersfield, the fans all but demanded that the manager put Ernie in the starting lineup for all the games. The *Oakland Tribune* started calling him "Bombo" Lombardi for the distance and frequency of his hits. Despite his slow start, he ended the 1930 season with an average of .370, third best in the league, and 22 home runs.

After three outstanding seasons in the Pacific Coast League, Ernie Lombardi had nothing left to prove. He was the best-hitting catcher, and one of the best hitters, in the minor leagues, and he was ready to take a step up on the baseball ladder. Besides, the Depression had begun, and the Oaks decided to cash in some of their stars. They sold Buzz Arlett to the Philadelphia Phillies and infielder Johnny Vergez to the New York Giants. Ernie was next. His value was never higher, so on January 19, 1931, the Oaks traded him to the Brooklyn Robins of the National League. Brooklyn sent Hank DeBerry and Eddie Moore to the Oaks, along with a reported $40,000.

2

Brooklyn

"Oakland will send four stars to National and American league clubs. Leading the hitting and eating attack will be Ernie Lombardi, huge catcher, who hit .377 and ate .950 in the coast league. He should be worth [the] $40,000 Brooklyn paid for him."[1]
—*Brooklyn Standard Union*, February 6, 1931

Ernie Lombardi was one of a growing number of Italian Americans to ascend to the major leagues. When the National League began play in 1876, there were plenty of Irish Americans on team rosters, but no Italians, and they were absent for more than two decades. The first of Ernie's ethnic group to reach the majors was Ed Abbaticchio, a Pennsylvanian who made his debut with the Philadelphia Phillies in 1898. In the decades that followed, more Italians—many from the Bay Area—entered top-level baseball, first in a trickle, then in a wave.

There was Ping Bodie, a San Franciscan whose real name was Francesco Pezzolo. He played the outfield for several teams in the 1910s and 1920s and told the press that, while a member of the New York Yankees, he roomed not with Babe Ruth, but with his trunk. There was Tony Lazzeri, also from San Francisco, who in 1925 belted 60 homers in the Pacific Coast League and jumped to the Yankees the following year. Young men with last names like DiMaggio, Fonseca, Lavagetto, Pinelli, Camilli, Crosetti, and many more emerged from the Bay Area and populated major league baseball during the 1930s. The most famous of these were the three DiMaggio brothers, all of whom were All-Stars while Joe, the middle brother, became one of the sport's greatest players and perhaps the most famous athlete in the United States.

It remained to be seen, however, how Ernie Lombardi would handle major league life. Italians were still a minority in the nation, and the razzing they received from the fans could be biting. Terms like "Dago" and "Wop" were frequently used slurs at the time, and much more commonplace than they are now. Most Italian ballplayers took it in stride—Ping

Bodie was "The Wonderful Wop" while Joe DiMaggio called himself "The Big Dago" in the privacy of the Yankee clubhouse—but Ernie was a sensitive sort. He was close to his family, shy around strangers, suspicious of the press, and eager to make good. He was three thousand miles from home and would remain so until the season ended in October.

Also, the Brooklyn club had no guarantees how Ernie's high batting averages in the Pacific Coast League would translate to major league competition. The PCL was a hitter's paradise, with the league leaders posting averages over the .400 mark and compiling single-season totals of over 300 hits and 200 runs batted in. Some outstanding Coast League hitters like Paul Waner and Tony Lazzeri became big league stars, while others like Paul Strand and Ox Eckhardt flamed out. Would Ernie Lombardi be another Waner or another Strand?

Brooklyn management ordered Ernie to report for spring training at Clearwater, Florida, in mid–February of 1931, but the young catcher hesitated. He knew that the club had paid $40,000 and two players for his services, and he figured that the Oakland Oaks should pay him a slice of the purchase price. So Ernie remained in Oakland while the rest of his new team assembled in Clearwater. Not until the last day of February did Ernie board a train for the five-day cross-country trip to Florida. He had, almost certainly, never traveled farther west than Ogden, Utah, in his life up to that point.

Ernie as a second-string catcher for the Brooklyn Robins, 1931 (National Baseball Hall of Fame Library, Cooperstown, New York).

Ernie Lombardi arrived in camp on March 6, 1931, and the newspapermen, always on the hunt for something to write about, took notice of this large, ungainly-looking newcomer. "Ernie Lombardi travels light," said Quentin

Reynolds in the *World-Telegram*. "He carries nothing but a blue serge suit, a well-worn cap, a small leather bag, the biggest schnozzola ever seen in baseball circles and a .370 batting average."

Reynolds continued,

> He weighs 200 pounds right now but he isn't fat. He stands six foot two and his hands are like two enormous hams hanging at the end of his arms. He totes a 42-ounce bat, the heaviest on the club, and as far as any of the players could recall the heaviest in the league ... [his new teammates] raised incredulous eyelids at the strange apparition.[2]

The story goes that Lombardi marched up to Brooklyn manager Wilbert Robinson and announced, "I'm Lombardi, from Oakland." Robinson looked over his new catcher and stated that the name Lombardi was too difficult to remember. From now on, he said, he would call the rookie Lumbago. Robinson then asked "Lumbago" if he had brought his golf clubs.

Ernie scoffed at the very idea. He was not there to play golf. He was there to play ball.

Wilbert Robinson, whom everyone knew as "Uncle Robbie," ran the loosest ship in baseball. A star catcher for the three-time league champion Baltimore Orioles of the 1890s, Robinson took over the Brooklyn club in 1914 and won pennants in 1916 and 1920. A friendly, easygoing man, Robinson was so popular in Brooklyn that the papers called the team the Robins in his honor.

However, the team fell on hard times after losing the 1920 World Series to the Cleveland Indians. A string of second-division finishes, interrupted only by a surprising second-place showing in 1924, thrust the Robins into irrelevance in the National League. In 1925, after team owner Charles Ebbets (builder of Ebbets Field) died, Robinson became team president while remaining as manager.

Perhaps the responsibilities of his dual roles overwhelmed Robinson, because the Robins sank in the standings as the front office—with competing factions evenly split between Ebbets' heirs and co-owner Steve McKeever—bickered endlessly. During this era, the team took on the "Daffy Dodgers" persona, as stories of the wacky goings-on surrounding the Brooklyn ballclub gained currency.

The Robins may or may not have had three baserunners on third base at the same time.

The manager may or may not have handed the umpire a laundry list instead of a lineup card.

The manager may or may not have told his team not to cheer so loud, because a pitcher was taking a nap on the bench.

Babe Herman, the Robins' hard-hitting but poor-fielding outfielder, may or may not have been hit in the head by a fly ball. Herman always denied the claim. "On the shoulder, yes," he said. "Never on the head!"

Relieved of his post as team president in 1929, Robinson led the 1930 team to its best showing in years, leading the league from May until August before fading to a fourth-place finish. Things were looking up in Brooklyn, though Robinson, at age 67, was running out of time to produce a winner. The front office was bitterly divided between the Ebbets heirs, who wholeheartedly supported the manager, and the McKeever family, who had been trying to oust him since the mid–1920s. Only a pennant would quell the boardroom turmoil and secure the aging manager's position.

Robinson, a former catcher, assembled a veritable fleet of promising catchers at the 1931 spring training camp. In addition to Ernie Lombardi, the Robins employed Al Lopez, who batted .309 in 1930 and claimed the regular starting job at the age of 22. Val Picinich, a 34-year-old veteran, served as backup to Lopez and spent most of his time in the bullpen, while Paul Richards, a prospect from Waxahachie, Texas, also earned a look. Though the Brooklyn club's pitching and infield defense needed improvement, the catching corps looked to be a strong point for the 1931 Robins, especially if Ernie Lombardi lived up to his billing.

As training camp unfolded at Clearwater, Florida, in March, Robinson paid close attention to his new catcher. "I haven't used Picinich yet," he told Tommy Holmes of the *Brooklyn Eagle*, "and these older chaps are apt to feel insulted and slighted unless they get in there once in a while. But I know what Val can do, and I'm still curious about old Lumbago."[3]

Ernie's strange way of holding a bat was already well known to the Brooklyn writers. As Tommy Holmes wrote in February, before spring training commenced,

> Ernie's grip on a baseball bat resembles what golf professionals and glib gentlemen still trying to break 120 call an "interlocking grip." He places his pinkie of his right hand between the index and second fingers of his left hand as he dares the pitcher to throw one over. He must have hands like hams to apply this grip, no great trick with the thin shaft of a golf club, on the comparatively thick end of a Louisville Slugger.
>
> Lombardi's "interlocking grip," which he probably learned out on some California golf course, is a more radical departure than [Ty] Cobb's grip and entirely in the opposite direction. Far be it from me to condemn a scientific theory unseen and untested, but I cannot imagine what benefits Lombardi derives from his particular system. Maybe Bobby Jones could tell you in several thousand words.[4]

Ernie impressed the Brooklyn press with his hitting. In one game between the regulars and the rookies, Lombardi whacked three hits, including a double and a triple as the rookies won the game 8 to 3. Another three-hit game against the barnstorming House of David nine helped establish Ernie as a threat at the plate. He had work to do on defense, however. The *Eagle* called Ernie "an extremely presentable catcher apart from his lack of ability to corral high fouls. In this particular department, his deficiency is nothing short of startling."[5]

However, Wilbert Robinson liked his new catcher, and Ernie was a lock to open the season in Brooklyn. The Robins had paid $40,000 and two players for him, and perhaps the manager could teach him to catch foul pop-ups. Besides, the fact that he was a right-handed batter was one reason the Robins bought him from Oakland. "The Robins," said the *Eagle*, "need a driving, right-handed pinch hitter even more than they do another catcher."[6]

Wilbert Robinson, manager of the Brooklyn Robins from 1914 to 1931. He was Ernie's first major league manager (George Grantham Bain Collection, Library of Congress).

The nation's sportswriters had a field day with the newest Robin even before he saw Brooklyn. The *Brooklyn Standard-Union* made fun of his nose; "Ernie Lombardi ought to be a great target for the pitchers to toss at. What a schnozzle!"[7] Abe Kemp of the *San Francisco Examiner* painted a picture of Lombardi as a cartoonish character, immature and diffident:

> Ernie Lombardi, whose sale by Oakland to Brooklyn has just been completed, broke in under Ivan Howard, and he was the bane of Ivan's existence.
> Ernie lacked ambition in those days and no end of coaxing or threats could stir him. He had his own ideas and his own ways and refused to change.
> One of Lombardi's pet stunts was to stretch himself full length in front of the stand during the batting practice and go sound to sleep.

Kemp then claimed that Ernie once belted a ball all the way to the wall but stopped at first. He saw it was still rolling, so he walked to second and sat on the bag, refusing to advance any further. When Howard demanded to know why he didn't take third, Ernie answered, with "his charming simplicity," that "I only hit it for two."[8]

Kemp's stories about Ernie ring false, because the young catcher was determined to succeed in professional baseball and aimed for the major leagues all during his time with the Oaks. He showed the Robins that he was willing to work hard and improve on both offense and defense. As William McCullough wrote in the *Times-Union*, "It has been his ambition to be a major leaguer since he was a kid on the sand lots of Oakland. His dream is now realized and he is determined to remain under the big tent for years to come."[9]

The National League experienced an offensive explosion in 1930, with the league as a whole (pitchers included) batting .303 and scoring a record 5.68 runs per game. The pitchers were overwhelmed, so the league adopted a less lively ball for the 1931 season in an attempt to rein in the offense. But either no one told Ernie about the new deader ball, or he didn't notice, because during a batting drill, "taking a swing that would have lifted a house from its foundation," he walloped a long home run that landed 450 feet from the plate, rolled for a while after that, and only stopped when it bounced against the side of a church.

Joe Becker, a scout who recommended Ernie to the Brooklyn team in 1928, was ecstatic. "I look to him to succeed [Babe] Ruth as the leading home run hitter," said Becker. "Say, that ball he drove to the church was as long as any Babe ever hit on the nose."[10] No one knows how much farther the hit would have traveled if the 1930 ball was still in use.

Ernie made the team as the second-string catcher, with Al Lopez as the starter and Val Picinich mostly in the bullpen. Lopez expected to get most of the playing time, with the newcomer pinch hitting and playing the second games of doubleheaders, especially against the weaker teams. As Lank Leonard wrote in the *Brooklyn Citizen* in early May,

> Ernest Lombardi, the young Italian catcher who is breaking into the big show with the Brooklyn Dodgers, may not be of any great help to the club this summer, but he certainly appears to be a brilliant prospect for the future.
>
> Brooklyn is very well equipped behind the plate with Al Lopez and Val Picinich on hand, but Lombardi will will be given an opportunity to pick up knowledge against such teams as the Phillies and the Reds.
>
> Ernie has plenty of rough spots that must be smoothed over, but at least he has no false ideas about himself, and an ambitious youngster able to hit as he can hit and throw as he can throw is bound to improve.[11]

Leonard also pointed out Ernie's resemblance to Larry McLean, another large catcher of a generation before. McLean, who played for the New York Giants in the early 1910s, was also over six feet tall and weighed over 200 pounds. McLean also, said Leonard, "looked down at you from either side of a comic valentine nose, and Lombardi's 'schnozzle' is one of the largest on record."[12]

Ernie had to learn how major league players presented themselves. Apparently, young men dressed differently in the eastern states than they did in California, and the other players told Ernie that major leaguers don't wear caps. Said Paul Richards, "He reported with a little cap on and a satchel about the size of one a doctor would carry. The ballplayers put together some money to buy him a hat. Everybody liked him."[13] But Ernie never liked wearing a hat, so he went bare headed.

Ernie had a lot to learn in his first year in the National League. The pitchers discovered that Ernie liked to swing at the first pitch, so they stopped throwing that pitch over the plate. The new catcher had to adjust to that. By mid-season, the pitchers found that Ernie had trouble with the fastball up and in. He had to learn to recognize the pitch and bring his 42-ounce bat around quicker. Also, he saw the tricks that pitchers like to play. One day, while facing Jesse Haines of the Cardinals, Ernie saw Haines motion his outfielders to shift to the right. "I'm a right-handed hitter," recalled Ernie, "so I got to figure he's pitching me outside. I leaned away over the plate. That's just what Jess wanted." Haines' next pitch drilled Ernie in the elbow. "But he made sure he would get me with the first pitch by setting me up for it."[14]

The other Robins soon recognized the new catcher's toughness. In May, he was assigned to catch Dazzy Vance, the veteran Brooklyn strike-out artist who still possessed a good fastball. As Paul Richards described it, "Somebody swung at a ball and Lombardi ducked and the ball hit him on top of the head and bounced all the way back to the bench. A blow like that would have knocked out an ordinary man, but Lombardi just crouched down and gave another sign, as if nothing had happened."[15] The papers reported that the blow staggered Ernie, but after the catcher regained his footing, he waved off his teammates' offers of help and resumed the game. That was a tough day for Ernie, as he got lost in the subway on the way to the ballpark, but the Robins beat the Reds 2 to 1.

Though Al Lopez owned the starting job, Wilbert Robinson liked what he saw from his new catcher, and started using him in clutch situations. On May 6, the Robins and the rival Giants were scoreless in the seventh when Brooklyn's Rube Bressler reached third with one out. Though right-hander Ray Phelps had shut out the New Yorkers for seven innings, Robinson decided to play for one run. He sent Ernie Lombardi up to pinch hit for the pitcher. Many in the crowd booed, but Robinson knew that Ernie could produce a long fly to score the runner. After fouling off a few pitches, Ernie delivered. He sent a high fly ball to Mel Ott in center field, scoring the only run of the game in a 1–0 win. Robinson always enjoyed beating the Giants and his former teammate and bitter rival, manager John McGraw, especially when strategy was involved.

The pitchers liked seeing Ernie behind the plate. "He's so darned big," said Joe Shaute, "that he gives the pitcher a target that hardly can be missed. You know a pitcher aims at his catcher and not at the plate and a big catcher helps me, at least, in the matter of control."[16]

Watty Clark revealed one of Ernie's tricks. Ernie used a small glove, not much larger than his hand, and the pocket of the glove left only leather, and no padding, to cover his palm. When Clark's fastball hit Ernie's glove, it sounded like a gunshot. "Maybe it's my imagination," said Clark, "but pitching to Lombardi gives me a feeling of power. He makes me think that I can throw a ball through a house."[17]

The pitchers had to get used to him, though. "I hope the big boy don't cripple some of our pitchers," said Shaute in April. He showed a bruised right palm to a *Brooklyn Eagle* reporter. "Look at that. Just from Lombardi throwing the ball back to me. I had to ask him a couple of times if he was trying to show me up. He throws a cannon ball."[18]

Ernie added his own chapter to Brooklyn lore when he made a double play and an error on the same play. On May 5, in a game against the Giants, Ernie went in to catch after Al Lopez suffered a split finger. In the ninth inning, with no outs, the Giants had Shanty Hogan on first and Johnny Vergez on third when Freddie Fitzsimmons hit a grounder to third baseman Wally Gilbert. Gilbert threw home, and the "giant Italian catcher" caught Vergez in a rundown and eventually tagged him. As Hogan dashed for third, Ernie ran down the baseline and tagged him too.

That's when Vergez, Ernie's former Oakland teammate, sprang a trap on the rookie catcher. Though Ernie had tagged him out, Vergez broke for home anyway. Ernie threw the ball to Del Bissonette covering the plate, but the ball hit Vergez and bounded away. Fitzsimmons made it all the way to third on the bad throw, and the scorer gave Ernie an error. Had he thrown the ball to third to catch Fitzsimmons sliding in, the Robins might have completed a triple play.

The Robins won only three of their 13 games in April, but a solid May kept them from falling too far back, and in June a 15–2 streak boosted the Brooklyn crew into third place, within four games of the lead. Ernie made his contributions, as both a starter and as a pinch-hitter. On July 27, before 33,000 fans in Brooklyn, the Robins swept a doubleheader from the Cardinals. Al Lopez caught both contests, but when the two teams entered the bottom of the ninth inning of the second game tied at 3, Ernie pinch hit for pitcher Jack Quinn. With runners on first and second and one out, Ernie drilled a line drive off the right field fence to drive in the game-winning run.

2. Brooklyn

Brooklyn's high point of the season came in a July 4 doubleheader against the rival Giants. Before 42,000 fans, the largest crowd in Ebbets Field history up to that time, the Robins shut out McGraw's Giants twice by scores of 4–0 and 5–0. Ernie caught the second game and mashed a two-run homer in the fourth inning to give the Robins a 3–0 lead, while Babe Herman's two-run shot in the eighth sealed the victory.

However, the St. Louis Cardinals, the defending champions, were too talented and too deep for the rest of the National League. The Cardinals grabbed first place on Memorial Day and never relinquished it, fighting off the Giants, Cubs, and Robins. By late July they had opened up a nine-game lead on their way to 101 wins, the best record in team history up till then. Wilbert Robinson, after 11 years without a pennant, would have to aim for 1932.

In early August, during a brutally hot three-game series against the Braves in Boston, manager Robinson found himself short of batting practice pitchers. Lombardi volunteered to help out, and for twenty minutes he buzzed fastballs past his teammates. His fellow Robins were impressed with what they saw, and veteran reliever Jack Quinn, who had seen it all since his major league debut in 1909, suggested to Lombardi that he should pursue a mound career. For several weeks thereafter, most of the usual ribbing directed to the big catcher centered on his presumed future shift to the mound.

Uncle Robbie stoutly denied that he planned to convert Lombardi into a pitcher, and Ernie himself had shot the idea down several years before. He said,

> One time when I was playing in the Pacific Coast League, the manager tried to convert me into a flinger. But I quickly put a stop to his intentions by announcing that I would resign from the team first. He didn't bother about the idea any longer.
>
> I'm a good hitter, and maybe some day I'll become a real major league star, but when and if I do, it will be as a catcher.[19]

Ernie shocked the Reds in Cincinnati on September 11 when he beat out a bunt along the third base line. "Will the age of wonders never cease?" asked the *Brooklyn Standard Union*. "Can you imagine Ernie Lombardi, he of the mastodonic build and protruding nose, beating out a bunt?" Ernie played down his accomplishment. "Of course I know ball players don't beat out bunts every day," he said, "but I prefer not to talk about it. When I steal my first base then it will be time enough to brag."[20] Perhaps Ernie forgot that he stole a bag on May 18, also against the Reds. That was his only steal of the year.

Ernie hit at a .448 clip in August, but mostly rode the bench after that, playing only eight games in September. Still, he finished the 1931 season with a credible .297 average in 50 starts and 24 pinch-hitting appearances. Lombardi also enjoyed the unwavering support of his manager. Said the Brooklyn field boss in September, "With a year [of] major league experience under his belt, I look for Ernie to be a big asset to the Robins in 1932. His hitting during the past two months bears out my contention that his Coast averages weren't padded, and his fielding, especially in catching foul flies, has vastly improved of late."[21]

The St. Louis Cardinals ran away with the 1931 pennant, finishing 13 games ahead of the second place Giants. The Robins, with a record of 79–73, came in fourth, 21 games behind the Cardinals. It was a good season for Brooklyn, but not a great one, and manager Robinson expected his team to make a move to the top in 1932.

However, Uncle Robbie's tenure in Brooklyn was over. For years, the four-man board of directors of the Brooklyn club, evenly divided between the McKeever family and the heirs of Charles Ebbets, had battled over Robinson's future. The McKeevers, citing Robinson's lax approach to spring training and in-season discipline, wanted the 67-year-old manager out, only to be blocked by the Ebbets faction. The boardroom squabbling became so heated that the National League stepped in and appointed a fifth director, a former Yale pitcher named Walter Carter. Carter sided with the McKeevers, and on October 23, 1931, the club announced Robinson's dismissal. Max Carey, the former Pittsburgh outfielder and current third base coach of the Robins, signed a one-year contract to manage the club.

Carey's appointment cast doubt on Ernie's future in Brooklyn. He had performed well and was so popular with the city's ethnic fans that an Italian Elks club in Brooklyn held a banquet in Lombardi's honor in May, before Ernie had completed two months in a Robins uniform. But as a player, Max Carey was a speedy base stealer, not a lumbering old catcher like Wilbert Robinson. With his status uncertain, Ernie went home to Oakland.

3

Cincinnati

> "The Reds are not in healthy condition, either physically or financially. The team lost a chunk of money last year. It wound up in eighth place. There is not even a prospect of soaring to seventh place this season."[1]
> —*Miami News*, March 31, 1932

Max Carey wanted to remake the Brooklyn club, now renamed the Dodgers with Wilbert Robinson gone, and Ernie Lombardi did not fit in his plans. Carey knew that Al Lopez was a superior defensive catcher and a good hitter, and the new manager intended to build his team around speed, which Ernie noticeably lacked, and defense. Ernie reported to camp at Clearwater, Florida, and trained with the Dodgers for three weeks, all the while knowing that a trade was in the works. On March 14, 1932, the Dodgers traded Ernie, third baseman Wally Gilbert and outfielder Babe Herman to the Cincinnati Reds for second baseman Tony Cuccinello, catcher Clyde Sukeforth, and third baseman Joe Stripp.

Many Brooklyn fans were sorry to see the popular Lombardi go. "Herman and Lombardi may not be the greatest ballplayers in the league, but they undoubtedly possess oodles of color, and for that reason were of great value to the Dodgers and will be the same to the Reds," columnist Murray Robinson wrote in the *Brooklyn Times-Union*. "Stripp, Cuccinello and Sukeforth lack the ingredients which made the eccentric Babe and the lumbering, good-natured 'Bocci' the targets of the customers' jibes."[2]

But the new Dodger manager felt it was a win for his club.

"The deal should help both clubs but it will benefit us more than the Reds," Carey told the *New York Daily News*. "You may think I've sacrificed some hitting strength in letting Herman go but as a matter of fact I've gained. Stripp will outhit Gilbert, Sukeforth will outhit Lombardi and last year Cuccinello outhit Herman and drove in more runs when runs were needed."

The deal made sense for both teams. The Reds wanted a better-hitting catcher than Sukeforth (who batted .256 and failed to hit a homer in 1931), and the Dodgers had no room for Ernie with Al Lopez, Val Picinich, and Sukeforth behind the plate. Besides, Carey, a former National League base-stealing champion, believed in speed, which neither Lombardi nor Gilbert could provide. "We unloaded two players who were not to figure in my plans this year,"[3] Carey told the press. "I had no intention of using either Wally Gilbert or Ernie Lombardi." Cuccinello and Stripp had both batted over .300 for the Reds and were expected to solidify the Brooklyn infield, while the Reds replaced them with Gilbert at third and George Grantham at second.

The biggest name in the trade was Herman, one of the stars of the National League. Though Herman had batted .393 in 1930 and played solidly again in 1931, the Dodgers were tired of his annual holdouts and famously poor fielding. The Reds wanted Herman to provide a jolt of power to the lineup and to replace veteran outfielder Edd Roush, who retired at the close of the 1931 season.

Herman was a temperamental sort, but Reds manager Dan Howley had coached him at Detroit a decade earlier and got along well with him. Howley had even given Floyd Caves Herman his nickname. Herman had called himself "Lefty" as a young man, but Howley rejected the moniker as "too common." When the outfielder mentioned that a female fan had called him "Babe," Howley quickly replied. "From now on, you're my Babe."

Dan Howley got along with everybody. A baseball veteran who caught a few games for the Phillies in 1913, Howley worked his way through the minors as a coach and manager for more than a decade. In 1927 he landed in St. Louis as manager of the sad-sack Browns. He pushed the team into the first division, topping the .500 mark in 1928 and 1929, then left to manage the Reds. Unfortunately for Howley, the talent-poor Reds were in no condition to climb the standings. They lost 95 games in 1930 and 96 in 1931, finishing at the bottom of the league in the latter season. Still, Howley never lost his positive attitude. As Cincinnati shortstop Leo Durocher explained, "We'd lose eight straight and after every game Howley would say, 'Don't worry, boys, we'll get 'em tomorrow.' Then we'd win one and he'd do everything except throw a party for us."[4]

The majority owner of the Reds, a local automobile dealer named Sidney J. Weil, was a rabid baseball fan who bought enough stock on the open market to gain control of the team in the fall of 1929. Unfortunately for Weil, the stock market crashed a few weeks later, and his dreams of glory for his beloved Reds faded, as did his financial prospects. The underfunded team finished in seventh place in 1930 and dead last in 1931, bleeding money all the while. Ernie Lombardi now found himself on the weakest, most unstable team in the National League, one that had joined the circuit in 1890 and owned only one pennant to show for it.

Still, Weil was determined to build up the Reds, and he tried everything to do so, given his financial limitations as his automobile business withered. In 1930 he bought Leo Durocher, a poor hitter but one of baseball's best fielding shortstops, from the Yankees to anchor the infield defense. Weil persuaded Edd Roush, star of Cincinnati's World Championship team of 1919, to come out of retirement and play one more season, and claimed Harry Heilmann, a four-time American League batting champ, from Detroit on waivers. The aging Heilmann hit .333 in 1930 (with a team record 19 home runs) but was so slow in the outfield and on the bases that his nickname "Slug" now referred not only to his batting. Heilmann sat out the 1931 season but returned as a part-timer in 1932. The 1931 Cincinnati club hit only 21 home runs all year, but with Heilmann, Babe Herman, and Ernie Lombardi in the lineup, Weil expected a power increase in 1932.

The pitching staff, however, was a mess. The Reds had finished last or next to last in the league in almost every pitching category in 1931, and their pitching showed no sign of improvement. The workhorses of the staff were Si Johnson (11–19 in 1931) and Red Lucas (14–13). Lucas may have been the best player on the team; not only did he lead the league in complete games, but he made an incredible 68 appearances as a pinch-hitter in 1931. The veteran of the staff, 41-year-old left-hander Eppa Rixey, was once a star but now made most of his starts against Pittsburgh, the one team he could beat reliably.

In a bid to improve the Cincinnati offense, Weil made a deal with the Cardinals to land the National League batting champion. Chick Hafey, a bespectacled outfielder with a cannon arm, was one of the mainstays of the St. Louis offense for several years and batted .349 in 1931 to gain the batting title. But Hafey and Cardinals business manager[5] Branch Rickey continually feuded over contract issues. When Hafey performed so poorly in the 1931 World Series that he rode the bench in the deciding seventh game, and then sat out spring training in another contract dispute, Rickey decided that he was expendable. On April 11, 1932, the day before the season began, Rickey sent the hard-hitting Hafey to the Reds for pitcher Benny Frey, some cash, and a player to be named later.

Defensively, the 1932 Reds appeared strong in some places and weak in others. Leo Durocher was a Gold Glove-level shortstop, but the new second baseman, George Grantham, was a good hitter but a poor fielder. Grantham was a ten-year veteran acquired from Pittsburgh, where the fans called him "Boots." Chick Hafey was solid in left, but Babe Herman, the new right fielder, was infamous for his misadventures in the outfield. Ernie Lombardi was expected to add offense, but his defensive value was still a question mark.

Ernie reported to the Reds' spring training base in Tampa, Florida, in fine condition, and hit the ball hard from the first day in his new uniform. In his first game at Cincinnati's Redland Field, an exhibition contest against Babe Ruth and the Yankees on April 5, Ernie smacked a sharp single and two doubles. The second double, in the eighth inning, rocketed off the wall in left center, two feet from going over the fence. The Yankees won the game on a homer by Lou Gehrig, but Ernie's performance made the fans take notice. Perhaps the Reds were the winners in the trade with Brooklyn after all.

Dan Howley, who needed all the offense he could muster, was satisfied. "Lombardi is certain to be in the catcher position," the manager told the *Cincinnati Enquirer*, "and will probably start every game behind the bat so long as he keeps his health and strength."[6] Howley's theory was that a big man like Lombardi needed lots of work to stay in shape, and because backup catchers Clyde Manion and Bob Asbjornson contributed little at the bat, Ernie held a solid grip on the starting position.

The Cincinnati club opened the 1932 season at home against the Chicago Cubs, and more than 25,000 fans braved the chilly weather to see the newest edition of the Reds. Ernie Lombardi batted sixth in the lineup that day, and after the Cubs scored twice in the first, Ernie came to bat in the second and belted a single, his first hit as a Red. Estel Crabtree then forced Lombardi at second to end the inning. Ernie went out his next two times up and the Reds could muster little offense against Cubs right-hander Charlie Root. After eight and a half innings, the Cubs owned a 4–1 lead.

In the bottom of the ninth, while thousands of fans made their way to the exits, the Cincinnati bats came alive. George Grantham led off with a single, and Mickey Heath worked Root for a walk. Ernie then smashed a line drive straight at Root. The pitcher deflected the ball with his hand, and both runners moved up as Ernie hustled to first. Root was unable to continue, so the Cubs brought Guy Bush in to pitch while Leo Durocher pinch-ran for Lombardi. Ernie left the field to a loud ovation from the remaining fans. Red Lucas then batted for Joe Morrissey and cracked a double to score two runs and cut the Chicago lead to 4–3. After an intentional walk, Taylor Douthit delivered a two-run single to win the game.

The Reds lost the next day, and though Ernie contributed a single, drove in one run and scored one, disaster struck in the eighth inning when a foul tip smacked into the index finger on his throwing hand. Ernie finished the game, despite the pain and swelling. After the game, the Reds discovered that Ernie's finger was broken. He sat out for the next two weeks while his injury healed, robbing the team of one of its strongest hitters.

By the time Ernie rejoined the club on May 4, the Reds had managed to remain afloat, holding third place before three losses in a row to the Cardinals dropped them into fifth position, two games under the .500 mark. Ernie returned with a failed pinch-hitting assignment in a 7–0 loss at St. Louis but started the next game at home against the Boston Braves. He picked up where he left off, belting a triple and a homer, driving in four runs and scoring twice in a 9–8 win. The next afternoon, in a 14–1 destruction of the Braves, the big catcher contributed two more hits, both doubles, to raise his batting average to .444.

On May 7, Ernie Lombardi cemented his popularity with the Cincinnati fans. With 5,500 in the stands, the Reds built a 5–1 lead as Ernie contributed a double in the second inning and a single in the fourth, eventually scoring on a sacrifice fly by Mickey Heath. Lombardi ended a rally in the fifth by grounding into a double play, but in the seventh he followed a triple by Estel Crabtree with a run-scoring double, his third hit of the day.

Cincinnati starter Larry Benton held the Braves at bay for the first seven innings but allowed two runs in the eighth and two more in the ninth to send the game to extra innings. No one scored in the first two extra frames, despite another single in the 11th by Ernie. Then the roof fell in, as the Braves pounded reliever Biff Wysong for three runs in the top of the 12th to take an 8–5 lead. The contest was now more than three hours old, and once again, many of the remaining fans headed to the exits.

In the bottom of the 12th, Andy High and Taylor Douthit reached base on walks, but a strikeout and a fly ball left the Reds down to their last out. The game should have ended when Joe Morrissey grounded to short, but Bill Akers booted it, loading the bases. That brought the veteran Harry Heilmann, the onetime Detroit batting champion, to the plate. Heilmann drilled a single to right that scored two runs and cut the Boston lead to 8–7.

Now it was all up to Ernie Lombardi.

With Cliff Heathcote, who pinch-ran for Heilmann, on first and Morrissey on third, Tom Zachary pitched carefully to the big catcher. Ernie worked Zachary to a 3–2 count, and with the game on the line, delivered. Ernie slammed a line drive that ricocheted off the top of the fence in right-center field, scoring Morrissey and Heathcote for a walk-off, 9–8 win.

Ernie Lombardi had not only caught the entire 12-inning game, but also belted five hits in seven plate appearances, including the game-winner. The Cincinnati fans had found a new hero, and as the veteran Boston shortstop Rabbit Maranville told the papers, "how'd you get the idea around here that that two-legged whale behind the bat for the Reds is named Lombardi. All wrong. His real moniker is Bombardi."[7]

Ernie's hot streak did not end there. Two days later, he pounded a triple and a home run, his second of the season, and drew a crucial walk in the ninth inning of a 4–3 walk-off win against the Phillies. On May 14, a three-hit game against the Dodgers led the Reds to a 5–3 win and raised Lombardi's league-leading average to .524. This victory left the Reds at 16–14 and clinging stubbornly to third place, only four games out of first. Though the bottom of the order struggled at the bat, the hitters in the second through fifth positions—George Grantham (.306), Babe Herman (.325), Lombardi, and Chick Hafey (.443)—gave the Reds a powerful attack. They held on to third place to the end of May, and on Memorial Day, a win over Pittsburgh in the first game of a doubleheader left the surprising Reds two games above the .500 mark.

Aside from the 17 games he missed due to his broken finger, Ernie did most of the rest of the catching for the Reds in 1932. The second-string backstop was Clyde Manion, a 35-year-old career backup who spent most of his career in the American League. Manion was no offensive threat, batting only .207 in 1932, but Ernie needed a rest sometimes, so Manion made 38 starts. Ernie, who started 105 contests, became a workhorse because the talent-challenged Reds had few options.

Ernie loved playing for the Reds. "I'd like to catch every day if Dan [Howley] would let me," he said. "I'm strong enough. That's why I couldn't get started in Brooklyn. I couldn't get enough work. It's the only way to get a thing down pat—work at it."[8] He appreciated the advice that Howley, a former catcher, provided. "I could always hit good, but I've had to learn how to catch. Dan has given me a lot of tips. He taught me how to pull the glove down on my hand. I used to go under the bat with it just hanging on my fingers."[9]

He learned to adjust to his home park, Redland Field. Built in 1912, the Cincinnati ballpark was one of the smallest in the major leagues, with seating for 25,000. It was a nightmare for right-handed power hitters, with a left field fence 360 feet down the line. It was so far away that the park was nearly ten years old before any batter managed to hit an over-the-fence homer to left.[10] But the spacious outfield with its faraway fences yielded more than its share of doubles and triples. Ernie, who specialized in sharp lines drives rather than long fly balls, would never be a home run hitter in Cincinnati, but singles and doubles could keep his batting average high.

Dan Howley was an optimist. The Reds lost the second game on Memorial Day and lost again the next afternoon to the Pirates, leaving their record at an even .500, but Howley exuded confidence. "The Pirates caught us when we were off our stride and also at a time when they were playing to the limit of their ability," he said. "I still maintain no club is going to run away with this pennant.... I look for my team to get straightened out any day now and am confident it will be one of the flag contenders toward the finish."[11]

Ernie fields a pop-up. He needed a lot of work on pop-ups when he reached the major leagues (National Baseball Hall of Fame Library, Cooperstown, New York).

"Any day now" never happened, and the pitching-poor Reds never had a chance in 1932. The two losses to Pittsburgh started the Cincinnati club on a ten-game losing streak that dropped them to the bottom of the league by June 10. They won only seven of their 28 games in June, and at the end of the month a nine-game skid cemented their hold on the cellar. Chick Hafey, counted on to lift the offense, missed the entire month of June with influenza and suffered a relapse in July that kept him out of the lineup for two more weeks. He hit well but played in only 83 games.

Perhaps the only point of interest for Cincinnati fans in 1932 was the emergence of their new catcher, Ernie Lombardi. Lombardi's average peaked at .397 on June 10 after belting three singles against the Giants. He solidified his hold on the starting catching job with his bat, though his defense needed work. Despite all his training in Oakland with the Oaks, Ernie was still weak on pop-ups, he led the league in passed balls, and his range remained below the league average for a catcher. Also, the jury was still out on his ability to handle pitchers. The Cincinnati staff was so short on talent that it was difficult to get an idea of how well Ernie called the pitches.

Still, Ernie emerged as a fan favorite. Though he said little to the press—some writers complained that a grunt from Ernie was the extent of his communication with them—the Cincinnati fans enjoyed this large, oddly-shaped player with the strange batting grip, huge hands and prominent nose. The fans could see that Ernie smiled on the field and in the dugout and got along well with his teammates. And he accepted the jokes about his nose from both fans and teammates without complaint. "They first began kidding me about the nose and calling me 'Schnozz' back in the Coast League," he said. "But the funny thing was, I didn't get too much razzing from the bench jockeys. Mostly, it came from the fans."[12]

"Schnozz" was only one of his nicknames. Others included Lom, Muss (because his teammates liked to muss his thick dark hair), Lumbago, Schnozzola, Dago (then not considered an ethnic slur—even Joe DiMaggio called himself that), and, more poetically, the Cyrano of the Iron Mask. The fact that his nose extended outside of his mask, and was sometimes scraped and bruised by foul tips, made Lombardi seem even more human. But back home in West Oakland, he was Botch, the nickname he picked up on the baseball fields at Bay View Park.

Lombardi was a very big, muscular man, and might have presented himself as a highly intimidating character had he chosen to do so. Instead, as Bill James wrote in his *Historical Baseball Abstract*, Ernie, by both size and temperament, took on the persona of the "gentle giant." He was, said James, the man whose sheer physical presence made him feel unthreatened, and magnified any threat he might happen to project.

The world calls upon such men to put on a benevolent face, and Lombardi responded. He was quiet, taciturn, yet fully engaged in the clubhouse give and take, handing out vaguely insulting nicknames and accepting them with grace. Dick Bartell [a National League shortstop] reports that he was often the butt of practical jokes, a kind of clubhouse equivalent of school kids teasing the elephant.[13]

In June, Cincinnati team owner Sidney Weil decided to follow the lead of most other major league teams and put numbers on the backs of the players' uniforms. The New York Yankees were the first to do so on a permanent basis in 1929, and the numbers proved so popular that other clubs followed suit. In a Sunday doubleheader against Pittsburgh on June 26, the Reds wore numbers for the first time. The *Cincinnati Enquirer* applauded the move with the comment "The fans will now be able to distinguish Ernie Lombardi from Leo Durocher without much trouble."[14] Ernie took the field in 1932 with a 7 on his back, but his number really didn't matter to him. He wore six different numbers during his tenure with the Reds.

The last three months of the 1932 season were a lost cause for the Cincinnati Reds. While the Cubs, Cardinals, and Pirates battled for the pennant, the Reds stumbled along, winning barely a third of their games in the second half. Ernie's bat cooled off, too. Nine of his 11 home runs came in the first half, and he batted only .238 during the last three months. Dan Howley, whose contract expired at season's end, fought to keep his job, but could not get the team out of its rut.

After falling into last place on June 10, the Reds never climbed out of the National League cellar, even for a day, and ended the season on a 2–11 skid. They wound up with 60 wins and 94 losses, 30 games behind the pennant-winning Chicago Cubs. None of their starting pitchers won more games than they lost, with only the ancient Eppa Rixey, at 5–5, reaching the break-even mark.

Babe Herman proved his value, leading the team with a .326 average, 16 homers and 87 runs batted in. Herman also led the league with 19 triples and gained a few votes in the Most Valuable Player balloting. The rest of the offense was mediocre, with Leo Durocher (.217) and Wally Gilbert (.214) providing almost nothing at the bat. Chick Hafey spent much of the campaign on the sidelines, while the once-dangerous Harry Heilmann saw action in only 15 contests before quitting the team at the end of May.

Ernie Lombardi, however, had a very good year. He hit .303 with 11 homers and 68 runs batted in, finishing second on the team to Babe Herman in all three categories. Despite his lack of speed, Ernie also belted nine triples, eight of which came at home in the spacious Redland Field.

Because the batters behind him in the lineup were so weak, Ernie led the major leagues with 12 intentional walks, an unusual result from a player in his first full season.

He showed off his throwing arm, catching 16 of the 32 runners who tried to steal on him, an excellent success rate. He did, however, hit into 16 double plays, commit 14 errors and allow a league-high total of 17 passed balls. So Ernie ended the 1932 season on a positive note, but on the defensive side, he knew he had room for improvement.

4

"The Giant Italian Catcher"

> "The big catcher is a picturesque and colorful figure on the field, and with his power and precision at the plate he should develop into a valuable back-stop. However, he has to battle every winter with his increasing poundage and bulk."[1]
>
> —*Brooklyn Eagle*, January 8, 1933

Dan Howley had failed to lift the Reds out of last place, and his three-year contract had expired, so on November 10, 1932, Sidney Weil released Howley and hired Owen (Donie) Bush as his new manager.

Donie Bush was a light-hitting, good-fielding shortstop with the Detroit Tigers during their pennant-winning seasons of 1908 and 1909. He was a small man, nicknamed "the midget" in the newspapers, but his enthusiasm and fielding skill kept him in the Tiger lineup for 13 seasons. He was routinely described as "scrappy" and "fiery" and, like his teammate Ty Cobb, turned every baseball game into a battle of wills. He gave his maximum effort in every game, and always demanded that his fellow Tigers do the same.

His tenure with the Tigers ended in 1921 when Cobb became manager and hired Dan Howley as his coach and main assistant. Bush and the usually friendly Howley grew to hate each other, arguing so vociferously that other players often had to separate them. To relieve the tension on the club, the Tigers sent Bush to the Washington Senators later that year.

Bush's playing career ended in Washington, and team owner Clark Griffith named Bush to manage the team two years later. Though he lifted the 1923 Senators from sixth place to fourth, Griffith released him at season's end. Hired to lead the Pittsburgh Pirates in 1927, Bush led them to the National League pennant, though the team was utterly demolished by the Yankees in the World Series. But some of his personnel decisions weakened the team. He benched star outfielder Kiki Cuyler for the last half of the 1927 season in a personal dispute, then traded him to the Cubs. Bush also gave up on young shortstop Joe Cronin, who surfaced in the American League and wound up in the Hall of Fame.

Bush remained in Pittsburgh for two more years, and nearly became manager of the Reds in 1930 before Sidney Weil bought controlling interest in the club and put his own choice, Dan Howley, in the post. Bush managed Minneapolis of the American Association to the pennant in 1932, and when Howley's contract ran out that fall, Bush was the leading candidate to succeed him.

Weil expected Bush to light a fire under the Reds in contrast to the easygoing Howley, but he faced a daunting task. "No bed of roses awaits the new manager here," said one paper. "He falls heir to a run-down team, with little financial backing and a quick-to-criticize public."[2] Reportedly, Weil toyed with the idea of having Bush run the team without the assistance of a coach. In the end, Weil agreed to sign Jewel Ens, Bush's right-hand man and successor in Pittsburgh, as his chief assistant. Also, the cash-poor Reds signed the new manager to a one-year contract. This put Bush under pressure to deliver a winner, and quickly.

Bush's task became much more difficult on November 30, when Weil traded Babe Herman, the Reds' leading hitter in 1932, to the Chicago Cubs. The Reds received four players—catcher Rollie Hemsley, pitcher Bob Smith, and outfielders Lance Richbourg and Johnny Moore— and probably some cash too. The Cubs had offered to buy Herman in a straight cash deal, but the talent-deprived Reds needed depth. Hemsley, a well-regarded defensive catcher, was expected to battle Ernie Lombardi for the starting position.

After acquiring Chick Hafey from St. Louis the year before, Weil turned once again to Cardinals general manager Branch Rickey for offensive help. On December 17, 1932, Rickey sent his star first baseman, Jim Bottomley, to the Reds for two little-used players. Bottomley, a perennial .300 hitter with power, was a

Donie Bush, who managed the Reds in 1933 (George Grantham Bain Collection, Library of Congress).

key figure in four pennant-winning seasons for the Cardinals and once drove in 12 runs in a single game. But Bottomley would be 33 years old in 1933 and was often sidelined with injuries during the previous two seasons. Still, many wondered why the Cardinals disposed of Bottomley so cheaply, especially as the first baseman, whose nickname was "Sunny Jim," was much easier to get along with than the temperamental Babe Herman.

Ernie spent the winter of 1932–33 at the family home in Oakland, as always, and at Christmastime was bedridden with a severe case of tonsillitis. Teammate Taylor Douthit, who also lived in Oakland, stopped to visit and found a very sick catcher. "I heard Ernie was sick so [I] went over to see him and he was a sad sight," said Douthit. "When a fellow as big as Ernie gets sick there's a lot of him to be miserable and he was sick all over."[3] Ernie, at his doctor's suggestion, had the tonsils removed and was ready for spring training.

Sidney Weil tried to make spring training enjoyable. On St. Patrick's Day, he and the new manager divided the team into the Irish and the Dutch and set them to play each other, with 50 cigars as the winning prize. The Dutch (or "Deutsch," of German ancestry) were led by Wally Roettger, who grew up speaking German and issued commands on the field in German. Leo Durocher, whose parents were French-Canadian, nonetheless directed the Irish and claimed the Cuban pitcher Oscar Tuero, who took the name Casey for the afternoon.

What about the big Italian catcher? Roettger christened him "Johann von Lombardi" for the day, and the Dutch won the cigars, scoring a 6–3 win in a six-inning contest.

Donie Bush ran a tighter spring camp than Dan Howley. He set the team to work right away with fielding and hitting drills, all the while proclaiming his belief in "hustle." He put up a sign on the outfield wall in the Tampa ballpark that read, "No Loafing." As Bush told the Associated Press, "The Reds lost a flock of games by one run [in 1932], nearly 50 of them. Now that is simply murder and if hustling can overcome that habit I believe the boys will furnish it. I sincerely believe the Reds no longer will be push-overs."[4] Actually, the Reds lost 34 one run games while winning 19. Still, the new manager's expectations were modest. He expected his Reds to move up to fifth or sixth place.

The *Brooklyn Eagle* wasn't so optimistic and wrote, "Cincinnati is going to lose a lot of games at one time or another this season and they might just as well get the bad news to the good burghers along the American Rhine quickly."[5] Perhaps it was an omen when the new manager fell ill with blood poisoning from an infected blister on his foot. The foot swelled up so much that Bush could not put a shoe on it, so he went to Cincinnati for treatment and missed the last two weeks of spring training. Coach Jewel Ens took over the club and brought it north to start the season.

The Reds played at a .500 pace in April and May, and after a split of a Memorial Day doubleheader against the Pirates, they stood in third place, only four and a half games out of the lead. But the turning point of the 1933 season came in early May when, for once, Branch Rickey approached Sidney Weil with hat in hand. The Cardinals desperately needed a shortstop after their starter, Charlie Gelbert, suffered a gunshot wound in a hunting accident that put him out of action for two years. Rickey wanted Leo Durocher, and on May 7, Weil sent Durocher and two minor players to the Cardinals for pitcher Paul Derringer and two more minor players.

The Cincinnati fans were outraged. Durocher never hit much, but his outstanding shortstop play anchored the Cincinnati defense. Rickey, according to rumor, had coveted Durocher for months, and some local reporters wondered in print if the deal was made to even the scales for the Bottomley transaction several months before. However, the trade wound up helping both clubs. Durocher sparked the Cardinals to a World Series championship in 1934, while the Reds obtained a future star in Paul Derringer.

Derringer, a 26-year-old right-hander, was once the top prospect in the Cardinal farm system. In 1931 he won 18 games as a rookie and appeared to be the team's ace of the future. However, Derringer lost both games he pitched in the 1931 World Series and went 11–14 in 1932. With the emergence of Dizzy Dean as a right-handed starter, Rickey decided to trade Derringer to fill his most urgent need.

More ill fortune befell the Reds in mid–May. Donie Bush became ill once again, this time with a combination of pneumonia and pleurisy. The illness was so severe that Bush returned to his home in Indianapolis and remained bedridden for four weeks. Jewel Ens took control of the team again, but Bush's absence made it impossible to implement his program in his first year as manager.

All the while, Ernie Lombardi struggled mightily out of the gate. His average stood at .103 at the end of April and remained under the .200 mark well into June. Nonetheless, Bush kept Ernie in the lineup, waiting for his hitting to improve. Rollie Hemsley and Clyde Manion were no better, so during the first few months of the season, the Reds received almost no offensive production from their catchers. As Tom Swope of the *Cincinnati Post* wrote of Ernie's slump, "The first time Ernie Lombardi of the Reds gets into his stride and socks a fair ball over some fence, he's likely to have a bronze plate erected on the fence to commemorate the event."[6] Ernie finally connected for his first home run of the season on May 2 in Boston, a 400-foot shot that provided the margin of victory in a 2–1 win over the Braves.

Ens kept the team afloat for a while, but in June, the Reds totally collapsed. The team held fourth place, 6.5 games out of first, with a record of

27–26 on June 13 after winning the first four games of a five-game home series against the Cubs, but managed only two hits in the last game, a 7–0 loss. The league-leading Cardinals then traveled to Cincinnati and walloped the Reds by scores of 17–2 and 13–1. The veteran Eppa Rixey threw a complete game win against the Cardinals in the final game of the series, scattering 13 hits, but the Reds went on the road and dropped nine of their next 10. By July 11 they had fallen behind the Phillies into last place.

Donie Bush was so desperate to find some offense that he decided to sacrifice some defense to get it. He had benched George Grantham for a while because of his poor defense but restored "Boots" to a regular spot at second base. He also increased Ernie Lombardi's workload, moving the better-fielding Rollie Hemsley to backup status. "Our pitching has become so uncertain," said Bush to *The Sporting News*, "[that] we have reached a point where we must try to overpower the opposition and Grantham and Lombardi have the batting skill to help in that direction if they only can break loose at the plate in their old-time form."[7]

Paul Derringer, though he pitched well, established himself as the unluckiest pitcher in baseball. Due to anemic run support, Derringer lost 27 games (25 with the Reds after losing two with the Cardinals) with seven wins. No major league pitcher has lost that many decisions in a season since, as of the close of the 2022 season. Red Lucas (10–16) and Si Johnson (7–18) fared little better, mostly due to poor run support. The Reds scored only 496 runs, the lowest total in the league, and also finished last in batting average, runs, hits, and home runs.

Bush's latest moves didn't help much. Red Lucas, the always-dependable pitcher, lost seven decisions in a row from mid–May to mid–July. One of those defeats was Cincinnati's worst loss of the season, a 17–2 stomping at the hands of the St. Louis Cardinals, in which Lucas lasted only one inning. To break his personal losing skid, Lucas threw a 15-inning, nine-hit shutout for a 1–0 win over the Giants on July 16. Perhaps the effort took a lot out of his arm, for Lucas won only three of his final 12 decisions in 1933.

Unlike the richer, more successful teams like the Yankees and Cardinals, the Reds simply did not have the manpower to overcome injuries. Whenever Lombardi was out of action, Rollie Hemsley filled in, but batted so poorly (.190) that the club traded him in August to the St. Louis Browns. Clyde Manion, who batted .167 in 1933, was no improvement. Another disaster occurred on August 3, when George Grantham broke his leg while sliding into third. Grantham was out for the season, leaving the light-hitting Joe Morrissey to man second.

The Reds were so short on talent that they signed Eddie Hunter, a former minor league infielder who in 1933 was playing amateur ball. Hunter made it into one game as a late-inning replacement at third base, in which he saw no fielding chances and did not come to bat. That was the extent of Eddie Hunter's major league career. On July 31, the Reds sent pitcher Bob Smith the Braves for the waiver price. Smith had pitched well for the Reds, mostly in relief, but Sidney Weil needed the money more than he needed a relief pitcher. Weil even signed the 49-year-old Jack Quinn, the oldest player in baseball and one of the last remaining spitball pitchers in the majors. Quinn, recently released by the Dodgers, lasted only two months before he was dropped, no doubt to save on his salary.

The Reds were not hitting, the loss of Leo Durocher damaged their infield defense, and the team sank further into the National League cellar. Donie Bush tried everything, but a 10-game losing streak in late July, and another 10-game skid in mid–August, left the Reds gasping for air. The fans lost interest as well, and crowds of less than 1,000 people became common on weekdays. Sidney Weil, trying desperately to stave off bankruptcy, looked at the attendance figures with alarm. Weil had used his stock in the ballclub as collateral for loans to keep his ailing businesses afloat, and the disastrous performance of the 1933 Reds spelled trouble for the financially stressed team owner.

Ernie's worst injury of 1933 came on July 21, when a collision at the plate damaged his left side and put him out of action for 13 games. He finally re-entered the lineup on August 8 in an exhibition game in Huntington, West Virginia. Lombardi pounded one of the longest homers ever seen in Huntington that day, and resumed his good hitting until September 6, when Tony Cuccinello of the Dodgers spiked Ernie in the left knee at the plate. He sat out a few games, then caught almost all the games the rest of the way.

Ernie Lombardi's record tailed off a bit in his second season with the Reds. This time, he hit poorly in the early stages of the campaign but found his stroke as the summer wore on. He ended the year with a .283 batting average, down 20 points from the year before, and scored only 30 runs in the 107 games he played. His total of triples fell from nine to one, though his count of stolen bases—two—would prove to be a career high. Ernie also grounded into 26 double plays, leading the league by five. He performed well, especially in the second half, but he could not yet be called a star.

Also, the jury was still out on Ernie's catching. The *Brooklyn Eagle* said that Lom "defensively is pretty sad, especially on low balls,"[8] and he won no points for his handling of the woeful pitching staff. His passed balls dropped from 17 in 1932 to nine, though his range factor still remained well below the league average. The *Eagle*, in a post-season analysis, laid the problems in Cincinnati at three positions—second base, shortstop, and catcher. "Durocher, the great shortstop, was traded to the Cards. George Grantham, second baseman, broke his hand. And Ernie Lombardi proved to be the worst defensive catcher in the majors."[9]

Still, the other National League teams respected Ernie's bat. When Ernie suffered a thumb injury from a foul tip on July 11 and was unable to play against Philadelphia two days later, the papers reported that Phillies manager Burt Shotton wore a smile on his face. "That's a break for us," said Shotton. "We won't have to be worrying how to keep him from breaking up the game with his bat."[10] The Reds won the game anyway.

By the end of the 1933 campaign, Ernie had established himself as a major league starter with identifiable strengths (hitting for average, arm strength) and faults (lack of speed, passed balls). Perhaps the league did not yet take him seriously; his entry in the annual book *Who's Who in Major League Baseball* for 1933, which identified him as Ernest Natali "Snozz" Lombardi, spent the first few paragraphs talking about his nose. But the Cincinnati fans loved their "giant Italian catcher," as the papers called him, and, as one of the team's few offensive threats, his position with the Reds looked secure.

Lombardi's photo from *Who's Who in Major League Baseball, 1933* (author's collection).

The problem was that the attendance at Redland Field was falling with each passing year. The Reds drew slightly more than 218,000 fans in 1933, less than 2,800 per game, far too few for the team to even dream of turning a profit. Sidney Weil was losing money hand over fist, and various rumors circulated that the club was close to being sold, folded, or taken over by the National League. When Ernie went home to Oakland in October, he had no idea what the fall and winter months would bring for his team.

5

The Crosley Era

"All season long, [Lombardi]'s just about murdered our pitching. He's just another hitter to most clubs but to us he's been poison."[1]
—Bill McKechnie, Boston Braves manager,
August 1933

Sidney Weil could no longer keep up with the financial demands of owning the Reds. To keep his failing businesses afloat, he had used his shares of the team as collateral for loans from the Central Trust Company, and when he defaulted on his loans in the fall of 1933, he was forced to give up the club. The bank took control of the last-place team and cast about for a baseball man to operate the Reds while the bank searched for a new owner.

The bank directors wanted to hire Branch Rickey, but Rickey was reluctant to leave his post with the St. Louis Cardinals. Instead, Rickey recommended Leland Stanford (Larry) MacPhail, who had operated the Cardinal farm club in Columbus, Ohio, with great success, for the job of rebuilding the Reds. In November of 1933 the bank hired MacPhail and gave him full control of the baseball operation.

Larry MacPhail was a 43-year-old lawyer and World War I veteran who brokered the sale of the failing minor league team in Columbus, Ohio, to Branch Rickey and the Cardinals. Rickey made MacPhail the business manager of the team, and MacPhail restored the team to health, by installing lights for night games and financing the construction of a new, modern stadium. Attendance soared, even at the height of the Depression, and in 1932 the Columbus team outdrew the parent Cardinals, 310,000 to 279,000. But MacPhail was a loud, abrasive, and aggressive man who drank heavily, and he and the teetotaling, church-going Rickey clashed repeatedly. Rickey fired MacPhail in 1933, but recognized his talent, and knew that MacPhail could resuscitate the moribund Reds.

MacPhail set to work in remaking the talent-poor roster and began his tenure by putting every Red—even Ernie Lombardi, the team's best hitter and most popular player—on the waiver wire. This allowed MacPhail to determine which of his players were wanted by the other National League teams, and the new general manager made a slew of deals, with several players (including George Grantham, Red Lucas, Otto Bluege, and more) leaving and others arriving. Most of those deals, as before, were made with the Cardinals. "No other team will do business, so why shouldn't we trade with the Cardinals if we figure we can strengthen our team?" asked MacPhail, somewhat defensively. "The Cardinals own an army of ball players and always are willing to do business."[2]

In an effort to gain attention for his new club, the publicity-conscious MacPhail floated a rumor that he might hire Babe Ruth as Cincinnati's playing manager. Ruth, though still a home run hitter at age 39, was on the downside of his career with the Yankees and failed to get along with manager Joe McCarthy, whose job he openly coveted. Ruth himself was willing to entertain the idea, but Yankees owner Jacob Ruppert was not. Ruppert believed that MacPhail and the Brooklyn Dodgers were conspiring to bring Ruth to Cincinnati, after which the Reds would deal him to the Dodgers to compete with the Yankees in New York.[3]

Nothing came of the Ruth rumors, and other reports said that MacPhail wanted to trade Ernie Lombardi to the Phillies for catcher Jimmie Wilson, who would then become the Reds' playing manager. Wilson was eight years older than Ernie and highly respected in baseball circles; he had caught for the National League in the first All-Star Game in 1933 and had a good reputation for handling pitchers. But the Phillies turned down the proposed swap, keeping Wilson and hiring him as their manager. In January, MacPhail made a trade with the Cardinals that brought in veteran catcher Bob O'Farrell, who had managed St. Louis in 1927. MacPhail installed O'Farrell as his new manager and catcher.

Bob O'Farrell was a highly regarded catcher who began his major league career as a teenager with the Cubs in 1915. Traded to the Cardinals in 1925, O'Farrell enjoyed the year of his life in 1926, leading St. Louis to its first pennant and winning the National League Most Valuable Player award. In the ninth inning of the last game of the World Series, O'Farrell threw out Babe Ruth, who tried to steal second, ending the Series and giving the Cardinals their first world title.

When playing manager Rogers Hornsby and team owner Sam Breadon had a falling out over contract terms at season's end, Breadon stunned the baseball world when he traded Hornsby to the New York Giants and named O'Farrell to succeed him. Though O'Farrell's charges finished the 1927 season in second place, only a game and a half behind the pennant-winning Pirates, Breadon fired O'Farrell at season's end, then traded him to the Giants. The ex-manager eventually made his way back to the Cardinals, and now, seven years after his firing, O'Farrell received his second chance to make good as a manager.

While MacPhail wheeled and dealed, the downtrodden team remained in limbo for several months until MacPhail could find a buyer. In time, MacPhail zeroed in on one of the wealthiest men in Cincinnati, a businessman and baseball fan named Powel Crosley Junior. Crosley had passed on the opportunity to purchase the Reds several years before, but MacPhail used all his considerable powers of persuasion to convince Crosley that he, and only he, could save baseball in Cincinnati. On February 4, 1934, after several meetings with the insistent MacPhail, Crosley paid $240,000 to buy control of the team from the bank.

Unlike Sidney Weil, Powel Crosley Junior had plenty of money. The 47-year-old Crosley made his fortune in manufacturing radios, compact cars (the first in the nation), refrigerators, auto parts, and more. In 1922 he founded Cincinnati's first radio station, WLW, and by 1934 the 500,000-watt station boasted the most powerful transmitter in the United States.[4] Crosley was a director of the bank that took over the Reds after Weil's bankruptcy and bought the team mostly out of civic pride. With the team now financially stable for the first time in years, team management put Crosley's name on the ballpark. Redland Field became Crosley Field, the name it carried until the park closed in 1970.

Crosley's arrival met with approval from Reds fans, who knew that the team might have been moved out of Cincinnati or taken over by the league had he not saved it. The papers described Crosley as a smart businessman with a $15 million fortune who played polo and raced cars in his spare time. The *Cincinnati Enquirer* reported,

> He's very much interested in engines. He has an automobile he has driven 118 miles an hour and he thinks it will do 125. He drives alone, for obvious reasons. His hobby is speed.
>
> So he's in for a quick shock the first time he sees his big catcher, Ernie (Schnozzle) Lombardi, running bases.[5]

MacPhail also started building a farm system. The St. Louis Cardinals had jumped to the top of the National League with a pipeline of talent from a network of minor league teams, so MacPhail convinced Crosley to invest in player development. In 1933 the Cardinals had seven minor league teams in their system, while the Reds had only two (in Topeka, Kansas, and Rock Island, Illinois). MacPhail signed a working agreement with Toronto of the International League, giving the Reds a team at the top level of the minors for the first time.

O'Farrell, who like MacPhail was not impressed with Lombardi's defense, stated that he planned to catch as many as 100 games in 1934,

5. The Crosley Era

using Ernie as a backup catcher and pinch-hitter. MacPhail even told the newspapers that Ernie would benefit from dancing lessons to improve his footwork behind the plate. The new general manager explained that Jake Daubert, a two-time batting champion and star of the Reds in their 1919 Championship season, became a fine fielding first baseman after he learned to dance. Ernie's reaction to this suggestion was not recorded.

Lom reacted negatively, however, to the contract that MacPhail sent to him during the winter. The money-losing Reds were slashing salaries wherever possible, and Ernie's contract called for a $2,500 cut. The big catcher refused to sign and made plans to travel to spring training in Tampa in late February to negotiate with MacPhail personally. Not wanting to have a holdout drama play out in camp, MacPhail instructed Reds scout Charles Chapman, who lived in Berkeley, to meet with Lombardi and hammer out a deal. On February 23, the two men agreed to a contract with a cut of $1,250, and Lombardi boarded a train to Florida for the start of spring training.

In a bid to uncover talent, and to populate the new farm system, MacPhail and O'Farrell gathered more than 50 players, many of them raw and untried, to the training camp. One invitee was Beattie Feathers, an All-American running back at the University of Tennessee. Feathers failed to make the club as an outfielder and elected to play pro football instead. That fall, playing for the Chicago Bears, he became the first man in NFL history to rush for over 1,000 years in a season. Another familiar face in camp belonged to Dazzy Vance, the onetime strikeout king of the Brooklyn Dodgers. Vance, at age 43, was at the end of the line, but O'Farrell believed that he had one more comeback left in his arm.

However, Eppa Rixey, a 21-year veteran, was finished. Rixey was not happy with Donie Bush, who pitched him mostly against Pittsburgh in 1933, so he told MacPhail that he wanted to take the mound against other teams as well. MacPhail told Rixey that it was O'Farrell's decision, not his, so Rixey, at age 43, announced his retirement after 13 seasons with the club. Rixey is, as of the 2022 season, still Cincinnati's all-time leader in wins by a pitcher. Jack Quinn, now 50 years old, also hung up his glove. At least the average age of the Cincinnati pitching staff would be much lower in 1934.

With his starting job on the line, Ernie hit the ball at a ferocious pace at training camp. He had stayed in shape by playing in charity games in the Bay Area, and he was ready for action. On his first day in Tampa, he took batting practice against Dazzy Vance and pounded three home runs on the first three pitches. O'Farrell, who also hit well in the spring, was not ready to concede the starting position. He told the papers that he would catch Paul Derringer and Si Johnson, while Ernie would work with Dazzy Vance and Larry Benton.

The new manager also welcomed the news that the National League had adopted a new, livelier baseball for the 1934 season. "If Lombardi continues to plaster that livelier ball," said O'Farrell, "I won't be able to keep him out of there."[6] But O'Farrell was determined to share the catching job, though Ernie's potent bat was sorely needed in the lineup.

More than 30,000 fans, energized by new ownership and a strong spring performance, jammed the newly-named Crosley Field for the season opener on Tuesday, April 17, only to see the Chicago Cubs dominate the Reds. With O'Farrell catching and Ernie on the bench, the Reds put up a good fight until the sixth inning, when the Cubs scored four runs off Si Johnson to take a 5–0 lead. All the while, Lon Warneke mowed down the overmatched Cincinnati batters, striking out 13 men and carrying a no-hitter into the ninth. Ernie, inserted as a pinch hitter, struck out to lead off the final frame, and then Adam Comorosky broke up the no-hitter with a single. The Cubs won the game by a 6–0 score as Warneke completed a one-hit shutout.

Ernie poses before a game on the road. Notice the interlocking grip he uses on his bat (National Baseball Hall of Fame Library, Cooperstown, New York).

It was mostly downhill from there. The Reds won only one of their first seven games, and on June 9 they stood in last place with nine wins and 32 losses. Ernie did his part, pushing his batting average over the .300 mark after a slow start, but the Reds remained in the cellar as attendance dwindled. There would be no quick fix; it would take several years for MacPhail's new farm system to produce talent, and the Reds would remain at the bottom of the league until it did so.

Dazzy Vance failed in his comeback bid, and after six undistinguished appearances was released on waivers to the Cardinals. Hard-luck right-hander Paul Derringer did not win his first game until May 22, a 10–4 victory over the Braves in which Chick Hafey and Ernie Lombardi belted home runs.

Ernie played the longest game of his career on July 1, a brutally hot day in Cincinnati. In the first game of a doubleheader, pitchers Tony Freitas of the Reds and Dizzy Dean of the Cardinals battled through 17 innings, with neither team scoring between the tenth and 16th frames. With the score tied at 5, Joe Medwick belted a homer off Freitas to give St. Louis the lead in the top of the 17th, but the Reds tied it off Dean in the bottom of the inning on a double by Tony Piet and a single by Gordon Slade. Paul Derringer, in relief of the exhausted Freitas, gave up three runs in the 18th, and though the Reds loaded the bases in their half of the inning, Medwick made a fine running catch in the outfield to end the game. Ernie, who caught the entire game, went to bat nine times and produced two singles.

By this time, Ernie was catching on a regular basis, as O'Farrell suffered a charley horse on June 16 and restricted himself to a few games a week. The regular work revitalized the big catcher, and on July 6 he whacked five hits, including a triple and a homer, and drove in six runs in a 16–15 win at St. Louis.

By mid-season, with the Reds firmly in possession of the National League cellar, MacPhail understood that rebuilding the team would take several years, not just one. Even with all the upheaval in the roster, Ernie Lombardi and the two aging ex-Cardinals—Chick Hafey and Jim Bottomley—remained the only reliable hitters on the club, and the lack of offense frustrated the pitching staff. Paul Derringer lost 21 games in 1934, while Si Johnson lost 22, and every pitcher on the club (save for reliever Don Brennan at 4–3) compiled a losing record. The Reds won only 30 of their first 90 games, and attendance at Crosley Field fell to 1933 levels, ensuring the new management group of an operating loss for the 1934 season.

MacPhail also lost patience with his manager. MacPhail was a boisterous and aggressive executive, but the soft-spoken and calm O'Farrell seemed to exude a distinct lack of dedication. MacPhail certainly noticed that after many games, whether the Reds won or lost, O'Farrell grabbed his golf clubs and bolted out of the clubhouse to get a few holes in before sunset. After a long, miserable road trip which saw the Reds win only nine of 25 games (including an embarrassing 18–0 loss to the woeful Phillies) MacPhail decided that Bob O'Farrell was too laid back to get the best out of his players.

The Reds had spent the 1930s alternating, as many teams do, between "nice guys" and "taskmasters." When nice guy Dan Howley failed, taskmaster Donie Bush took over, and when Bush failed, nice guy O'Farrell took the reins. MacPhail decided that it was time for another taskmaster. He fired O'Farrell and replaced him with Charlie Dressen.

Ernie at the bat during the mid-1930s (National Baseball Hall of Fame Library, Cooperstown, New York).

Dressen was familiar with Cincinnati, having played third base for the Reds during the late 1920s. His background bore many similarities to that of Donie Bush. Dressen was never a star, but was a feisty, hustling ballplayer who could be counted on to bring a jolt of energy to the ballclub. He managed Nashville in the Southern League for two seasons before being called up to the New York Giants as a backup infielder in September of 1933. The Giants won the pennant that year, but Dressen saw no action in the World Series against the Washington Senators. His playing career over, he returned to Nashville as manager in 1934.

Dressen made his reputation as a bold, decisive field leader in the 1933 Series. In the fourth game at Washington, the Giants held a 2–1 lead in the bottom of the 11th inning, but the Senators put two men on with only one out. After an intentional walk to load the bases, the Senators sent Cliff Bolton up to pinch hit for their pitcher, and the Giants' infielders gathered on the mound to discuss their next move with first baseman and manager Bill Terry. Accepted baseball strategy, then and now, dictated that the Giants move the infielders in close and hope for a ground ball to force the lead runner at the plate.

Dressen, uninvited, bounded out of the dugout and joined the conference. "I know Bolton from the Southern League," he told Terry. "Set the infield back. He's slow, and if the infield is back you can get two." Terry agreed and ordered the infield to play back. Just as Dressen predicted, Bolton smacked a grounder to short, and the Giants turned the double play and ended the game. Larry MacPhail, who attended the game that day, took note of Dressen's take-charge attitude.

The new manager was a talkative man, always free with his opinions and open to the local reporters. He had a healthy ego; one story says that when the Reds were behind one day, Dressen called out to his players, "Don't worry, boys, I'll think of something!" Pee Wee Reese, who played for Dressen years later with the Dodgers, said, "He drives, drives, and drives some more. If you make a mistake he'll criticize you in front of the players, thinking that the whole team should learn a lesson."[7] This was the attitude that MacPhail wanted to bring to the Reds.

Perhaps this attitude—and the departure of O'Farrell, his rival for playing time—energized Ernie Lombardi, for the big catcher went on a hitting tear under the Dressen regime. Ernie belted 15 hits in Dressen's first eight games and raised his average by 22 points in just over a week. He played in all but seven of the team's 102 remaining games in 1934, and a hot August pushed his average up to .310 at month's end.

The Reds showed signs of life in late August when they swept a four-game set at home against the Phillies, but they reverted to form in September. The Reds lost 11 of their final 12 games, with the last four losses coming in St. Louis as the Cardinals battled the Giants for the pennant. On Thursday, September 27 the Cards defeated the Reds 8 to 5 to pull within half a game of the league lead, and then the Dean brothers took over. Dizzy Dean shut out the Reds on Friday, Paul Dean beat the Reds 6 to 1 on Saturday, and Dizzy, on one day of rest, dominated the overmatched Cincinnati club with a 9–0 shutout on Sunday to clinch the flag. Dean scattered seven hits to win his 30th game of the season.

The 1934 campaign was another disappointing one for the Reds, who lost 99 games and finished 42 games behind the pennant-winning Cardinals. The attendance fell to 206,773, which was 12,500 less than the year before. But the Cincinnati franchise was financially stable for the first time in years, thanks to Larry MacPhail and Powel Crosley. The team lost money but was no longer in danger of being moved or folded.

And the Reds now owned a potential star in Ernie Lombardi. He caught in 111 games, batting .305 with nine homers and 62 runs batted in. Ernie was 26 years old, with his prime years ahead of him, and both he and the Reds had nowhere to go but up. As the always optimistic Charlie Dressen told the papers, "We ain't exactly a Red menace. But if these clubs up ahead of us stop too often for gas, we'll go right by 'em."[8]

6

Night Baseball

"Slow as he was, Lom was a good base runner. I know that sounds weird, but being a good base runner doesn't mean just stealing bases or being fast. It means never getting thrown out on a silly try. It means knowing how far you can go on a play, and making it. Lom never made any bad moves on the bases, even though it might take three singles to get him home."[1]

—Dick Bartell, National League shortstop

Leon (Goose) Goslin, a star outfielder and one-time batting champion, played all his career in the American League, but he and Ernie became friends when their teams met during spring training in Florida. Goslin joined the Tigers in 1934, the year the Detroit club opened its training camp in Lakeland, and Goslin's Tigers and Ernie's Reds (who trained in Tampa) played often. The Tigers and Reds then played exhibitions on their way North to start the season, traditionally ending with a two-game set in Cincinnati on the weekend before Opening Day.

Goslin owned perhaps the biggest nose in the American League, while Ernie's was the undisputed champion of the National, and the two men enjoyed ribbing each other. One of Goslin's favorite lines was, "Ernie, you're the only man I know who could smoke a cigar in the shower and not get it wet." Lombardi responded in kind, with barbs like "You could get by on one breath a day," and their banter lightened the mood during the training sessions.

In April of 1934, the Tigers and Reds played their final exhibition game at Crosley Field on a Sunday, two days before the season openers for both clubs. Goslin was at bat when he swung and missed an outside pitch. The force of his swing made him spin all the way around. Unfortunately, Ernie chose that moment to try to pick off a runner at second base. As he threw, his hand struck Goslin square in the face.

As Goslin bled on the ground, Ernie stood over him. "That settles it," he said. "You've got the bigger nose." Goslin lost so much blood that he spent the night in the hospital, but the injury never affected their friendship. It also gave Ernie a new insult to use. "You've got such a damn big nose," said Lombardi, "I can't even throw to second base."[2]

Ernie, a big, friendly giant of a man, was popular with his teammates, but no one ever wanted to be his roommate on the road. Chick Hafey was assigned to room with Ernie in 1934, but the big catcher's snoring drove the veteran outfielder batty. Hafey tried everything. One night he stuck a clothespin on Ernie's nose to no avail, and on another occasion, Hafey tied Ernie's big toe to the bedframe with one of his ties. That didn't work either, and when Ernie awoke, he tumbled to the floor. Ernie took his roommate's efforts in stride, and in later years, he praised the outfielder's prodigious throwing arm. "I saw him pick Pepper Martin off rounding second on a single twice in one game," Ernie said. "Pepper didn't have a chance. He was nailed by two feet."[3]

Ernie knew that he snored, and he knew that his nose was a source of amazement and humor. Yet, he never complained, at least in public, about his nickname. He'd been called "Schnozz" or "Schnozzola" since his Pacific Coast League days, and he didn't let it bother him. Comedian Jimmy Durante, a fellow Italian American with the biggest nose in show business, once compared his proboscis to Lombardi's. "His is bigger," proclaimed Durante, "but mine is more educated."[4]

However, on the field, Ernie was a very proud man. He absolutely hated to be shown up. As National League infielder Tony Cuccinello recalled, "There was a close play at second and I missed (Lombardi) sliding in. The pitcher was standing nearby. While Ernie's getting up I told the pitcher to stay off the rubber. I had the ball in my glove. The pitcher went toward the mound, picked up the rosin bag and looked in at the catcher like he's looking for the sign and Ernie walked

A 1934 Goudey Big League Chewing Gum card of Ernie (author's collection).

off the bag. When I had enough room I ran over to him and showed him the ball. Oh, he was mad. He said to me, 'You tag me and I'll punch you right in the nose.' I never tagged him. He just walked back to the dugout."5

Larry MacPhail and Powel Crosley had rescued the Cincinnati franchise, but the fans demanded a winner, and the Reds ended the 1934 season in last place. The attendance of 206,773 was the lowest in Cincinnati since the war-shortened 1918 campaign, so more work was needed to put the Reds on solid ground. MacPhail believed that a total of 400,000 paid admissions would put the team in the black, and he had an idea to achieve that goal and rekindle enthusiasm for baseball in the Queen City.

MacPhail's solution was night baseball.

Minor league clubs had installed lights and played at night for several years. One of the earliest teams to adopt night baseball was MacPhail's own Columbus team in the American Association. In 1932, MacPhail put in permanent lights and worked with engineers and lighting experts to produce the best possible result. The permanent lights were a huge success, and attendance in the Ohio city more than doubled that year.

Night baseball had its detractors, and not all previous attempts were successful. In 1930 the Kansas City Monarchs of the Negro National League put up a string of temporary lights and played a night contest against the Homestead Grays. The ball was so hard to see that Grays starting pitcher Joe Williams struck out 27 batters in a 12-inning game. His mound opponent, Chet Brewer, struck out 19. But MacPhail's installation in Columbus delivered top-notch lighting, and he knew that the concept would succeed in Cincinnati as well. At the league meetings in December of 1934, the other National League owners gave the Reds permission to stage seven night games in the upcoming season. The vote was close, with five teams supporting it and three (the Giants, Dodgers, and Pirates) in opposition.

Charlie Dressen, in his first spring training camp with the Reds, was determined to make his team younger and livelier. He and MacPhail convinced Powel Crosley to spend money for talent, so once again they made two deals with Branch Rickey, purchasing right fielder Ival Goodman from the Cardinals for $25,000 and third baseman Lew Riggs for $30,000. They also bought two minor league catchers, Gilly Campbell from Los Angeles of the Pacific Coast League and Hank Erickson from Louisville of the American Association, to challenge Ernie Lombardi for the starting position. Dressen was still not sold on Lombardi as his starter, and Campbell, often described as "peppery," appealed to the manager.

Crosley and MacPhail also laid out money to buy outfielder Sammy Byrd from the New York Yankees. Byrd spent six seasons in New York, where his main duty was to replace Babe Ruth as a pinch-runner and defensive substitute in the late innings. The writers called Byrd "Babe Ruth's Legs," but Ruth was no longer a Yankee, having been released to the Boston Braves in February of 1935. Ruth's departure made Byrd expendable, so the Reds bought him and gave him a regular starting spot for the first time in Byrd's career.

The Reds nearly acquired a future Hall of Famer to man the right side of the Cincinnati infield. Johnny Mize, a 22-year-old first baseman, was the star prospect of the St. Louis Cardinal farm system. Mize had battered opposing pitching at Rochester for two years, but a painful groin injury limited his playing time and cast his future in doubt. The Reds bought his contract from St. Louis for $55,000, but with the option to return him to the Cardinals if he could not perform. Mize hit well for the Reds, but his groin problem, coupled with spurs on his pelvic bone, caused the Reds to cancel the deal. Only after the St. Louis team physician, Dr. Robert Hyland, performed surgery on the youngster was Mize able to return to the field. He joined the Cardinals in 1936 and quickly became one of the stars of the National League.

Ernie was determined to prove himself in 1935, and though he had not yet signed his contract, he and fellow Bay Area resident Chick Hafey reported to the training camp in Tampa on March 11 after a long train ride from Oakland. Lombardi then huddled with Larry MacPhail, and after a few days of tough negotiations, hammered out a deal, most likely one that restored the cut he received the year before, with a small raise attached. The papers reported that Ernie looked fit and ready upon his arrival, and he cracked out line drives from the first day of batting practice.

MacPhail believed in speed, and he arranged a series of footraces for the Reds, with prizes awarded to the winners of two groups, with pitchers and catchers in one group and all the other players in the other. Among the catchers, Gilly Campbell easily outraced Hank Erickson and Ernie, who surprised no one by finishing last. Campbell had caught Charlie Dressen's eye, and due to his superior speed, Dressen gave Campbell every opportunity to claim the starting job.

Indeed, Campbell fully expected to supplant Ernie as the regular catcher. His bosses in Los Angeles, where he played in 1934, allowed Campbell to choose which major league team he wanted to join, and Campbell picked Cincinnati because he thought that he had a better chance at a starting job with the Reds than with any other club. But Ernie hit so well during training camp that Campbell knew he had a battle on his hands. "I'll either catch most of this club's games or make a great catcher out of someone,"[6] Campbell told the *Cincinnati Post*.

Ernie took the challenge from Campbell seriously. He worked hard in Tampa, not only on his hitting, but on his defense as well. "Whether competition is putting new pep in Lombardi or the big Italian is coming into his own is difficult to decide," reported the *Post*. "The main thing is that Lombardi is a much smoother workman back of the bat this year than in the past and that, regardless of whether he or Campbell does the more catching, the Reds appear well heeled in this department."[7]

Campbell got his chance in the season's opening game, a 12–6 loss to the Pirates, when Ernie took a foul tip off his knee in the ninth inning and had to leave the game. The painful bruise that resulted kept Ernie out of action for three days. When Lombardi returned, he and Campbell shared the catching position, with Campbell getting most of the starting assignments in April and Ernie pinch hitting. Ernie started slowly at the bat, but on May 8, in a 15–4 rout of the Phillies in Philadelphia, Ernie belted four doubles off four different pitchers. His four doubles in one game tied the major league record, which still stands, and lifted his batting average from .136 to .286.

This performance put Ernie back into the number one position, and he started most of the games for the rest of the month. Nine hits in four games in late May pushed his average toward the top of the league listings, while Campbell held his own on offense and defense and Hank Erickson filled in where needed. For all the team's other problems, the Cincinnati catching corps was one of the most solid in the league.

Lombardi's hitting surge was welcome news for the Reds, who lost one of their stars in early May. Chick Hafey, the starting center fielder, was the team's best hitter in April, but a bout of influenza knocked him out of the lineup. The flu, combined with his chronic sinus problems, kept him away from the team for three weeks. He returned in late May but suffered a relapse, after which he decided to go home to California. Hafey sat out the rest of the 1935 season, leaving a hole in the Cincinnati lineup.

MacPhail tried his best to improve the offense. On June 21 he re-acquired Babe Herman, buying the hard-hitting but troublesome outfielder from Pittsburgh in a straight cash

Chick Hafey, the former Cardinal star who played his last few seasons for the Reds (National Baseball Hall of Fame Library, Cooperstown, New York).

transaction. In less than four years, Herman had bounced from the Dodgers to the Reds to the Cubs to the Pirates and, now, back to the Reds. Two weeks later, MacPhail scooped up Hazen (Kiki) Cuyler, who had just been released by the Chicago Cubs. Cuyler was once one of baseball's brightest stars, but a serious leg injury in 1934 robbed him of his speed, though he could still hit.

To some, these transactions reeked of desperation. The Cincinnati roster was full of former stars like Jim Bottomley, Chick Hafey, and now Herman and Cuyler, men in their 30s who were recognizable names but were now on the downside of their careers and were unwanted by other teams. It also appeared that the powerful St. Louis Cardinals used the Cincinnati club as a dumping ground for players they no longer needed. But MacPhail's farm system was just getting started. In a few years, reasoned the Cincinnati general manager, the farm would provide new, rising stars to replace the old, fading ones.

Soon after Hafey's departure, Ernie turned on the power. He hit no home runs in April or May, but beginning on June 9, Lom belted six homers in six games, all on the road. The Reds lost five of those contests, but the only win, on June 11 at the Polo Grounds, featured a homer and two singles by Ernie, who scored twice in a 4–1 victory. On July 3, with the Reds and Cubs tied at 3 in the bottom of the ninth at Crosley Field, he belted a walk-off four-bagger to win the game for Paul Derringer.

In the meantime, Derringer began to fulfill his promise. After losing 27 and 21 in his previous two seasons, Derringer won 22 games in 1935 and established himself as the team's number one starter.

Also, after mid-season, the Reds had a solid outfield, with Babe Herman in left, Sammy Byrd in center, and rookie Ival Goodman in right. Goodman, at age 26, led the Reds in runs scored, runs batted in, and stolen bases. The pitching staff needed improvement, but the Reds, while not yet a first division club, were no longer the worst in the National League. They spent the last half of the season fighting with the Dodgers and Phillies for the fifth, sixth, and seventh positions.

The Cincinnati club was saved from the cellar by the total implosion of the Boston Braves. The Braves, under manager Bill McKechnie, had enjoyed some success, finishing fourth in 1933 and again in 1934 with an undermanned, poorly funded ballclub. But in 1935 team owner Emil Fuchs hired Babe Ruth as a player, vice president, and assistant manager. This signing turned into a disaster, as Ruth could no longer play and believed that he would soon take McKechnie's job. Ruth's ambitions caused friction with McKechnie and turmoil in the clubhouse. The controversy, and the news that Fuchs was nearly bankrupt, caused Ruth to quit the team in June. In August Fuchs gave up control of the club, and the demoralized Braves lost 115 games.

6. Night Baseball

A finish in the top four was out of the question by August, but the Reds fought the Dodgers and Phillies for fifth position. On August 10 Ernie provided the offense in a 2–0 win over the Pirates; he homered in the second inning and in the fourth, he doubled, took third on a sacrifice, and scored on a fly ball. On August 26 Lombardi drove home two runs and contributed three hits against Brooklyn before Babe Herman's home run won the game in the ninth for Derringer. Herman and Lombardi, the team's two best hitters, and Derringer, its ace pitcher, kept the Reds in the fight for fifth place.

A foul tip off his elbow knocked Ernie out of a game at Chicago on September 2, but when Gilly Campbell took to the bench with a sore arm and Hank Erickson was severely injured in an auto accident, Ernie wrapped his elbow tightly and continued to play. As it turned out, the elbow was chipped, and Ernie needed an operation to remove the floating piece of bone. But the Reds had no healthy catchers, so Ernie played through the pain as the Reds fought for fifth place. In the end, the Reds gained the fifth position during the last week of the season, but two losses to the Cardinals and one to the Pirates dropped the Reds back to sixth, where they finished the campaign.

Ernie beat out a bunt on the last day of the 1935 campaign, a feat that made the pitcher, Claude Passeau, livid with anger years later. Passeau made his major league debut for the Pirates that day, with Lee Grissom on the mound for the Reds. But Charlie Dressen planned, once the Reds gained the lead, to bring in Paul Derringer to help him gain his 22nd win. Larry MacPhail had promised Derringer a $1,000 bonus for every win over twenty, and Dressen wanted his star pitcher to get it. The problem, related Passeau, was that his Pittsburgh teammates were in on it too.

"The first major league hit made off me," recalled Passeau in 1947, "was a bunt by Ernie Lombardi. Can you imagine that—a guy who couldn't catch a bad cold at the North Pole in a dirty undershirt. The Pirates were just giving those Reds hits. If a ball wasn't smacked right at somebody, it was good for a safe one, and there I was pitching my first game and sweating blood."

The Reds took the lead, and according to plan, Dressen removed Grissom in the fifth inning and brought in Derringer, who went the rest of the way and won the game. Passeau, a tough competitor, never forgot it. "I've spent years looking all those Pirates up and telling them just what I think of them—in words of one syllable and sometimes two," he said. "They were just giving Derringer that $1,000. I still want to fight when I think of it."[8]

For the Cincinnati Reds, the 1935 season was one of slow progress. Night baseball was a huge success, driving the total attendance for the year to over 448,000, more than double the year before. Paul Derringer was an All-Star for the first time, Ival Goodman led the league in triples, and Ernie Lombardi finished with a .343 batting average, fourth best in the league.

Charlie Dressen was not yet ready to make Ernie the undisputed number one catcher. Lombardi started 76 games in 1935, almost half the games on the schedule, with Gilly Campbell making most of the rest of the starts. Dressen also used Ernie as his main bat off the bench, giving him 43 pinch-hitting assignments. But Ernie proved his toughness, playing in pain during September. On October 1, two days after the close of the season, Ernie underwent an operation in Cincinnati to remove the chipped bone. The operation was a success, and Ernie returned to Oakland to spend the winter.

7

An All-Star Year

> "[Lombardi] used to hit screamers, and most of 'em were sinking line drives. Lom was the only man I ever was afraid would hit a line drive back at me and kill me. The third baseman always wanted me to pitch him outside. I finally said the hell with that—I was only 60 feet away from Lombardi. All the other guys were way back on the grass."[1]
> —Carl Hubbell, New York Giants pitcher

The 1935 Reds finished in sixth place, and the 1936 Reds would have to go on without one of its few good hitters. Chick Hafey left the team in May of 1935 after only 15 games, suffering from the flu, and after three weeks of rest he rejoined the club. A sudden relapse put him on the sidelines again, and in mid-season, with his health still uncertain, he decided to sit out the rest of the campaign. In early 1936 Hafey informed the Reds that he had decided to retire. Charlie Dressen tried to coax him back to the Reds, but Hafey's condition had not improved. "If I get to feeling better, I'll check in late in May," said Hafey. "But the way I feel now, I'll never play again."[2]

The Reds also lost Jim Bottomley, traded to the St. Louis Browns during spring training. Bottomley's production had tailed off sharply in 1935, so Larry MacPhail sent him to the American League, receiving infielder Johnny Burnett in return. MacPhail then made a deal with the New York Yankees to acquire George McQuinn, a young first baseman who was blocked in the Yankee system by Lou Gehrig. Both MacPhail and Dressen expected McQuinn to be an improvement on the aging Bottomley.

So desperate were the Reds for power in the lineup that MacPhail reached out to the most powerful hitter of all. Babe Ruth's career with the Yankees ended after the 1934 season, and he opened 1935 as the starting left fielder for the Boston Braves. But the Babe was finished, and aside from one memorable game in Pittsburgh in which he walloped three homers, Ruth proved that he could no longer play. He batted .181 in 28 games and the Boston pitchers threatened to go on strike if he continued to stumble around in the outfield. Ruth quit the Braves in May, but in March of 1936

MacPhail offered the 41-year-old Ruth a contract. Nothing came of the offer, and reports stated that the Babe was willing to suit up for Cincinnati, but his wife talked him out of it.[3]

In the meantime, two of Cincinnati's best hitters decided to hold out for better pay. One was the always-difficult Babe Herman, who battered the ball at a .335 clip after MacPhail brought him in from Pittsburgh to replace Chick Hafey.

The other was Ernie Lombardi.

Ernie's 1935 season was the best of his career so far. His .343 average (fourth best in the league) and outstanding plate discipline (he struck out only six times all year) convinced Ernie that he deserved not only a raise, but a substantial one. He had, for the first time, gained some votes in the Most Valuable Player balloting. He had proven his toughness, playing in pain during September and holding off his elbow surgery until the season was over. Also, thought Ernie, he deserved some credit for helping Paul Derringer blossom from a 20-game loser to a 22-game winner in 1935. Lombardi, at age 27, was a star on the rise, and probably the key performer on the Cincinnati team.

Though Charlie Dressen still boosted Gilly Campbell's prospects as a starting catcher, Ernie's holdout made the manager nervous. "We'll look pretty sick in the slugging column without some of Ernie's long distance swats,"[4] he told the Associated Press in February. But Ernie was a determined sort, and when spring training began, neither Ernie nor Babe Herman was present. So MacPhail made a deal with Oakland to acquire Billy Raimondi, who succeeded Ernie at catcher for the Oaks, on a conditional basis.

MacPhail had always been fascinated with Latin America and the Caribbean, and in early February he gathered his Reds, some in New York and the rest in Miami, for what *The Sporting News* called "the most adventurous spring training program ever undertaken by a ball club."[5] The Reds flew from New York and sailed from Miami for a series of games in Puerto Rico. The Reds played local all-star teams in San Juan and Ponce, then played two more games in the Dominican Republic before resuming their spring practice in Tampa. The Latin American crowds were large and enthusiastic, though the most popular Red was nowhere to be found. Ernie Lombardi was still in Oakland, waiting for MacPhail to offer a salary he thought he deserved.

Ernie was less than thrilled about going to Latin America anyway. He had been to Cuba once before, when the Brooklyn club trained there for two weeks in 1931, and the big catcher had no burning desire to see the Caribbean again. "Larry MacPhail asked us to report to Puerto Rico on the fourth of January," he said years later. "Imagine that? Ival Goodman and I refused to go that early." Pitcher Ray (Peaches) Davis didn't like it either. "[Davis] wrote a letter to MacPhail, and guess what he said? He said he'd agree to go to Puerto Rico if MacPhail would let him drive there."[6]

As the holdout dragged on into March, MacPhail grew frustrated. One reporter asked what would happen if Lombardi and Herman held out all the way into 1937; MacPhail grumpily replied that they could hold out until 1987 for all he cared. In mid–March, the general manager asked both Lombardi and Herman to come to Tampa and negotiate in person. Ernie agreed and set out on a cross-country trek, driving all the way from Oakland to Tampa in five and a half days.

Most observers believed that Ernie's holdout was nearing its end, but the big catcher remained defiant. He arrived in Tampa on March 17, but told the papers that if his negotiations failed, he would be happy to turn his car around and drive the five and a half days back to Oakland. This attitude annoyed MacPhail, but on March 19 Ernie and the Reds finally came to terms. The exact figures were not disclosed, but Ernie received a healthy raise; some claimed that his pay jumped by 40 percent, putting him in the $10,000 range for the first time. He was now, by general consensus, the second-highest paid catcher in the National League behind Chicago's Gabby Hartnett, who was eight years older.

Ernie was never worried about his physical condition in the spring. "I was always heavy," he said, "but I still needed only two or three weeks to round into shape. After that, we'd play exhibitions, which I think a player needs. You can't get your timing when someone just lobs the ball up to you in batting practice. Only actual game competition sharpens the eye."[7] Besides, he played in exhibition games in the Bay Area before heading east, so he always believed that he had a head start on teammates who came from colder climates.

Still, Ernie's speed, or lack of it, was still an issue. In 1935 he scored only 36 runs in 120 games, and though he grounded into 11 double plays, a career low, he failed on both of his stolen base attempts. Several years earlier, the Oakland Oaks hired a track coach named Walter Christie to work with Ernie during the off-season. Christie claimed that he could make Ernie faster by "two or three steps." The attempt failed miserably. "I showed up one day," said Ernie, "did what he told me, and then spent the next week in bed. I decided I was fast enough."[8]

Ernie was ready for the season to start. In an exhibition game against the Detroit Tigers in Florence, South Carolina, in early April, Ernie walloped a ball off Tigers starter Schoolboy Rowe that, as the *Cincinnati Enquirer* reported, "not only cleared the left field wall, but landed clear across the street outside of left field, finding a final resting place among the houses."[9] However, the ballpark was a tiny one, and the Reds and Tigers agreed before the game to count balls hit over the short fences in left and right field as doubles. It was the longest double Ernie ever hit.

At the end of training camp, Ernie and Gilly Campbell claimed the two catching jobs. The Reds sent Billy Raimondi back to Oakland, where he spent the rest of his career without ever playing a single major league game. Raimondi, a San Francisco native, and Ernie were friends from Bay Area baseball circles, and their paths would cross again a dozen years down the road.

Charlie Dressen made no promises, but he aimed to break into the first division in 1936. The top tier of the National League had consisted of the same four teams—the Giants, Cubs, Pirates, and Cardinals—for several years, and the Reds would have to find a way to dislodge one of those clubs. But the sixth-place finish of 1935, after four last-place finishes in a row, gave the Cincinnati fans cause for optimism. At long last, the Reds appeared to be headed in the right direction.

Charlie Dressen became manager of the Reds in July of 1934 (National Baseball Hall of Fame Library, Cooperstown, New York).

To keep his players focused, Dressen instituted a system or fines and rewards for his men. Dressen decreed that if a batter failed to drive in a runner from third with less than two out and less than a four-run lead, the player paid two dollars into Dressen's fund. But if that batter succeeded, he received two dollars. Likewise, a pitcher who failed to lay down a bunt to advance a runner was fined two dollars, but one who succeeded was given two dollars from the fund. For the first few days, it worked so well that Dressen had to make up the difference when one pitcher paid into the fund while several batters received payouts.

Ernie Lombardi needed no monetary incentive. Batting in the cleanup spot behind Babe Herman,

7. An All-Star Year

Ernie started the season hot, batting .439 in April and keeping his average among the league leaders through May. Ernie also followed Dressen's example and became more assertive to the umpires. In late May, the Reds became enraged at Babe Pinelli's decision on a ground rule double. Pinelli had recommended Ernie to the Oakland Oaks many years before, but Ernie not only pushed the much smaller umpire, but kicked Pinelli's mask all the way to the backstop. Somehow, Ernie avoided the first ejection of his major league career that day.

He also provided some unintentional comedy on May 13, when Jimmie Wilson, manager and catcher of the Phillies, ordered his pitcher to walk Lom intentionally. Wilson did not bother to put on his mask while receiving the four outside pitches and left it lying on the ground in the batter's box. Lombardi absent-mindedly picked it up and stood at the plate with the mask in one hand and his bat in the other as he watched the first two pitches go by. Then he realized that Wilson's mask was in his hand, and he tossed it aside in embarrassment.

Sammy Byrd, an outfielder who joined the Reds in 1935 after six years as a reserve with the Yankees, hit only two home runs in 1936, but one of them made history. On May 23, the Reds trailed the Pirates by a 3–0 score in the bottom of the ninth at Crosley Field. Pirate pitcher Bill Swift had throttled the Reds all day, but in the ninth Cincinnati's Lee Handley and pinch-hitter Calvin Chapman singled, and pinch-hitter Gilly Campbell walked to load the bases with none out. Pittsburgh manager Pie Traynor brought in Cy Blanton to close it out, and Charlie Dressen sent Byrd, the third pinch-hitter of the inning, up to bat for Don Brennan.

Byrd drilled Blanton's first pitch over the right field fence for a game-ending, walk-off grand slam to win the game. The blow was an "ultimate grand slam," turning a three-run deficit into a one-run win, and it was the third such homer in baseball history, the first by a Cincinnati Red, and the first in the National League since 1881.[10]

In June, the Reds called up first baseman Les Scarsella from their Toronto farm club. Scarsella, 23 years old, was an Italian American who was born in Santa Cruz and grew up in Richmond, just north of Oakland. He was a fan of the Oakland Oaks as a teenager, and his favorite player was none other than Ernie Lombardi. Now the two men, the only two Italians on the team, were teammates and became close friends. Scarsella filled the first base slot after George McQuinn failed to hit in April and May. Ernie and Scarsella were such good buddies that in late September, when Scarsella got married at a Cincinnati church, Ernie served as his best man.

The high point of the season came on the Fourth of July, when the Reds swept the league-leading Cardinals in a doubleheader. Ernie won the first game when he walloped a homer in the seventh inning to break a 2–2

Paul Derringer. He had an unusually high leg kick (National Baseball Hall of Fame Library, Cooperstown, New York).

tie and provide the winning margin in a 3–2 win. Gilly Campbell caught the second contest, and all looked lost when the Cardinals' Roy Parmalee took a 9–5 lead into the ninth. But after Lew Riggs tripled, Hub Walker walked, and Les Scarsella singled Riggs home, the Cardinals brought in their ace, Dizzy Dean, to relieve Parmalee. Dean struck out Babe Herman, but Ernie Lombardi pinch-hit for Billy Myers and delivered a two-run single to cut the Cardinal lead to one. Calvin Chapman's single tied the score, and the Reds scored off Dean in the tenth to win it.

The doubleheader sweep gave the Reds nine wins in their last 10 games and not only knocked the Cardinals out of first place, but also left the Reds in third position, seven games above the .500 mark. But 1936 was one of the hottest years on record in the United States, and the temperature in Cincinnati exceeded 100 degrees eight days in a row in early July. The Reds wilted in the heat, and the Cardinals gained revenge in a Sunday twin-bill on July 5, winning by scores of 8–6 and 17–7. Cincinnati lost 10 of 13 at home, falling back to the .500 mark and settling into fifth place, where they remained for the rest of the summer. By August, their pennant hopes for 1936 were, for all practical purposes, over.

One game in particular stood out. On July 26, in the first game of a doubleheader against the Giants at the Polo Grounds, Ernie hit into a triple play. With Kiki Cuyler on second and Les Scarsella on first, Ernie smashed a ball off Carl Hubbell into the deepest part of the outfield, a blow that would have been a homer in almost every other park. But center fielder Hank Lieber caught the drive and relayed the ball to Jo-Jo Moore, who dropped it. When Charlie Dressen, coaching at third, saw the ball drop, he waved the runners on, but Moore recovered and threw the ball in quickly. The relay throw caught Cuyler at third. Scarsella tried to take second and was thrown out there for the third out.

Still, the Reds entered the ninth inning with a 4–2 lead, but three Giants singles off Paul Derringer brought in one run, and Derringer then balked home another run to tie the game. Don Brennan relieved Derringer and, with Jo-Jo Moore on second, gave up a single to Lieber. Rather than throw home to get the runner at the plate, Reds left fielder Babe Herman merely lobbed the ball back to the infield as Moore scored the winning run.

Dressen was so angry that he fined Derringer $200 for issuing a balk and Herman $200 for not trying to throw Moore out. "Babe may have gotten away with things like that for other managers, but I told him he could not do it under my direction," he told the papers. "Had he thrown he might have caused Moore to stop at third. He might have retired him at the plate and he might not have done any good at all. But at least he would have been trying. And since he did not try he's out $200."[11] Herman was a famously lackadaisical fielder, and his carelessness might have been acceptable for Wilbert Robinson in Brooklyn, but not for Dressen in Cincinnati.

Derringer, a temperamental sort, was a problem for Dressen all year. In May the pitcher hit a double against the Giants with two out, and when Kiki Cuyler followed with a single, Dressen, coaching at third, waved Derringer home. It looked to Derringer that he would be out easily, so the pitcher did not bother to slide. But Jo-Jo Moore's throw from the outfield was off line, and because Derringer came in standing up, catcher Gus Mancuso was able to grab the ball and apply the tag to end the rally. The Reds eventually lost the game in 11 innings.

After the game, Dressen and Larry MacPhail suspended Derringer indefinitely. "Paul Derringer could be the best pitcher in the National League if he so desired ... [but] any player who does not give the team the best in him can't put on a uniform for me," said Dressen. "That goes for the highest paid player down to the greenest rookie."[12] After four days the manager reinstated Derringer, who told his teammates that he spent his suspension working on his golf game. Though Derringer was Cincinnati's ace, Reds management let it be known that they would listen to trade offers for the star pitcher.

However, Ernie Lombardi gained a significant honor for the first time that summer. He was named as a reserve to the All-Star team. He and third baseman Lew Riggs made the trip to Boston, as did Charlie Dressen, selected as a coach. Ernie did not get into the game, as Chicago's Gabby Hartnett caught the entire contest, but his presence was a nice bit of recognition of his value to the Reds.

Baseball was a tough game during the 1930s, and with recognition came more rough play from other teams. One day, Cardinals pitcher Jesse Haines, with Ernie at bat, motioned all his fielders to shift to the right. That made Ernie lean over the plate for an outside pitch, and Haines drilled the Reds catcher in the elbow. Brushbacks and hit batsmen were a fact of life then, as Eddie Joost, a young infielder from the Bay Area, discovered. As Joost remarked to Ernie soon after joining the team, "What kind of a league is this? Every time I came to bat I was down on my back."[13]

More rough play took place on August 24 at Chicago. Ernie Lombardi whacked three singles and a double off the Cubs' Lon Warneke in a game that was tied at 1 after eight innings. After Ernie led off the ninth with a single, Alex Kampouris came in to pinch-run. The Reds failed to score, and in the bottom of the ninth Gilly Campbell went in to catch.

Campbell didn't last long. In the tenth, Campbell reached base on a forceout and was soon forced at second himself, sliding hard into Cubs shortstop Billy Jurges. Jurges took exception to the slide and tagged Campbell on the head, then punched the Reds catcher as he lay on the ground.

7. An All-Star Year

This started a fight between the two and resulted in ejections for both. But with Ernie out of the game, the Reds were left without a catcher. Outfielder Hub Walker volunteered to put on the mask and pads and caught the bottom of the tenth, in which the Cubs scored on a single and two errors to win the game.

Perhaps Charlie Dressen should have left Ernie in. The man that the papers routinely referred to as "the big Italian catcher" enjoyed a hot streak in late August, with 15 hits in 25 times at bat to jump his average to .358. He hit so well that all during September and October, Ernie's name popped up in trade rumors that had him going to the Giants, Dodgers, or Cardinals. But Ernie was popular in Cincinnati, and the Reds had no intention of trading their best and most consistent hitter.

Lombardi put on another power surge in September. On September 10, Ernie's home run broke a 1–1 tie and led to a 7–2 win over the Giants, and five days later in Boston, Ernie's three-run shot started the scoring in a 6–0 win over the Bees (formerly called the Braves). The big catcher also stole a base that day, his only steal of the season, having accepted a bet to do so from his teammates. Both these victories came with Paul Derringer on the mound, and despite the star pitcher's behavioral issues, he and Lombardi made a great team. Derringer's competitive fire rubbed off on Ernie, and Ernie's calm demeanor helped keep Derringer on track.

While the Reds failed to crack the first division, finishing in fifth position, Ernie put together another fine year. He batted .333 to finish in seventh place in the batting race, and once again drew a few Most Valuable Player votes. He was the best hitting catcher in the National League in 1936, and his count of passed balls dropped to seven, though that figure was still enough to lead the league. At the age of 28, Ernie had entered his prime years, and both he and the Reds looked forward to more improvement in 1937.

8

Back to Last Place

"It would get so hot in Cincinnati during the summer. I remember Ernie came out to the mound when I was struggling late in the game and it was hot as hell. He looked at me and said, 'Chrissake Si, finish this game so we can get a beer.'"[1]

—Si Johnson, Reds pitcher

Larry MacPhail and Powel Crosley had saved the Cincinnati Reds, but tension between the two men escalated as the 1930s wore on. MacPhail was a prodigious drinker, and as his grandson Andy, later a respected baseball executive himself, said, "My grandfather was bombastic, flamboyant, a genius when sober, brilliant when he had one drink and a raving lunatic when he had too many."[2] MacPhail, despite his many accomplishments, had richly earned his nickname "The Roaring Redhead," and his drunken exploits embarrassed Crosley and the team. In a conservative town like Cincinnati, his behavior could no longer be tolerated, and in October 1936 MacPhail resigned under pressure.

To replace MacPhail, Crosley once again asked Branch Rickey for advice. Rickey recommended Warren Giles, who had served under Rickey as general manager of the Cardinal farm clubs at Syracuse and Rochester since 1926. The 40-year-old Giles also spent part of the 1936 season as president of the International League. Giles knew his baseball, and though he had recently signed a five-year contract to head the Rochester club, Rickey decided not to stand in the way of a promotion to the major leagues. On November 1, 1936, Crosley hired Giles as the new general manager of the Reds.

Giles immediately began to look for help on the trade front, and as usual, Ernie Lombardi's name featured prominently in the discussions. Rumor had it that the Cardinals were ready to trade their star right-hander Dizzy Dean to the Reds for Lombardi and several others. The talented but unpredictable Dean, who won 24 games in 1936, was not only holding out for more money, but he and his wife were blasting Rickey every day in the newspapers. Rickey denied the story, but instead sold catcher Virgil (Spud) Davis and shortstop Charlie Gelbert to Cincinnati.

Gelbert, who sat out the 1933 and 1934 seasons while recovering from a hunting accident, was still on the comeback trail, while Davis left St. Louis because he did not get along with Dizzy Dean. Dean refused to pitch to Davis, and Rickey decided that one of the two had to go. The acquisition of Davis, a good hitter and mediocre fielder, gave rise to more rumors that Ernie was headed to the Giants, the Dodgers, or one of several other clubs.

New York Giants manager Bill Terry had long coveted Ernie, whose right-handed line drive swing would have been a perfect fit for the Polo Grounds. In early 1937 Terry, who needed a catcher, met with Giles. "I stopped off at Cincinnati on my way to New York," said Terry, "and tried to make a deal with Warren Giles for Ernie Lombardi or Virgil Davis. Giles wanted [Giants center fielder Hank] Leiber, but so do I." Terry elected to keep Leiber, and the deal was off, though the new Cincinnati boss proved that Ernie, the most popular Red, was not untouchable.

Giles decided to keep Charlie Dressen as manager for 1937, though he had a candidate of his own. Bill McKechnie, who had won pennants with the Pirates in 1925 (winning a seven-game World Series against the Senators) and the Cardinals in 1928, was Giles' manager at Rochester in 1929 before landing in Boston to lead the moribund Braves in 1930. McKechnie achieved modest success in Boston under trying conditions, and Giles saw McKechnie as a perfect fit for the Reds. Dressen was Larry MacPhail's man, and Giles wanted to put his own stamp on the team. However, McKechnie was not yet available, as his contract with Boston had one more year to run. Giles stayed with the incumbent field leader, though his desire to hire McKechnie was one of the worst-kept secrets in baseball.

The Reds had made progress under Dressen. After a last place finish in 1934, the Cincinnati club was going in the right direction, rising to sixth position in 1935 and fifth in 1936. So Giles signed the manager to a one-year contract with a salary bump and gave Dressen the right to choose his coaches, make trades, and select the roster. The 1937 campaign would be a make-or-break season for Dressen, and he needed to guide the Reds into the first division to have a future in Cincinnati.

In response, Dressen decided that the Cincinnati ballclub needed to play the Dressen way—hard, aggressive, and unsparing. In spring training, the manager had his charges bowling over infielders to break up double plays, pitching opposing batters high and tight, and earning the name "the Roughhouse Reds" from the local newspapers. He also hired a new third-string catcher named Gus Brittain, who was better known for his fighting skill than for his baseball talent. Brittain played in only three games for the 1937 Reds, but Dressen kept him around. He believed that

National League pitchers were taking liberties with the Cincinnati hitters, and he wanted the muscular Brittain close by in case a fight broke out.

Brittain, a North Carolinian who left a trail of fights and suspensions behind him in the minors, was only too happy to oblige. "First they tell me I gotta quit fighting to stay in baseball," he said, "and now I go to the big leagues because I get into fights. Boy, oh boy! If it's fights they want I'll supply 'em."[3]

The papers were filled with mentions of the new "Roughhouse Reds," but the players were slow to buy into it. Reportedly, many of the Reds viewed Dressen's new attitude as a desperate bid to save his job, and before long the players were mocking their manager behind his back. And Gus Brittain got into only one fight all year—against his own teammate Paul Derringer in the dugout. Derringer took exception to a sarcastic remark and smacked Brittain in the head with a catcher's mask, after which Brittain tackled the Cincinnati ace and pummeled him before the other Reds could pull him off.

The tempestuous Derringer had other problems. His wife filed for divorce in March of 1936, and in June of that year he got into a drunken fracas at a hotel in Philadelphia, and a warrant was issued for his arrest. For a while it looked as if the All-Star pitcher might face a prison term, but he avoided that fate, though he lost the case at trial and had to pay $8,000 in damages to a man he injured. The Reds helped him pay part of the settlement. But on the mound Derringer was all business. Most likely the turbulent pitcher benefited from having an even-keeled, friendly catcher like Ernie Lombardi to keep his emotions under control.

Still, the 1937 Reds had reason for optimism, as the farm system that Larry MacPhail built started to pay dividends. Frank McCormick, a big infielder from New York City, batted .381 in the Piedmont League in 1936 and looked ready to hit big league pitching. Other up-and-coming major leaguers included outfielder Harry Craft, shortstop Eddie Joost, and pitchers Whitey Moore and Red Barrett. Most would remain in the minors in 1937, but their time was fast approaching.

Perhaps the prize of the Cincinnati system was a hard-throwing left-handed pitcher named Johnny Vander Meer. A native of New Jersey, the 22-year-old Vander Meer won 19 games in the Piedmont League in 1936, striking out lots of batters while walking nearly as many. He was ticketed for Syracuse for 1937, but baseball men were already comparing him to Lefty Grove, the strikeout king of the Philadelphia A's. If Vander Meer could improve his control, he could blossom into one of the top pitchers in the game.

In early January, Ernie Lombardi traveled to Sarasota, Florida, to prepare for the upcoming season, though the start of spring training was

Johnny Vander Meer threw two consecutive no-hitters. He always gave a large share of the credit to his catcher, Ernie Lombardi (National Baseball Hall of Fame Library, Cooperstown, New York).

more than a month away. He told the Associated Press that he had decided to take his job more seriously, by doing four things: laying off the night life, training harder than ever before, cutting out the "monkey business," and signing his contract without a holdout for once. "I want to be the leading catcher in the National League," said Ernie. And how did he intend to do that? "I want to duck all the parties my friends want to give me," he said. "All they do is put on a lot of excess poundage."[4]

However, the papers said that Ernie did not touch a baseball until he arrived at the spring camp in Tampa on March 4. Instead, Ernie spent nearly two months living in a beach cottage on the gulf with a friend from Oakland. Ernie spent his days fishing, swimming, sunning himself, and doing his best to lose weight. He also attended the Professional Ball Players' Golf Tournament in Sarasota; Ernie did not play golf himself, but he followed Sammy Byrd, a Reds teammate, around the course. His goal, he told the papers, was to get his weight down to 216 pounds by the start of the regular season.

On February 13, the Reds announced that Ernie had, indeed, signed his 1937 contract. Warren Giles, no doubt with a sense of relief, declined to reveal the salary figure, though most of the sportswriters surmised that the big catcher received at least a small raise in pay. Giles told the papers that he "didn't mind paying the fellows that have showed they could earn what they're getting." Ernie was happy with the arrangement. "It seems strange not to be squabbling over salary differences,"[5] he told the *Cincinnati Enquirer*.

It was not as easy as Lombardi made it sound. As Giles told the newspapers a few weeks later,

> I'll never forget the night I decided to sign up Ernie Lombardi. I put in a long distance telephone call from my home in Cincinnati to Lombardi in Sarasota, Florida. Well, for 45 minutes, I talked and argued with him. I tried every avenue of attack I knew, groping for his weak spot. I talked in circles, felt the fellow out and finally got him to agree to our salary figure.
>
> When I finished my arms were so tired I could hardly lift them. Mrs. Giles was laughing. She told me she'd never, never believe me again as long as she lived.[6]

This would not be the last contract battle between Ernie Lombardi and Warren Giles.

The Reds lost an outfielder that spring, when Sammy Byrd left the club to try his luck on the professional golf tour. Byrd, who had already played in sanctioned PGA events, won the baseball players' tournament in Sarasota that January by 14 strokes, while the other players grumbled that he was simply too good to take part in the competition. When the Reds chose to send him to Rochester for 1937, Byrd instead retired to become a full-time golfer.

The team nearly lost another outfielder during an exhibition game against the Detroit Tigers on April 1, when Kiki Cuyler suffered a broken cheek bone in a basepath collision. Cuyler recovered well enough to open the season, but the injury bothered him all year. Cuyler, who batted .326 and led the Reds in runs batted in, hits, and runs scored in 1936, hit poorly in 1937 and cost the team some much-needed power. Also, Babe Herman's time in Cincinnati was over. Herman was 33 years old, prone to injury, and did not get along with Charlie Dressen, so the Reds put him on waivers during spring training. In April, the Reds sold Herman to the Detroit Tigers, the team that had originally signed him.

Ernie Lombardi hit as well as ever in spring action. He was noticeably lighter than usual when he reported to Tampa, and he drove the ball hard from the first day. Perhaps the presence of Spud Davis, a catcher with similar talents, lit a fire under Ernie, because Giles was not sold on Ernie as his starter. In early February, when asked whether Davis or Lom was the top catcher, Giles replied, "They're both No. 1."[7] So Ernie announced his claim on the starting job when he mashed a grand slam homer against the Red Sox in Danville, Virginia, on April 15 in a 10–5 win.

Johnny Vander Meer, the rookie pitcher, and Ernie became good friends, but the youngster was confused during spring training when his catcher said that he could not wait to see his "old friend Mr. Hudie." As Vander Meer recalled years later, "Naturally, I'm curious. What makes this guy so special with Ernie, I'm asking myself." He didn't learn who Mr. Hudie was until the team broke camp and traveled north to start the season. As the Reds' train crossed the Ohio River into Cincinnati, Ernie put his arm around Vander Meer and pointed to an advertising sign for Hudepohl beer.[8]

Dressen and the Reds exuded the usual optimism during spring training, but the Cincinnati club crashed to earth almost immediately at the start of the campaign. In the season opener, played against the Cardinals in front of 34,374 fans at Crosley Field, the Reds reached Dizzy Dean for 13 hits (two by Lombardi) but no runs. Cincinnati's Peaches Davis matched zeroes with Dean through nine innings, but the Cardinals scored twice in the tenth to win. This loss was the first in a skid that left the Reds in the league cellar with a 1–9 record before the season was two weeks old.

Their first win, on April 28, came against the Cubs and was partly due to Ernie's talent for hitting line drives. In the first inning, Ernie hit a liner straight at the head of pitcher Larry French, who tried to deflect it with his glove. The ball missed the glove and broke a bone on French's hand, driving him from the game after he pitched to three more batters. The Reds piled up 14 hits on French and his successors to score a 10–3 win.

In April and May, the Reds had trouble scoring runs, while their pitchers struggled to make up for the lack of support. Among the losses was a 19–9 drubbing by the Phillies in Philadelphia's Baker Bowl on May 22. Ernie helped the cause with a two-run single, but pitchers Al Hollingsworth, Peaches Davis, and Whitey Moore could not stop the rampaging Phillies. The debacle ended when rookie left-hander Johnny Vander Meer pitched the last three innings, allowing seven runs on seven hits while hitting two batters and not striking out anyone.

The old, decrepit Baker Bowl was Ernie's favorite park for hitting. It was built in the 1890s and crammed into a single city block, and it featured a huge left field area and a tiny right field, with the fence only 270 feet down the line. Lombardi, a right-handed pull hitter, made sure to hit the ball to left, because the right fielder at the Baker Bowl was so close to the infield that he might throw Ernie out at first on a single. Ernie batted .387 during his career at the Baker Bowl, his highest average in any park by far. When the Phillies left the Baker Bowl and moved into Shibe Park with the Athletics in 1938, Ernie was sorry to see the old place go.

Lombardi rarely struck out, but on April 22, a rookie Pirate pitcher named Russ Bauers made headlines when he struck out Ernie twice in successive innings. Lombardi's pride was wounded, and Ernie, who seldom spoke more than a few words to the press, felt the need to explain himself to the *Cincinnati Post*. Ernie said, a bit defensively,

> It was the first time I ever saw Bauers pitch, and his delivery is a little out of the ordinary. His curve breaks right in front of the plate and I didn't have it timed quite properly the first two times I hit against him.
>
> After those two strikeouts I hit the ball solidly although not getting one safe. I hope he pitches against us in Cincinnati, I not only believe I'll hit him, but that our whole team will have better success against him the second time we see him that the first one.

The *Post* concluded, "Anytime anyone mentions it to Ernie the massive Italian just says, 'He won't do it again.'"[9]

The Reds played their share of wild games in 1937. On May 10 in Philadelphia, Ernie belted four singles and two doubles in six trips to the plate, while Alex Kampouris walloped three homers (the first Red to do so since 1897) in a 21–10 rout. Ernie's six hits broke his 0 for 14 slump and pushed his average over the .300 mark. On June 15, Johnny Vander Meer walked 11 Dodgers but allowed only three hits in eight innings at Brooklyn, carrying a 4–1 lead into the ninth. But Vander Meer filled the bases with a double and two walks, forcing Dressen to bring in Al Hollingsworth to close it out. Hollingsworth gave up a groundout and a single to score two runs, but with two out, Brooklyn's Gibby Brack made an ill-advised attempt to steal home. Ernie took the throw from Hollingsworth, blocked the plate, and tagged Brack out to end the game.

8. Back to Last Place

Charlie Dressen needed to produce a winning season to keep his job, but aside from Ernie, the Reds could not muster enough offense to win games. Kiki Cuyler was finished at age 38, Chick Hafey battled injuries and illness once again, and Charlie Gelbert, the shortstop acquired from the Cardinals, batted only .193 and was sold to Detroit in July. Several younger men from the farm system, including Frank McCormick, Harry Craft, and Eddie Joost, made appearances for the Reds, but they were not yet ready to step in.

One bright spot for the Reds was the sudden emergence of left-hander Lee Grissom. Though Grissom compiled a 12–17 record, he led the National League in shutouts and earned a spot on the All-Star team. Dressen had worked with him extensively in spring training to improve his control, and the effort paid off as Grissom, at age 29, burst into stardom.

Grissom, a talkative, eccentric pitcher in the Dizzy Dean mold, liked to draw attention to himself. When the Ohio River flooded to record levels in the spring of 1937 and left Crosley Field under 21 feet of water, Grissom and pitcher Gene Schott were photographed rowing a boat across the outfield. (Though some accused Grissom of grandstanding, the stunt was conceived by Reds management for publicity purposes.) Grissom also bragged about his pitching skill and publicly begged Dressen to let him pitch both ends of a doubleheader. "If [Grissom] can live up to what he says, as Ol' Diz does, the writers will forgive him, but they are inclined to believe that he is quite a distance from the Dean class,"[10] said the skeptical *Sporting News*.

Grissom gave Dressen the fighting spirit he wanted to see. On April 23 Grissom and Pittsburgh's Al Todd threw punches on the field when Todd objected to a knockdown pitch, and on July 14 Grissom tangled with Brooklyn's Babe Phelps after a hard collision at the plate. During spring training, Grissom also punched a clubhouse attendant and a taxi driver in separate incidents, and Dressen had to ask him to tone it down. But Dressen's penchant for aggressive play did not translate into wins, and in July the Reds settled into seventh place, fighting desperately to stay out of the cellar.

Because Ernie was virtually the only Red hitting well, Giants manager Bill Terry named the big catcher to the National League All-Star team as a reserve; he and Lee Grissom were the only two Reds to make the trip to Griffith Stadium in Washington for the contest. Grissom pitched an inning, but for the second year in a row Ernie never got into the game, warming up pitchers in the bullpen as Chicago's Gabby Hartnett and New York's Gus Mancuso shared the catching duties. "Unless he took a peek at the Washington Monument," said one paper, "the trip was a total loss."[11] But the next year's game was set to be played in Cincinnati, which provided incentive for Ernie to continue climbing the ranks of National League catchers.

The Reds fought their way into sixth place in early August, but the low point of the season occurred on August 13 in Chicago, when the Cubs dismantled the Reds by a score of 22 to 6. Cincinnati pitchers allowed nine runs in the third inning and, long after the game was out of reach, six more in the eighth. The Reds fielders made eight errors in a contest that the *Enquirer* described as "putrid" and a "travesty on [the] game." Dressen always preached about the importance of hustle and effort, but the Reds looked totally uninterested that day. From a fan's perspective, it appeared that Dressen's players had tuned him out.

The local papers were disgusted with the Reds' poor performance. After ripping the manager, the pitching staff, and the infield defense, the *Enquirer* zoomed in on the team's best hitter:

> This brings us to the catching situation. The less said about it the better. Ernie Lombardi is strictly a hitter, and a big target to throw at behind the dish. But there is no fight and hustle in him like Gabby Hartnett, and neither is he the shrewd, cold, calculating type like Gus Mancuso. Spud Davis, along with being equally as slow as Lombardi, if not a trifle slower, can't begin to shellack the ball with Schnoz.

The paper added, "General Manager Giles refuses to say 'yes' or 'no' as to whether Dressen will be retained as field general of the 1938 Reds."[12] Indeed, the rumor mill was already spinning, and reports said that Reds management had already decided to sack Dressen at season's end. One item claimed that Warren Giles offered to trade Ernie Lombardi to the Giants for another large, veteran Italian catcher, Gus Mancuso, who would then become the playing manager of the Reds. But most agreed that Bill McKechnie, whose contract with the Boston Bees was soon to expire, was still the leading candidate to lead the Reds in 1938.

Perhaps Ernie took the criticism of his "fight and hustle" to heart, because on August 21 the usually mild-mannered catcher was ejected for the first time in his career. In a close game against the Pirates, Ernie whacked two doubles and two singles, and in the eighth inning he advanced from second to third on a fly ball. But the Pirates appealed, claiming that he had left the base early, and umpire Beans Reardon called Ernie out. Ernie protested so vehemently that Reardon tossed him from the game.

In later years, Reardon enjoyed telling the story of that play. "I didn't bother watching that slow moose, and when I looked around after the catch, Lombardi was halfway to third. 'Out,' I calls. 'You left the base too soon.'" When Ernie protested, Reardon replied, "When I see you halfway to third after a short fly, I don't have to see it," he said. "I KNOW you left the base too soon!"[13] At the end of September, Ernie was tossed by umpire Lee Ballanfant for arguing balls and strikes. Though the Reds were losing with regularity, at least Ernie showed some fighting spirit.

Ernie was ejected only six times during his career, and he could never be too offensive in his language to the umpires. One of his ejections came later in his career on a called third strike, when he told umpire George Magerkurth, "Sir, you are a meathead." For the short-fused Magerkurth, that was enough to give Ernie the boot.

After the 22–6 defeat, the Cincinnati club rallied briefly, winning their next three games against the Cubs and scoring nine or more runs in all of them. But the Reds followed up by losing six of their next seven, all at home, as part of a 1–11 skid that dropped them to last place. And for some reason, the Reds simply could not beat the Pittsburgh Pirates. The Pirates played 22 games against the Reds in 1937 and won 21 of them, with Cincinnati's only win coming in the second game of a Memorial Day doubleheader. No one could explain it, and the Reds' futility against the Pirates played a major part in dooming the Reds' drive to the first division in 1937.

The last two months of the season were painful to watch. Lee Grissom fell to earth, losing his last six decisions. Paul Derringer battled a hernia problem all year but continued to take his turn on the mound, holding off on surgery until after the season. Kiki Cuyler, who had managerial aspirations, decided to retire, as did Chick Hafey, who was no better than mediocre for the Reds in 1937. As the season wound down with the Reds in last place, the team played listlessly in front of small crowds.

Charlie Dressen was as disappointed as anyone over the Reds' lack of success in 1937, and the feisty manager certainly suspected he was on his way out of Cincinnati. Dressen decided to force the issue on September 13, a day after the Reds split a Sunday doubleheader against the Cardinals at Crosley Field. Their 5–4 win in the first game of the twin bill snapped a streak of six straight losses, three of them in walk-off fashion. With the Reds buried in last place, 27 and a half games behind the league leaders, Dressen marched into Warren Giles' office and demanded to know his standing for the 1938 season.

Giles addressed the matter with his characteristic bluntness. "All I could tell him," said Giles to the press, "was that we had determined some time ago not to re-hire him, and that he might as well leave the team now."[14] Dressen agreed, and just like that, Dressen and his coaches, Tom Sheehan and George Kelly, were out. Giles then hired Bobby Wallace, the Reds' chief scout, as interim manager for the last 25 games of the season.

The 63-year-old Wallace, a star shortstop with the St. Louis Browns three decades before, was ill-suited to the task of leading a demoralized last-place team. The listless Reds lost 20 of their 25 games under Wallace's direction, closing the 1937 campaign with 14 losses in a row and finishing 40 games behind the pennant-winning Giants. The fans gave up on the team as well, with the final homestand drawing as few as 500 or 600 people for weekday games. After the promise of 1936, it appeared that the team had fallen right back to where it started.

All the while, Ernie Lombardi kept swatting the ball. Playing in almost every game, Ernie slumped a bit during the final disastrous weeks of the season as his batting average fell from the high .340s and settled into the mid-.330s. At season's end, his still-impressive average of .334 led the team by a wide margin; no other regular on the club compiled an average above .282. He led the league in passed balls for the third year in a row, but grounded into 12 double plays, less than half as many as he had in 1933 and 1934. Though the team struggled all year, Ernie put together an All-Star season, and expected to be granted a sizable raise for 1938.

Even Dizzy Dean, the premier right-handed pitcher in the league, paid Ernie a compliment, though a backhanded one. Said Dean to the press, "That big guy [Lombardi] is the best catcher in the league, even if he is awkward."[15] Gabby Hartnett of the Cubs was the perennial All-Star starter, but Ernie was catching up to him. And the public was seeing more of Ernie. In 1937, Ernie began appearing on Wheaties cereal boxes, the first Cincinnati Red so honored.

Warren Giles, as usual, played hardball. Attendance at Crosley Field in 1937 fell by more than 55,000 from the year before, and neither Giles nor team owner Powel Crosley were much inclined to hand out raises to a last-place team. Giles sent Ernie a contract that called for no increase in pay. Ernie sent it back unsigned, and the two strong-willed men prepared once again for their annual winter battle.

In a tragic coda to the 1937 season, pitcher Benny Frey, who played for the Reds from 1929 to 1936, committed suicide at his sister's home in Michigan on November 1. Frey, as a reliever and occasional starter, won 10 games for the Reds in 1936, but Charlie Dressen never had much confidence in him. Dressen ignored the veteran pitcher at the 1937 training camp and released him to Nashville without ever letting him take the mound in an exhibition contest. Frey turned down the demotion and quit the game instead, but his relatives later said that Frey feared that "his arm was never going to be good enough again ... and that he spent several months despondent since his release."[16] The pitcher killed himself in a garage with carbon monoxide fumes from his car.

9

MVP

> "Bill's a great manager to work for. He took hold of me last year, saying, 'You're our catcher.' When the night games came in I believed I would be on the shelf again. Charlie Dressen didn't use me under the lights. But McKechnie said, 'Get in there and catch.'"[1]
>
> —Ernie Lombardi, 1939

With Charlie Dressen gone, Warren Giles had free rein to hire his own manager. Giles knew exactly who he wanted, and on October 7, 1937, mere days after the close of the season, Giles signed Bill McKechnie to manage the Reds.

McKechnie knew baseball inside and out. He made the major leagues as a utility infielder in 1907, at the age of 21, and while he was not a star, he made a reputation as a smart, dependable ballplayer. In 1915, when he played in the Federal League (a short-lived rival to the American and National circuits) the Newark Peppers made him their manager. When the Federal League collapsed, McKechnie returned to the National League and became manager of the Pittsburgh Pirates in 1922.

McKechnie's career up to 1938 was a mixture of success and bad luck. He directed the Pirates to a World Series title in 1925 but lost his job a year later in a front office power struggle. Hired by the Cardinals in 1928 (the third St. Louis manager in three years after Rogers Hornsby and Bob O'Farrell), McKechnie won the pennant but lost the World Series to the Yankees in a 4–0 sweep. Team owner Sam Breadon did not exactly fire McKechnie; instead, he sent McKechnie to Rochester and promoted Rochester skipper Billy Southworth to the main club. Rochester's business manager was none other than Warren Giles, with whom McKechnie formed a strong friendship.

Southworth got off to a bad start in 1929, so in mid-season Breadon switched the two men again, with McKechnie restored as Cardinal manager. At season's end, Breadon offered a one-year contract, but McKechnie seriously considered quitting baseball. He ran for public office in his native

Pennsylvania as a tax collector in his hometown but lost in the Republican primary. McKechnie was now 43 years old and looking for security, and when the Boston Braves offered him a four-year contract, McKechnie accepted it and joined the Braves in 1930.

Personally, McKechnie was a serious, fatherly sort; his nickname was "Deacon" because of his sober and stable demeanor. He did not care for theatrical clubhouse rants or on-field temper tantrums; instead, as he told *Look* magazine in 1944, "just treat them the way you'd like to be treated."[2] In a later interview he said, "A manager tries to pick his men carefully, keeping out the bad actors. But the average ballplayer plays [for] himself. He isn't hustling for the manager or the club owner. He's hustling for his own contract—his family and his future."[3] As historian and longtime Reds fan Lee Allen wrote, "McKechnie was a master handler of men. Some managers will never learn to handle personalities as long as they live. McKechnie in that department was without a peer."[4]

McKechnie was a taskmaster, but as Pirates star Paul Waner said, "he could be a father to you when he felt he had to be and a taskmaster when that was needed."[5] Unlike other Cincinnati field leaders of the recent past, McKechnie was a mature, experienced major league manager who owned a record of success. He had won pennants and knew how to win them. And he knew how to keep the players focused. As Ernie Lombardi said many years later, "I liked to play for Bill. He was quieter than other managers. But all he had to do was look out at you over the top of his glasses and you'd know you'd done something wrong."[6]

Bill McKechnie had seen Ernie Lombardi play against his Boston club many times. In that era, with an annual schedule of 154 games, each National

Bill McKechnie, who became manager of the Cincinnati Reds in 1938 and immediately tried to trade Ernie Lombardi (Library of Congress).

League team met its opponents 22 times a season, so McKechnie was well aware of Ernie Lombardi's abilities.

McKechnie was not impressed.

The new Cincinnati manager believed in a strong defense, but Ernie's passed balls and slow response to foul pop-ups did not fit with McKechnie's plans for his team. Ernie hit well for average, but scored few runs, grounded into too many double plays, and was forced out at second base too many times to count. He seldom struck out, but almost never walked. Besides, Crosley Field, with its far-away fences, was ill-suited for a right-handed line drive hitter like Ernie.

With this in mind, McKechnie made plans to rebuild the Reds. His first order of business was a simple one. He set out to trade Ernie Lombardi.

At the National League winter meetings in Chicago in December 1937, McKechnie let it be known that his All-Star catcher, the senior Red in years of service, was on the trading block. Lombardi's availability drew immediate interest from the Chicago Cubs, whose incumbent backstop, Gabby Hartnett, was nearly 37 years old and, despite a sterling 1937 campaign, would have to be replaced eventually. McKechnie and Giles huddled with Cubs manager Charlie Grimm and chief scout Clarence (Pants) Rowland, and soon Gabe Paul, the young Cincinnati publicity man, made an announcement. "We've just traded Lombardi to the Cubs," said Paul to a group of newsmen. "Or at least Bill McKechnie thinks he has. He's waiting now for confirmation."[7]

Grimm and Rowland were eager to land Ernie, but team owner Philip K. Wrigley was not. Reportedly, Wrigley believed that the Cubs did not need another catcher, especially as Hartnett, despite his age, had batted .354 in 1937 and finished second in the Most Valuable Player balloting. Wrigley turned the deal down, and Ernie, for the time being, remained a Red.

A few months later, with Ernie staging his annual holdout, the New York Giants made a play for the big catcher. Manager Bill Terry had always regarded Ernie highly, and the Giants' home park, the Polo Grounds, was built for a hitter like Lombardi. With the left field stands 279 feet down the line, topped by an overhang only 257 feet away, a powerful right-handed hitter like Ernie might see his home run total double in New York. The papers reported that Terry, whose own starting catcher Gus Mancuso was holding out too, offered Mancuso and outfielder Wally Berger for outfielder Harry Craft, infielder Dee Moore, and Lombardi. Berger, a home run hitter who made the All-Star team four times while playing for McKechnie in Boston, was unable to crack the starting lineup in New York. Giles turned Terry down, reportedly because he did not want to lose the highly-regarded Craft.

Another contender for Ernie's services emerged during the spring of 1938. Larry MacPhail, after leaving the Reds, spent a year out of baseball, then joined the Brooklyn Dodgers as general manager. He, too, coveted Ernie, and planned to use the big catcher in a tandem with rookie Babe Phelps. MacPhail had recently obtained first baseman Dolph Camilli from the Phillies in a trade and hoped to acquire another big bat to anchor his lineup.

In the end, Ernie came to terms with Warren Giles and signed his contract on March 8. McKechnie's trade efforts went for naught, so he retained Ernie as his starting catcher, with Virgil (Spud) Davis, a veteran acquired from the Cardinals the year before, as his backup. Giles and McKechnie also signed Willard Hershberger, a 27-year-old Californian who spent eight years in the Yankee farm system and had not yet played in the majors. The Reds purchased Hershberger's contract at the winter meetings, possibly as insurance in case they traded Lombardi.

The acquisition of Hershberger was a stroke of good fortune for the Reds. Most observers considered Hershberger to be the top catcher in the minor leagues. He had most likely been ready for major league action for several years but was stuck behind perennial All-Star Bill Dickey in the Yankee system. He was one of the key players on the pennant-winning Newark Bears in 1937, a team that included future stars Joe Gordon, Charlie Keller, Tommy Henrich, and more. Now, the Reds would give Hershberger his shot at major league stardom.

His new teammates soon found that Hershberger was friendly enough, but an extreme introvert. He kept to himself whenever possible, only rarely accepting invitations to dinner or the movies, and, though lots of young women in Cincinnati were interested in meeting the ballplayers, he never dated. He sent much of his paycheck home to his widowed mother in California, and on train rides, he spent his time looking quietly out the window and chain-smoking.

Hershberger's new teammates could not have known the reasons behind the young catcher's demeanor. They had no way of knowing that when Hershberger, an avid hunter, was 18 years old, he returned from the woods late one November evening and left his rifle and shells in the hallway, intending to clean the gun the next morning. Sometime after midnight, his father Claude, who had suffered through a series of financial reverses, wandered sleeplessly through the house. Claude Hershberger came across Willard's gun, took it into the bathroom, and committed suicide with it. Willard was the one who found the body.

Ever after, the young man carried a mixture of guilt, shame, and regret that prevented him from opening up to anybody, even his teammates. The tragedy may also have caused Hershberger to become a hypochondriac, as he haunted the trainer's office almost on a daily basis, worried about one imaginary illness or another. Still, his personal issues appeared to have no effect on his play. He hit well in spring training, and the Reds welcomed him to the team.

Hershberger had a different attitude than Gilly Campbell, Rollie Hemsley, and other Cincinnati catchers of the recent past. Just as Ernie Lombardi loved being the number one catcher, Willard Hershberger was more than happy to be his understudy. "No doubt in my mind he could have been a starter for most anybody," said pitcher Junior Thompson. "I don't think Hershey realized he was near as good as he was. We pitchers just thought he was outstanding. ... Most guys with Hershey's ability would say, 'Trade me. I want to go to a place where I can catch every day.' He had no confidence. He was satisfied (to be the backup)."[8]

Crosley Field had always been a pitcher's park, but before the 1938 season the team decided to reconfigure the playing field. Giles ordered the groundskeepers to move home plate 20 feet closer to center field, making the left field fence a more reachable 328 feet down the line. This move promised to help Ernie and the rest of Cincinnati's hitters, especially the right-handed ones. No Cincinnati Red had ever hit 20 home runs in a season up to this time, and perhaps 1938 would be the year that someone would break Harry Heilmann's club record of 19.

McKechnie then moved to tighten the Cincinnati defense. Frank McCormick was now ready to take over at first base; he was a fine glove man who hit for average with little power (only six homers at Syracuse in 1937), but Crosley Field's new dimensions might help him in that regard. Billy Myers, the regular at shortstop since 1935, was solid, but second base and third base needed upgrades. The new manager imported shortstop Lonny Frey from the Cubs and installed him at second base, and kept Lew Riggs, the regular for three years, at third. In the outfield, Harry Craft claimed center field, with Ival Goodman in right. Left field was unsettled, but these moves gave the Reds a much-improved defense and promised to help the Cincinnati pitchers.

Ernie Lombardi was not McKechnie's ideal as a defensive catcher, but his strengths outweighed his weaknesses. Ernie led the league each year in passed balls and his range factor was below the league average, but his cannon arm, which some rated the best in baseball, held the running game in check. Also, though he led the league in errors, his fielding average was at or near the league average. Backup Spud Davis, however, was a weak defender, and McKechnie had traded him away once, at St. Louis in 1928. Hershberger's addition not only aided the defense behind the plate but left the good-hitting Davis as trade bait.

Under the guidance of Bill McKechnie and Ernie Lombardi, Johnny

Vander Meer began to conquer his wildness. During spring training, Vander Meer uncorked a pitch far outside the strike zone, but Ernie simply reached out his arm, grabbed the ball with his bare hand, and fired it back. "Listen," yelled the pitcher, "if you're going to sit back there and catch me bare-handed, the least you could do is shake your hand a little like I had something on the pitch. You're making me look bad!"[9] McKechnie and coach Hank Gowdy, a veteran National League catcher, convinced the pitcher to throw straight overhand rather than sidearm in a bid to improve his control. Vander Meer appreciated his manager's patience. "I was able to concentrate on exactly what he told me," he said. "I knew I didn't have to rush or be afraid if I took my time."[10]

Vander Meer lost his first start of the season to Pittsburgh, after which McKechnie sent him to the bullpen for a while. Reinstated to the starting rotation, he beat the Pirates, lost to the Phillies (walking seven men), and blew a 5–1 ninth-inning lead to the Cardinals. Vander Meer then found his groove, and a 4–0 shutout of the Giants on May 20 started the left-hander on a nine-game winning streak. On June 11, he took the mound in Cincinnati against the Boston Bees, the team previously known as the Braves.[11]

Vander Meer was never in trouble against the worst-hitting team in the league. Gene Moore walked for the Bees in the fourth, but Ernie caught a pop foul from the bat of Johnny Cooney, then threw to first to catch Moore off the base. In the fifth, with the Reds ahead 1 to 0, Boston's Tony Cuccinello walked, but was picked off first by Lombardi's snap throw. In the Cincinnati sixth, a walk to Wally Berger (acquired from the Giants a few days before) and a line-drive home run by Lombardi increased the Cincinnati lead to 3–0. Though Vander Meer had given up three walks, no Bees batter had hit safely. Vander Meer breezed through the seventh and eighth, and a no-hitter looked to be within reach.

In the ninth, Boston manager Casey Stengel sent three pinch-hitters to the plate. Bob Kahle bounced out to first, Hal Maggert struck out, and when Ray Mueller bounced out to third, Vander Meer completed his no-hitter. It was the first no-hitter by a Cincinnati pitcher since the championship season of 1919.[12] Ernie and the Reds hoisted the pitcher on their shoulders and carried him off the field. "You watch him from now on," Stengel told the press. "They'll have trouble beating him."[13]

Pitching, however, was still a problem area for the Reds. Johnny Vander Meer's emergence gave the team two solid starters with staff ace Paul Derringer, but Lee Grissom regressed from his All-Star performance of 1937. Grissom suffered a throat infection, which led his doctors to perform a tonsillotomy (a partial tonsillectomy). The pitcher recovered slowly, sitting out almost all of May and June. He won only two games all year,

9. MVP

and his season ended on August 24, when he broke an ankle sliding into second on an ill-advised stolen base attempt.

While the Cincinnati fans celebrated Vander Meer's no-hitter, Bill McKechnie kept his eye on the future. His Reds stood only two games above the .500 mark on June 12, and while the team's showing so far was a major improvement from the last-place finish of 1937, McKechnie aimed higher. He wanted one more starting pitcher to solidify his staff, and he knew which pitcher he wanted.

One morning, McKechnie stepped into Warren Giles' office. According to historian Lee Allen, the manager got right down to business. "Warren," he said, "we need one more pitcher. If we get one, I think we might have a chance for the pennant." When asked who he had in mind, McKechnie replied, "Philadelphia has two of them—Claude Passeau and Bucky Walters. Of the two, I'd rather have Walters."[14]

Bucky Walters was, at the time, the unluckiest pitcher on the worst team in baseball. He was a hard-throwing right-hander, though he reached the majors in 1931 as a third baseman with the Boston Braves (managed by Bill McKechnie). He didn't hit well enough to earn a spot, so he returned to the minors, was sold to the Boston Red Sox, and then, after a thumb injury, was sold to the Philadelphia Phillies. In Philadelphia, manager Jimmie Wilson and the coaching staff suggested that he move to the mound, and Walters, who preferred to play every day, reluctantly did so.

The Philadelphia ballclub, during the mid–1930s, was every bit as unstable and underfunded as the Cincinnati Reds had been before Powel Crosley and Larry MacPhail took control of the team. Always at or near the bottom of the standings, their attendance was the worst in the National League, and team ownership operated the club on a shoestring, often selling off their good players to raise the necessary cash to stay afloat. Walters won 11 games in 1936 while losing 21, though baseball men recognized that his record might well be reversed with a decent team behind him. In 1937, though he won 14 and lost 15, Walters was named to the All-Star team.

The Phillies desperately needed money, so on June 12, 1938, after receiving permission from Powel Crosley for a large outlay of cash, Giles and Phillies owner Gerry Nugent finalized the deal. The Phillies sent Walters to the Reds and received pitcher Al Hollingsworth and $55,000 in return. In addition, Nugent insisted on a side agreement that, if Hollingsworth failed to perform to the Phillies' standards, the two clubs would undo the trade and send Walters and Hollingsworth back to their original teams. Commissioner Landis rejected the deal for that reason, and for a short while it looked as if it was all off. But the Phillies wanted the cash, so when Giles threw backup catcher Spud Davis into the mix, the Phillies dropped the side agreement.

With Walters' acquisition, Bill McKechnie now owned a starting pitching staff that gave the Reds a chance to win each day. The manager was also satisfied with his catching situation, as the steadily improving Willard Hershberger had proven himself capable of performing at a major league level. Ernie Lombardi's workload increased with Davis gone, but the big catcher had proven his durability, and McKechnie, after his initial reservations, had come to trust in Ernie's pitch-calling.

Larry MacPhail, the man who installed lights at Crosley Field in 1935, did the same for the Brooklyn Dodgers in 1938. Though many baseball men still opposed the idea of night baseball, MacPhail saw how the lights caused a sharp spike in Cincinnati attendance and convinced his bosses in Brooklyn to follow suit. On June 15, 1938, the Dodger team played the first night game in its history at Ebbets Field against the Cincinnati Reds. It turned out to be one of the most famous games in baseball history, but not because of the lights.

More than 38,000 fans—the second largest crowd ever at Ebbets Field up to that time—packed the ballpark that evening, not only to marvel at the lights, but also to see Cincinnati's starting pitcher. Johnny Vander Meer, four days after his no-hitter against the Boston Bees, was selected by McKechnie to start the contest. Vander Meer was opposed by Max Butcher, a 27-year-old right-hander who won 11 games that year.

As usual, Ernie Lombardi started for the Reds behind the plate. He rode the bench three years before when Crosley Field hosted its first night game, but McKechnie wanted Lombardi, not the rookie Hershberger, to catch Vander Meer's pitches. The Reds had no idea how good the lighting system would be, so the veteran got the starting nod. As it turned out, the lights drew nothing but praise. MacPhail had delivered the goods, just as he had in Cincinnati, though most players still preferred baseball during the daytime. "Night baseball isn't fun," complained Lombardi to the *Brooklyn Eagle* before the game. "It's hard work."[15]

At that time, the lights were considered most effective in total darkness, so the game did not begin until 9:20 p.m. Butcher allowed a leadoff single to Lonny Frey and a walk to Ival Goodman in the first, but retired Frank McCormick on a grounder and Ernie Lombardi on a fly to center. Vander Meer put the Dodgers down in order, and the two pitchers settled in.

Butcher and Vander Meer traded zeroes for the first two innings, but the Reds erupted in the third. After Butcher got the first two outs, Wally Berger singled, Ival Goodman walked, and Frank McCormick walloped a home run to put the Reds up 3 to 0. Lombardi walked and came home on singles by Harry Craft and Lew Riggs to make the score 4 to 0. Manager Burleigh Grimes brought in a relief pitcher, knuckleballer Tot Pressnell, who got the third out.

As the game went on, Vander Meer kept the Dodgers off the board. His control was not as good as it was four days earlier, as the Cincinnati left-hander issued walks in the second, third, and sixth, but no Dodger managed to land a safe hit, and the crowd buzzed with anticipation. Could Vander Meer complete a second no-hitter in a row, a feat no pitcher had ever accomplished in the major leagues?

The game stopped in the top of the seventh when Ival Goodman, with one out, drilled a liner off Pressnell's knee. Pressnell was helped off the field, and when the game resumed the new Dodger pitcher, Luke Hamlin, struck out McCormick, then walked Ernie Lombardi intentionally. Harry Craft singled Goodman home for the Reds' fifth run. In the bottom of the inning, Vander Meer walked two men with one out, but struck out Ernie Koy and retired Leo Durocher on a grounder. Now Vander Meer needed only six more outs to complete the impossible feat.

Vander Meer breezed through the eighth after the Reds scored their sixth run in the top of the inning. By now the Brooklyn fans had switched their allegiances; they were all pulling for Vander Meer to finish his second no-hitter. "They realized that they were about to see something that had never happened in baseball before," wrote Tommy Holmes in the *Brooklyn Eagle* the next day. "The fans had long ceased to root for the Dodgers. They were rooting for the new pitching star as the last of the ninth began."[16]

The Reds went out quickly in the ninth, with Lombardi striking out to conclude an 0 for 3 day at the plate, and now the stage belonged to Vander Meer. Buddy Hassett, the first Brooklyn batter in the ninth, tapped a weak grounder along the first base line; Vander Meer gloved it and tagged the runner himself. The Cincinnati pitcher then suddenly lost it, walking Babe Phelps, Cookie Lavagetto, and Dolph Camilli in quick succession. Vander Meer was clearly flustered, so McKechnie, Lombardi, and the infielders converged on the mound to discuss the matter.

Reports differ over what was said during the conference. McKechnie recalled that he gave Vander Meer, who had walked eight men that evening, the same advice he always offered the left-hander. "Forget everything else, John. Just pour that ball over the plate," the manager liked to say. "Those fellows are more afraid to swing at it than you are to throw it."[17] Another version has Lombardi imploring Vander Meer to simply pretend they were playing catch. "I'll hold up my mitt and you hit it. Forget there's anyone else in this ballpark but you and me.... You're either going to give up a hit or you're not, so blaze that fast one in there."[18]

The next batter was Ernie Koy, who had pounded three hits off Vander Meer two weeks before. Vander Meer, throwing only fastballs, got the speedy Koy to hit a grounder to Lew Riggs at third. Rather than try for a double play to end the game, Riggs threw to Lombardi at home to force the sliding Goody Rosen, who had pinch-run for Phelps. Now there were two outs, both the no-hitter and the shutout were still intact, and Brooklyn shortstop Leo Durocher stepped into the batter's box.

Durocher took a ball, then a called strike. He swung and missed the third pitch, and then belted a sharp line drive that curved foul into the right field stands. Vander Meer let loose again, and Durocher took a close pitch. The Reds jumped off the bench to storm the field in celebration, but umpire Bill Stewart called it a ball.

Ernie, who rarely argued with the umpires, jumped up and berated Stewart, who held his ground. "I had to call that one a ball," said the umpire after the game. "It was a little high as I saw it. Golly, I was pulling for the kid as much as anybody."[19] The dissatisfied catcher crouched again and called for another fastball. Durocher banged the next pitch to shallow center field, and the ball seemed to hover in the night sky as Harry Craft dashed under it. Craft caught it and set of a wild celebration in the middle of the field.

Johnny Vander Meer thus became the first, and only, pitcher in major league history to throw two consecutive no-hitters. It also made Ernie Lombardi the only man in baseball history to catch a pitcher in two consecutive no-hitters. Vander Meer's unprecedented feat made him a national sensation, though the pitcher said that his biggest thrill of the night was being congratulated by Babe Ruth, then a coach for the Dodgers. The pitcher always gave credit to Ernie for his accomplishment. "It was made possible," said Vander Meer nearly 30 years later, "by Ernie Lombardi not making a bad pitching call two games in a row."[20]

The home plate umpire concurred. "Give some credit to Lombardi," said Bill Stewart. "Sure, Vander Meer had to pitch perfectly to get his no-hitters. But what about the guy who told the kid what to pitch? If Lombardi had guessed wrong on one hitter, if he had called for a fastball when a curve was the smart pitch, Vander Meer never would've made it. Lombardi's judgment was just as perfect and just as important as Vander Meer's pitches."[21]

Vander Meer's two no-hitters cemented Ernie Lombardi's reputation as a handler of pitchers. From that moment on, few questioned Ernie's skill at pitch-calling. The double no-hitters made Johnny Vander Meer a household name, but also gave a huge boost to Ernie Lombardi's standing as a defensive catcher. He had come a long way from 1933, when the *Brooklyn Eagle* called Ernie "the worst defensive catcher in the majors." Now, only Chicago's Gabby Hartnett ranked ahead of Ernie among National League backstops.

Vander Meer's feat soon brought honors to both the pitcher and his catcher. On July 6, Crosley Field hosted the sixth annual All-Star Game, with Vander Meer as the starting pitcher and Ernie Lombardi as the starting catcher for the National League. Ernie had been selected as a reserve for the team in 1936 and 1937, though he did not play in either game. But now he would start in front of the home fans.

With 27,067 fans in attendance, Vander Meer pitched three shutout innings and gave up only one hit, while Ernie caught the entire game and contributed two singles. The first of his hits drove in Mel Ott of the Giants, who had tripled, with what proved to be the winning run. It gave the National League a 2–1 lead on their way to a 4–1 win.

The 1938 season was Ernie's best as a hitter. His batting average remained well above the .340 mark for most of the season, and on September 1, his .345 mark led the National League. His closest competitors for the batting title were Pittsburgh's Arky Vaughan at .329, Joe Medwick of the Cardinals at .324, and Ernie's teammate Frank McCormick at .323. With a 16-point lead in the race, it looked like Ernie would grab Cincinnati's first batting championship in 12 years.

But Johnny Mize, the 25-year-old slugging first baseman of the Cardinals, went on a tear. In tenth place in the race on September 1 with an average of .309, Mize batted .449 in September and zoomed into contention for the crown. Mize had a lot of ground to make up, but his average rose steadily until September 28, when his three hits against the Reds vaulted him past Ernie, .338 to .336. The next day, in a 7–4 Cincinnati win over the Cardinals, Mize went hitless while Ernie belted two singles to reclaim the lead by two points.

Mize faltered again on September 30, managing only one hit against the Cubs while Ernie smashed a homer, his 19th of the year, and a single against the Pirates in the first game of a twin-bill to raise his average to .340; an 0 for 3 showing in the nightcap dropped him to .338. On October 1, the next to last day of the season, Mize's five hits in a doubleheader jumped his mark to .340, but Ernie answered with a four-hit day of his own. The two men entered the final day of the season with Ernie ahead, .342 to .340.

Bill McKechnie asked Ernie if he wanted to ride the bench to preserve his title, but Ernie refused, preferring to win it on the field. After receiving a radio and a basket of flowers from the city's Italian fans in a pre-game ceremony, Lombardi caught the entire game. He belted one hit, a single, in four at-bats, but when Mize closed out the year with no hits in four trips, Ernie Lombardi clinched the National League batting championship.

It was a very good season for the Reds. They finished in the first division for the first time in 12 years, claiming fourth place, six games behind the pennant-winning Cubs. Warren Giles and Bill McKechnie had the Reds going in the right direction, and Cincinnati fans responded.

Attendance at Crosley Field jumped to 706,756, the highest in Cincinnati history.

The most popular Red, Ernie Lombardi, compiled his best season of his career to date. His 19 home runs, 95 runs batted in, and 60 runs scored set new career highs for the big catcher. He grounded into lots of double plays, setting a new all-time record with 30,[22] but also led the league with 21 intentional walks. As usual, he led the league in passed balls, but his 60 percent success rate at throwing out base stealers was the best in not only the National League, but in all of major league baseball.

The rise of the once-moribund Reds was headline news in the baseball world, and the big catcher came in for a large share of the credit. On October 31, the Baseball Writers Association of America named Ernie Lombardi as the National League's Most Valuable Player for 1938. He was the first Cincinnati Red, and the first Italian American, to win the honor.

10

Pennant

"The system I used on the Cubs last season [1938] was [to] give my pitcher the sign and then rush over and back up third base."[1]
—Cubs catcher Gabby Hartnett, when asked how to pitch to Ernie Lombardi

At the height of his popularity in Cincinnati, a lapse of judgement on Ernie's part led to an incident that colored the catcher's relationship with his general manager Warren Giles.

Cincinnati's Italian community was proud of its local hero, and on October 2, the day after the final game of the 1938 season, it threw a huge banquet at the Hotel Gibson to honor Lombardi. More than 800 people attended, including the mayor of Cincinnati, the Italian consul, local politicians, and several of Ernie's teammates. The menu was all Italian, and except for the mayor, the dais was filled with prominent Italian businessmen and community leaders. They loaded down their hero with gifts, including a shiny new blue and silver Buick.

Near the end of the evening, the master of ceremonies asked the guest of honor to say a few words. Ernie was never comfortable with public speaking, but he agreed to address the jubilant crowd. He had a few drinks. As he recalled a few years later, "The fans of Cincinnati decided to toss a big civic banquet for me. They did it up right. They gave me a brand new car and a load of other presents. Everybody from the mayor to the dog catcher made a speech. Finally it came to me. I hate speeches, but this is one I couldn't duck. I had to say something. I had to thank all those swell people."

Ernie nervously took his place at the podium. "Thanks for everything," he told the crowd.

> I don't know how to thank you all for all this. All I can say is I love Cincinnati, I love Cincinnati fans, I love everybody in Cincinnati....
> Except for Mr. Giles. Him I hate.[2]

Other accounts of Ernie's speech say that he called Giles an "old goat" and other uncomplimentary phrases as well. Ernie also declared, "I won't work for peanuts!"

Lombardi and Giles had talked salary a few days before. Ernie wanted $20,000 for 1939, but Giles was unwilling to go that high, and the catcher walked out without signing. Ernie had a habit of letting Giles explain his offers in great detail and shooting them down with two words—"T'aint enough." Now he had insulted Giles in public. "Then I sat down. The minute I did I knew I'd said something I shouldn't.... I knew the first bad season I had, Giles would get even with me."[3]

In the end, Ernie received his $20,000, in a way. In late October, he and Giles agreed on a base salary of $17,000, the highest of Ernie's career so far, and a bonus of $3,000 for winning the batting title and the Most Valuable Player award. Their agreement, finalized in early November, assured the Reds that Ernie would not be staging his annual holdout. But Giles never forgot Ernie's comments at that banquet.

Cincinnati's rise from last place to fourth, only one game out of third, was big news in the baseball world. As the *Spalding Guide* noted, "Cincinnati was the biggest surprise of the National League campaign of 1938 ... Most of the players were in possession of Cincinnati when McKechnie took charge and he was smart enough to permit them to stay. For instance, there was Lombardi, the giant catcher. The new manager gave him all the chance he wanted, and it seemed that all he wanted to do was work. He became one of the most valuable catchers in the league."[4] Perhaps John B. Foster, editor of the *Guide*, forgot that McKechnie tried to trade Ernie to the Cubs as soon as he took over the Reds. But all was forgotten now in the wake of Ernie's MVP season.

But there was more work to do. "You can't tell what a club like this—a young club—will do," said McKechnie to a reporter. "Our boys are overanxious sometimes. We beat ourselves in about half the games we lost. Steady clubs—veteran clubs—don't do that. Then there's another thing. Everybody was talking about us having four men up among the five leading hitters. I'll bet we're leading the league way off in men left on bases—must be leading by a hundred.... We haven't a great team, but we have the makings of a great team—maybe."[5]

Nonetheless, McKechnie believed that the revitalized Reds were now ready to challenge for a pennant. They had a strong catching corps with Ernie Lombardi and Willard Hershberger; a rising star in first baseman Frank McCormick; three top-flight starting pitchers in Paul Derringer, Bucky Walters, and Johnny Vander Meer; and solid performers in the infield and outfield. One problem area was third base, where starter Lew Riggs was fading, but that problem was solved with the acquisition of Bill Werber from the Philadelphia Athletics.

Bill Werber, a graduate of Duke University, was a highly intelligent and sometimes tempestuous man who had been a star in the American League. He led the league in stolen bases twice with the Boston Red Sox and once with the Athletics, and he was well known for his aggressive play and hard slides. Like Ernie Lombardi, Werber was never afraid to hold out for more money at contract time, and when he and Connie Mack clashed over salary, Mack sold him to Cincinnati.

Werber had a temper. While playing for the Red Sox, he became frustrated one day and kicked a water bucket in the dugout so hard that he broke his big toe. Werber had seen ace pitcher Lefty Grove kick that same water bucket many times; too late he realized that Grove always kicked it with the side of his foot. Werber's toe injury affected him for the rest of his career. But he solidified the third base position, completing perhaps the best infield in the National League.

Werber also brought his competitive enthusiasm to the Reds, labeling himself and his fellow infielders as the "Jungle Cats" and demanding the best from each one. Werber was the Tiger, second baseman Lonny Frey was the Leopard, and shortstop Billy Myers was the Jaguar. The three did not let Frank McCormick into the group at first; only when the big first baseman's play was deemed aggressive enough was he rewarded with the title "Wildcat."

One key facet of McKechnie's strategy, at least in the early part of the 1939 season, was to use Ernie Lombardi in nearly every game. Ernie caught 33 of the Reds' first 36 games and 45 of the first 49. He caught every contest of a 12-game winning streak in May that vaulted the Reds into the league lead. With Ernie hitting well, the infield stronger than ever defensively, and starters Paul Derringer and Bucky Walters winning nearly all their starts, the Reds grabbed first place and built a lead in the standings that reached five games in early June.

The other National League teams noticed the sudden rise of the Reds, the onetime doormat of the circuit. On May 17, in a particularly testy game against the Boston Bees at Crosley Field, Ernie complained to the umpires that Boston reliever Fred Frankhouse was throwing spitballs. Frankhouse struck Ernie out, but hit the next batter, Harry Craft, in the head and knocked him out of the game. The umpires agreed with Ernie (who knew spitballs, having caught them from Harry Krause with the Oakland Oaks many years before), and Frankhouse received a warning letter from Commissioner Landis a few days later.

For years the Reds had been the pushover of the league, and opposing pitchers knocked down the Cincinnati batters with impunity. Now the tables had turned, and Ernie called for more knockdown pitches than ever before. As Ernie put it, "Gabby Hartnett complained about it one time and I said, 'You guys handed it out. Now you can take it for a little while.'"[6]

The fans in opposing ballparks saw the Reds as a threat as well. Ernie was always a fan favorite in Brooklyn, but on June 10 Ernie struck out twice in a row at Ebbets Field and, possibly for the first time, heard boos and taunts from the Dodger crowd. He was still the most popular Red, though. Late in June his admirers presented him with a new shotgun in a pre-game ceremony against the Giants. And he belted two hits in the All-Star Game at Yankee Stadium, starting at catcher for the National League for the second year in a row.

One disappointment for the Reds in 1939 was the performance of Johnny Vander Meer. He was slow to recover from the flu that swept the training camp in Tampa, and various other illnesses and arm soreness rendered him ineffective. After his 15-win season in 1938, Vander Meer won only five games in 1939. But Lloyd (Whitey) Moore and Gene (Junior) Thompson, both products of Cincinnati's farm system, stepped up and completed the starting rotation, winning 13 games each. Another welcome addition was Lee Grissom, who rebounded somewhat from a poor 1938 campaign to win nine games.

On June 11, Lombardi was forced to the sidelines by an off-the-field injury. After the doubleheader in Brooklyn that day, Ernie stepped on a broken board in the shower at Ebbets Field and drove a large splinter deep into his left foot. He and Vander Meer had been invited to Cooperstown, New York, to take part in the dedication ceremonies for the Baseball Hall of Fame, but Ernie could not walk without limping, and was unable to make the trip. He remained out of action for eight games, returning on June 24 in a 7–2 loss to the Giants. In Lombardi's absence, Willard Hershberger filled in admirably, pushing his batting average well over the .400 mark as the Reds won five of the eight contests that Ernie missed. When Ernie returned on June 25, the Reds owned a four-game lead over the Cardinals.

With the Reds in a pennant race for the first time in years, tempers were apt to boil over during the hottest days of the summer, as they did on June 30 in Chicago. Ernie belted a homer to give the Reds a 1–0 lead in the second inning, but in the bottom of the frame Johnny Vander Meer could not find the plate. He struck out two but walked the bases full, arguing all the while with umpire Ziggy Sears about the strike zone. Another walk to Billy Herman, the fourth free pass of the inning, brought in a run and caused both Vander Meer and Lombardi to erupt, resulting in the pitcher's ejection.

Whitey Moore came in from the bullpen and walked Augie Galan to force home another run before finally getting the third out. But the Reds roasted Sears all day, and in the eighth, with the Cubs ahead by a score of 2 to 1, Ernie exploded at Sears again. Rip Russell was on third and Dick

Bartell on second when Stan Hack swung at a third strike. The ball rolled to the backstop, but Ernie believed that Hack had fouled off the pitch (as did Hack, who made no attempt to run to first), so Ernie did not bother to chase the ball. When Sears called "Strike Three!" Ernie turned to argue. While his back was turned, Russell and Bartell scored.

Sears had had enough of Ernie for one afternoon and thumbed him out the game, but the big catcher did not go quietly. As the *Cincinnati Enquirer* reported, "Big Schnoz gave the large Ladies' Day gathering a big laugh after being ordered out of the game. He tossed the mask, leg protectors, and chest protector high into [the] air, while giving Sears a final tongue-lashing. The big spaghetti-strangler really was sizzling."[7] Perhaps this fighting spirit invigorated the Reds, who won 22 of their 29 games in July and, after a doubleheader sweep of the Phillies at Crosley Field on July 30, extended their lead to 12 games over the Cardinals.

But the injury bug hit the Reds, with Lonny Frey, Harry Craft, and Billy Myers all missing time, while Ernie Lombardi fought through a series of nagging finger and hand injuries in July and August. McKechnie's men faltered in August with a 13–15 record and allowed the St. Louis Cardinals to climb back into the race. The Cardinals, powered by slugging Johnny Mize (the first baseman that the Reds had rejected four years before) whittled away at the Cincinnati lead and made a race of it.

The Reds needed Ernie's bat more than ever, and after hitting .190 in August, Lombardi found his stroke in September. "Lombardi is the batting bell-cow of the Reds," said *The Sporting News*. "When he hits, the club hits."[8] On September 3, Ernie belted a line drive that cleared the left field fence at Crosley Field and bounced off the front of the laundry building across the street. On September 7, in an 8–7 loss at Pittsburgh, Ernie socked two home runs and scored three times.

The Cardinals kept pace, lurking a few games behind in second place and waiting for the Reds to fade. On September 19, Johnny Vander Meer started against the Phillies but failed to get out of the first inning, giving up two walks and a single before McKechnie yanked him out of the game. The Phillies won an ugly 13–1 decision, dropping the Cincinnati lead over the Cardinals to two and a half games.

The 1939 season came down to a four-game set against the Cardinals at Crosley Field at the end of September. The Reds needed to win two of the four games to clinch the pennant, and they took the first game of a doubleheader on Tuesday, September 26 as Junior Thompson pitched a 3–1 victory. Ernie contributed a single, a double, and two intentional walks. But the Reds lost the second game with Willard Hershberger catching as Mort Cooper shut out the Reds on four hits, while Lee Grissom failed to complete the first inning. The next day, Bill McGee shut out the Reds again, defeating Bucky Walters, and cut the Cincinnati lead to two and a half games with four games left to play.

On Thursday, September 28, the Reds sent Paul Derringer (24–7) to the mound to face rookie Max Lanier. When Lanier allowed two runs in the first, St. Louis manager Ray Blades brought in the 22-game winner Curt Davis to contain the damage. The Cardinals tied the score on a home run by Terry Moore in the second, and the game seesawed for the next several innings.

Ernie Lombardi went hitless that day, but guided Derringer through the powerful Cardinal lineup. Derringer gave up 14 hits but worked his way out of one jam after another to keep the Cardinals off the board. The game was tied at 3 in the sixth when Derringer's sacrifice fly put the Reds on top again, and Harry Craft's home run in the eighth gave the Reds a 5–3 lead.

In the ninth, all Derringer had to do was to retire three Hall of Famers. He got Enos Slaughter on a pop-up to short and struck out Joe Medwick and Johnny Mize to complete his 25th win of the season and clinch the Reds' first pennant since 1919. The win set off a wild celebration, with fans swarming the field, Derringer's teammates carrying him to the clubhouse on their shoulders, and factory whistles blaring all over Cincinnati.

Ernie, bothered by nagging injuries all year, saw his batting average drop to .287, though his 20 home runs set a new personal high. He also led the league again with 19 intentional walks, proving that National League pitchers still feared his bat. Best of all, he was healthy at the end of the regular season and expected his hot hitting in September to carry over into his first World Series.

The Reds' success enabled Ernie's teammates to pull one of their many pranks on him. Upon returning from a road trip, the Reds learned that a throng of fans was waiting to greet them at Cincinnati's Union Station. So Ernie's teammates sent him a fake telegram, purportedly from the mayor of Cincinnati, asking him to make a ten-minute speech to the crowd. Ernie hated public speaking with a passion, but he was the senior Red in years of service and the club's most recognizable star.

When the train pulled into the station, Ernie was missing, but the crumpled telegram was left behind on his seat. A few minutes earlier, when the train stopped a few miles outside of town, Ernie grabbed his suitcase, hustled off the train, and took a cab home.

The 1939 season was Cincinnati's 50th in the National League. During that half century, the Reds had won the World Series only once.

And that title was a tainted one.

In 1919, the Reds, managed by Pat Moran and led by center fielder and batting champion Edd Roush, won their first National League pennant by nine games over the New York Giants. The 1919 edition of the Reds lacked stars except for Roush but featured a deep pitching staff and dependable starters at nearly every position. It was a solid team, if not a spectacular one, but they won 96 games and set a franchise record for winning percentage that still stands (as of the end of the 2022 season). They won eight more contests than their Series opponents, the Chicago White Sox of the American League.

The White Sox, on the other hand, boasted some of the most recognizable stars of the game in second baseman Eddie Collins, left fielder "Shoeless Joe" Jackson, and 29-game winning pitcher Eddie Cicotte. Most of the nation's sporting press made the White Sox the favorite, and few expected the Reds to put up much of a contest.

But the Reds won the Series in eight games (it was a best-of-nine affair at the time). A year later, the public learned that eight White Sox players, including Jackson and Cicotte, stood accused of taking money from gamblers to lose the Series. The eight players were indicted by a grand jury for their roles in baseball's greatest scandal, and though they were acquitted, they were banned from the sport for life by the new Commissioner of Baseball, Judge Kenesaw M. Landis.

Edd Roush and his teammates always believed that they would have won the Series even if the White Sox had played it honestly. As Roush told author Larry Ritter in 1964, "One thing that's overlooked in the whole mess is that we could have beat them no matter what the circumstances! Sure, the 1919 White Sox were good. But the 1919 Cincinnati Reds were better. I'll believe that till my dying day."[9] But the scandal cast doubt on the Reds' only championship, and it was up to Bill McKechnie and his charges to win a totally legitimate World Series title and put the taint of 1919 behind them.

It would not be easy. The American League champion New York Yankees were a juggernaut,

Bucky Walters, who came to the Reds from the Phillies in 1938 and became a 20-game winner (Wikimedia Commons photo repository at https://commons.wikimedia.org/wiki).

gunning for their fourth world title in a row. Managed by Joe McCarthy, the Yankees ran away with the pennant, winning by 17 games over the second place Red Sox and scoring 967 runs, more than six per game. Few observers, at least the ones outside of Cincinnati, gave the Reds much of a chance against one of the greatest teams of all time, and some thought that the Reds would be lucky to win even one game.

But the Cincinnati fans were thrilled. Their Reds were back in the World Series after a 20-year absence, and ticket sales were brisk. The bookies made the Reds the underdogs at odds of 13–5, but some believed that Cincinnati might give the Yankees a run for their money. It was a tall order, but if Bucky Walters, who won 27 games during the regular season, and Paul Derringer, who won 25, each won twice, the Reds would win the title.

In Game One, a 2–1 win for the Yankees in New York, Ernie went hitless in three trips to the plate against Red Ruffing, who allowed only four hits. The big catcher killed a potential Cincinnati rally in the second inning, grounding into a double play after a one-out single by Frank McCormick. In the fourth, after McCormick drove in the Reds' only run of the game, Ernie ended the inning with a weak tap to the pitcher, and in the seventh he again made the third out, this time with a foul pop-up. Still, the contest was tied at 1 until the bottom of the ninth, when Charlie Keller tripled, Paul Derringer walked Joe DiMaggio intentionally, and Bill Dickey drove Keller home with the winning run.

The next day, before 59,791 at Yankee Stadium, New York, right-hander Monte Pearson held the Reds to two hits in an easy 4–0 win. Pearson was nearly untouchable that day, and carried a no-hitter into the eighth inning when Ernie broke it up, rifling a sharp liner to center that fell in front of a hard-charging DiMaggio. It was Ernie's first hit of the Series, and the first Cincinnati hit since Harry Craft's single in the fifth inning of Game One.

Nothing came of it, as Frenchy Bordagaray pinch-ran for Ernie and remained on first as Craft struck out and Wally Berger grounded to the pitcher. Bill Werber reached Pearson for another single with two out in the ninth, but Lonny Frey forced him at second to end the game and give the Yankees a two-game lead in the Series.

Already, the Series looked like a mismatch, with the Reds apparently outclassed against the defending world champions. As one wag put it, "Not only does the National League get licked worse, it gets licked faster."[10] Hundreds of Cincinnati fans welcomed their heroes when their train pulled into Union Station on Friday morning, but even the most rabid Queen City loyalists could sense the impossibility of winning even one game against the mighty Yankees. The local papers reported that scalpers had trouble unloading their tickets, and the club admitted that half of the available standing-room tickets for Games Three and Four were still available.

The scene then shifted to Cincinnati on Saturday, October 7, for the first World Series contest in the Queen City in 20 years. In the top of the first Charlie Keller walloped a homer off Junior Thompson to give the Yankees a 2–0 lead, but the Reds answered in the bottom of the inning when, with two out, Ival Goodman and Frank McCormick singled off Yankee starter Lefty Gomez. Ernie then drilled a single to center to score McCormick and put the Reds on the board. In the second, after Bump Hadley replaced Gomez, the Reds took their first lead of the Series when four singles and a fielder's choice plated two runs and put the Reds ahead by a 3–2 count.

The lead disappeared in the third when Joe DiMaggio reached Thompson for a truly impressive two-run homer, a screaming liner to the deepest part of center field. Two innings later, Keller and Dickey belted homers of their own to drive Thompson from the mound and give the Yankees a 7–3 lead. Lee Grissom and Whitey Moore held the Yankees at bay the rest of the way, but Hadley was sharp, and the game ended with the Reds behind, three games to none.

That's when Joe DiMaggio went to work.

DiMaggio had missed most of May of 1939 with a torn calf muscle, but roared back in early June and dominated the American League as few batters ever have. Even the loss of Lou Gehrig, the slugging first baseman, to the incurable disease that now bears his name, barely slowed the Yankee juggernaut with DiMaggio at the helm. On September 9, after belting three hits against Washington, Joltin' Joe's batting average stood at .409. It sank like a stone thereafter due to an eye infection; Joe, ever the team player, refused to ask out of the lineup lest the local writers accuse him of protecting his .400 average. Sportswriters could be so vicious back then, as Ernie Lombardi would soon find out.

The man they called the "Yankee Clipper" finished the 1939 season with a .381 average, winning both the batting title and the Most Valuable Player award, but his season-ending slump gave the Cincinnati rooters some hope for an upset against the heavily favored Yankees. Unfortunately for the Reds, DiMaggio's eye infection cleared up, and he looked more like himself in the first three games of the Series.

Bill McKechnie probably knew that his Reds had no chance of winning four in a row against the mighty Yankees, but he sent Paul Derringer, the loser of Game One, to the mound on three days' rest for Game Four. Ernie belted a long drive to center in the second inning that threatened to score the game's first run, but DiMaggio hauled it in with a great running catch. The Reds scored once in the third, but when Bill Werber drove a long one to the wall, DiMaggio made another long running catch to end the Cincinnati rally.

For a while, the Reds made a game of it. Derringer blanked the Yankees for six innings but gave up two runs in the seventh on home runs by Charlie Keller and Bill Dickey. But the Reds answered with three in their half of the seventh. Frank McCormick reached on an error and then, after Ernie struck out, a double by Al Simmons, a groundout by Wally Berger, and singles by Willard Hershberger and Bill Werber gave the Reds a 3–2 lead. They made it 4–2 in the eighth when Ernie singled in Ival Goodman, who had doubled.

In the ninth, with Bucky Walters on the mound in relief, Keller and DiMaggio singled. Dickey grounded to second, but Billy Myers dropped the ball when DiMaggio slid into him at top speed to break up the double play. This allowed Keller to score, and a fly ball to right by George Selkirk advanced DiMaggio to third. Joe Gordon then bounced a ball to third. Werber gunned the ball home, but DiMaggio slid around Lombardi's tag and tied the game at 4. The Reds failed to score in their half of the ninth, and that set the stage for the tenth, the worst inning of Ernie Lombardi's life.

In the top of the tenth Frank Crosetti walked and was sacrificed to second by Red Rolfe. Keller reached on another error by Myers, putting runners on first and third with one out. This brought Joe DiMaggio to the plate with a chance to break the game open.

DiMaggio lashed a sharp liner to right, and when Ival Goodman bobbled the ball, Crosetti scored easily, and Keller came roaring around third and heading for home. Frank McCormick's relay throw reached the plate as Keller charged in, and what happened next has been the source of much conjecture since the afternoon of October 8, 1939.

Either Keller or the ball itself slammed into Lombardi hard. The blow, whatever its source, leveled the rock-solid catcher and left him lying dazed on the ground as the ball dribbled off a few feet away. As Ernie lay motionless in the dirt, DiMaggio dashed around third and tried to score. As DiMaggio ran for home, Ernie regained his senses, retrieved the baseball, and lunged for DiMaggio. But the Yankee superstar slid past Ernie and dragged his right foot across the plate as he passed. Three runs crossed the plate on DiMaggio's single, giving the Yankees a 7–4 lead. When the Reds went out meekly in the bottom of the tenth, the Yankees celebrated their fourth consecutive World Series title.

What happened? Today, high-definition television cameras would have recorded the play from every conceivable angle. In 1939, movie cameras caught the play from a distance. The film was not available immediately, so the reporters were left to interpret the play as they saw fit.

They called it "Lombardi's Snooze." They wrote that Ernie went to sleep at the plate. He did a "dying swan act." DiMaggio's run was virtually meaningless—it was the difference between a 6–4 win and a 7–4 win—but sportswriters, then and now, like to anoint a hero and blame a goat for the outcome of a major sporting event. The World Series was the biggest sporting event in the nation in 1939, and the writers, almost unanimously, gave the goat horns to Ernie Lombardi.

Ernie was now firmly ensconced in a list of baseball "goats" that included Fred Merkle (whose failure to touch second base cost the Giants a pennant in 1908), Hank Gowdy (who dropped a crucial foul pop in the 1924 World Series), and, much later, Bill Buckner (who saw a grounder go between his legs in 1986 and cost the Red Sox the chance to win the World Series). No matter that the Reds made four errors that day and blew a two-run lead in the ninth. The way the writers told it in the papers the next day, Ernie Lombardi lost the 1939 World Series all by himself.

On page one of *The New York Times*, John Drebinger wrote that DiMaggio scored "while the lumbering Cincinnati catcher still squatted on the ground, apparently brooding over the futility of it all."[11] In his "Sports of the Times" column, John Kieran said "DiMaggio ran home from third while Ernesto Cyrano de Bergerac Lombardi was brooding on the ground at the plate with the ball almost within reach of his hand."[12] Even the Cincinnati papers piled on, with the *Post* describing Lombardi as "imitating a wounded sea lion,"[13] and the *Times-Star* saying that DiMaggio scored "while Lombardi lolled around on the ground."[14] Ernie, a prideful man whose toughness had never been questioned in his 14 seasons of professional baseball, was now an object of scorn and ridicule. He would forever be remembered for his "snooze" at home plate.

None of his fellow Reds blamed Ernie for the play. Johnny Vander Meer described what he saw. "The throw from the outfield came in a short hop and hit Lom in the cup," said Vander Meer. "You just don't get up too quick. Somebody put out the word that 'Lombardi went to sleep, took a snooze.' He was paralyzed. He couldn't move. Anybody but Lombardi, they would have had to carry him off the field."[15]

DiMaggio saw it differently. "Ernie was wronged," recalled DiMaggio. "He was knocked out in a collision with Charlie Keller, who scored, and I saw immediately that something was haywire. I kept running and never stopped. Keller gave Ernie more than just a bump, as they described it. He put Ernie out of commission."[16] But Keller, interviewed at spring training the next year, claimed that he never touched Lombardi. The catcher, said Keller, merely fell backward for unknown reasons.

Bucky Walters, the losing pitcher, said, "It was a silly rap. But the Yankees beat us four straight and they had to pick on something, I guess. You can blame part of the thing on me. I was pitching, and I should have been behind home plate, backing up Lombardi. But the run didn't mean anything, anyway."[17]

Gabriel Schechter, a baseball researcher and author of several books on baseball history, studied the available film of the play in detail and states that most of the eyewitness accounts were wrong. According to Schechter, the ball could not have hit Lombardi in the groin, because it came in to Lombardi chest high. Schechter found that the ball beat Keller to the plate, but as Keller, who did not slide, extended his right leg to tag the plate, he made contact with Lombardi. The catcher was leaning forward to take the throw and thus was not solidly anchored on the ground. This contact, Keller's knee to Lombardi's ribs, is what caused Ernie to lose the ball and collapse at the plate.

Schechter also says, and a review of the film by this author backs him up, that Keller clotheslined Ernie as he passed. Keller was a strong, muscular ballplayer—his nickname was "King Kong"—and the combination of a chest shot and a head shot would have disabled any man, even one as tough as Lombardi. Joe DiMaggio, more than 40 years after the fact, agreed. Speaking in 1986, DiMaggio recalled, "They gave Lombardi an error, but it was wrong. Keller hit him on the head and stunned him. It was a short-count knockout."[18]

Ernie Lombardi carried the weight of that single play for the rest of his life. Though he won a batting title, earned a Most Valuable Player award, and led the Reds to the pennant, he became most famous for three things—his huge nose, his inability to run, and his "snooze" in the 1939 World Series. The play became an indelible, and unfair, stain on his reputation, one he could never shake off.

Perhaps baseball historian Bill James put it best. "Lombardi was now the Bill Buckner of the 1930s," wrote James, "even more innocent than Buckner, and Buckner has plenty of people who should be holding up their hands to share his disgrace."[19]

After the game, Ernie had little to say, but wanted to put the Series behind him as quickly as possible. "I'm going home to California right away," he said, "and do as much bass fishing as I can. I'm not even thinking about baseball for a while."[20]

11

Tragedy and Triumph

> "We certainly are not blaming Lombardi for the loss of the last world series game. As early as December 16 [1939] I wrote Lombardi, telling him I would like to have talked with him after that game and told him to forget about it."[1]
> —Cincinnati general manager
> Warren Giles, January 1940

Bill McKechnie shook hands with all his players after the last game of the World Series, but inwardly he was bitterly disappointed. Eleven years earlier, he led the St. Louis Cardinals to the National League pennant, was swept by the Yankees in the World Series, and was replaced shortly afterward. He knew that his job with the Reds was secure, thanks to his relationship with Warren Giles, but the frustration lingered. McKechnie told his coaches that had the Reds won Game Four, they had a chance to win the Series. "I don't care if they are the greatest team in baseball," he said. "We should have beat 'em and if we ever get another crack at 'em we will."[2]

He also refused to comment on the bizarre tenth-inning play that gave the Yankees a three-run lead. "You can't explain that tenth inning and that play with Lombardi. It's just one of those things,"[3] he said.

Lombardi himself said little about the play that made him infamous. Home plate umpire Babe Pinelli told *The Sporting News*, "Lombardi couldn't find the ball, and DiMaggio came home while he was hunting for it." Reached at home in Oakland, Lombardi hotly replied, "That's a lie. Pinelli told me he looked at me and my eyes were closed. Keller dazed me when he slid into me."[4] Otherwise, Ernie maintained his silence during the fall and winter. He played in all-star exhibition games in the Bay Area after the Series, as a teammate of Joe DiMaggio, and stayed away from the unpleasant subject of the "snooze."

Ernie never made excuses for himself, and in 1977, reporter Mike Lackey interviewed Paul Derringer about the play. Derringer's summation was probably the correct one. "Keller's knee hit [Ernie] in the ribs and knocked the breath out of him," said Derringer. "I finally got it out of him.

But he wouldn't tell a newspaperman a thing like that. Besides, they just wrote the first thing that came into their minds, without ever getting their facts straight."[5]

In January, Warren Giles sent Ernie a contract that called for a $6,000 pay cut. Ernie, predictably, sent it back unsigned. "I'm not mad," he told the papers, "but I can't figure where I'm entitled to a cut like that."[6] Giles explained that the cut was really only $3,000; he stated that Ernie should not count the $3,000 he earned for winning the 1938 batting title and Most Valuable Player award as part of his 1939 salary.

Asked by a reporter if the Reds were using his "snooze" against him at salary time, Lombardi played it cool. "I don't think so. No one on our club ever said anything to me about it. Our manager, Bill McKechnie, never opened his mouth. I guess they're cutting me because I didn't hit so well."[7]

Privately, Ernie was fuming. He didn't lose the World Series, and it looked to him as if Giles was using his unfair status as the goat of the Series against him in contract negotiations. After making another All-Star team, leading the team in home runs, and playing a key role in Cincinnati's first pennant in 20 years, reasoned Ernie, the team's most popular player should expect a raise, not a huge pay cut.

Due to Ernie's popularity in Cincinnati, Giles felt obliged to explain himself. "Ernie has done good work for the Reds," said the general manager.

> We want him to continue to do good work for the Reds and not for some other club, and I am hopeful that any differences of opinion respecting salary will be adjusted to the satisfaction of both parties in plenty of time for Ernie to be swinging his big war club in training when the first batting practice starts.
> Shortly after the end of the 1938 season in which Lombardi won the National League batting championship and also the league's most valuable player award the club presented him with $3,000 extra payment for his 1938 services. This was a bonus, not called for in his 1938 contract. He seemingly has confused this bonus with the salary he drew from the club in 1939.
> Our offer to Lombardi for 1940 contains provisions which make him reasonably certain of drawing as much money from the Cincinnati club for 1940 as he was paid by it for 1939. A small part of our offer for 1940 is contingent upon the Reds attracting approximately half as many admissions at home this year as last.[8]

So Ernie was a holdout, as usual, but he didn't stay one for long. On February 26, after a long talk with Bill McKechnie, he reached an agreement with Giles by phone and proceeded to Tampa. He was the last of the Reds to sign his contract, but he had something to prove in 1940. "I'm sure glad to be back with the Reds," he said, "and watch my smoke this year. I'm out to regain the batting championship, and also to prove to a few of the skeptical Cincinnatians that my batting sights aren't dimmed."[9]

11. Tragedy and Triumph

In March, while "wheezing like a contented walrus" on a training table in Tampa, Ernie gave his most detailed explanation of the disastrous World Series play to writer Bob Considine.

> Yeah, it sure raised a rumpus, me not tagging DiMaggio that day. Naw, I didn't mind what some of you fellows wrote. You gotta write 'em as you see 'em, I guess. But I'll tell you this much: Keller half knocked me cold when he hit me, when he scored the second run of that inning. They tell me he stepped on my arm with his spikes, but if he did I didn't even feel it, he hit me so hard.
>
> And DiMaggio? Heck, he was the third run of the inning. What if I didn't get him? Didn't hurt none. They only needed one run to beat us. Well, that's about all the people wanted to talk about when I got home. And, a funny thing, all that publicity seemed to get people interested in me, kind of got a ton of mail from fans during the winter, saying they were still with me and so on. Got 400 Christmas cards from Cincinnati people alone. Everything turned out all right.[10]

With that, Ernie put the "snooze" behind him, at least as far as he was concerned. He rarely talked about it ever afterward.

Though many writers, stunned by the Reds' failure to win a single game in the Series, predicted that they would drop to second or third place in 1940, Ernie disagreed. "We would have won two of those Series games with a little luck. The first and fourth. You can't tell what would have happened if we had ... but what I was saying was that experiences like we had in the Series won't hurt us. They teach things, especially to the young guys."[11]

The defending National League champions charged into the 1940 campaign. By the end of May, Cincinnati's 25–10 record left them in first place, two games ahead of the upstart Brooklyn Dodgers (the team run by two ex-Reds, manager Leo Durocher and general manager Larry MacPhail). Ernie, as usual, caught almost every game in the early going, and went on a tear in May with a series of two- and three-hit games. On June 1 his average stood at .345, near the top of the league, and he looked like a threat to recapture the batting title. On the few occasions that he took a day off to rest a bruised hand or an injured finger, Willard Hershberger filled in admirably, keeping his average well above .300 in his limited action. Hershberger's performance in relief of Lombardi led the *Cincinnati Enquirer* to label him "the best #2 catcher in baseball."

The Reds kept winning, but the pesky Dodgers kept pace, with the New York Giants close behind in what shaped up as a three-team race. But Brooklyn faltered in July, while Cincinnati went on an 18–2 run. Three consecutive wins against the Giants and three more against Brooklyn in late July virtually knocked both clubs out of the race, and by July 26, when

Paul Derringer defeated the Phillies for his 14th win, the Reds owned a lead of eight and a half games.

The Cincinnati lead might have been bigger had Johnny Vander Meer conquered his control problems. Derringer and Bucky Walters were headed for 20-win seasons, but Vander Meer could not find the plate, and in July McKechnie demoted the left-hander to Indianapolis to straighten himself out. But Junior Thompson and the newly acquired Jim Turner filled the third and fourth starting slots well, while Frank McCormick and Ernie Lombardi paced the offense.

Ernie was hitting as well as ever. On July 21, during a doubleheader sweep over the Giants at Crosley Field, Ernie mashed one of his longest home runs, which sailed over the left field fence and onto the roof of his favorite target, the laundry on York Street. Despite the nationwide heat wave which left the temperature at 98 degrees at game time, more than 33,000 fans came to cheer their Reds. McKechnie's men were now fully in charge of the race, and most of the nation's sportswriters already conceded the pennant to Cincinnati.

Ernie's teammates recognized the big catcher's contributions. "Lombardi is the best catcher in baseball and the most underrated, too," said Paul Derringer.

> He's a quick thinker, has a great pair of hands and is a swell hitter. He's really been cutting at that ball. I wouldn't be surprised to see Ernie lead the league in hitting as he did in 1938.
>
> The one thing he can't do is run. But his other abilities make up for that. Yes, Ernie is just about tops in his line.[12]

Others around the league agreed, as Ernie made the All-Star team for the fifth year in a row, his third time as the starter.

But on July 27, the injury bug struck when Ernie, batting a cool .320 at the time, sprained his ankle while running out a grounder in a pinch-hitting appearance in Philadelphia. Lombardi was expected to be out of action for more than a week during the most intense part of the schedule, with a string of doubleheaders coming up and the country gripped in a record-setting heat wave. So Bill McKechnie put Ernie's backup, Willard Hershberger, into the starting lineup, and all appeared to be well. "Hershey" had performed well when called upon, and a four-hit performance at Brooklyn on July 23 raised his batting average to .378.

Sadly, Willard Hershberger was not well. Some of his teammates told McKechnie that Hershberger talked about committing suicide on several occasions that season. To make matters worse, several Reds, including Hershberger, Derringer, and Ival Goodman, caught a bad case of dysentery in Philadelphia. With his illness, the heat wave, and the pressure of

Star-crossed catcher Willard Hershberger (National Baseball Hall of Fame Library, Cooperstown, New York).

replacing the Reds' All-Star catcher in a pennant chase, Willard Hershberger was falling apart.

Hershberger's mental state was deteriorating by the day. The games in Philadelphia and New York were played in brutal heat, and the papers reported that the backup catcher lost 10 pounds in a week. The Reds wobbled without Lombardi in the lineup, and though Hershberger tried his best, the Cincinnati club split four games against the Phillies, then lost two of three against the Giants in New York.

The final game against the Giants, played on July 31, was the most disappointing loss of all. Bucky Walters breezed through the first eight innings, scattering eight hits and carrying a 4–1 lead into the ninth. Walters retired the first two batters in the ninth, but then the roof fell in. As *The New York Times* described it the next day,

> Four times in a row Bucky Walters was one strike away from winning. Four times he failed.
>
> He had a 3–2 count on Bob Seeds and lost him by issuing a pass. He reached the same tally on Burgess Whitehead and Whitey slashed a home run just inside the right field foul line. He did it again before Mel Ott walked. Then up stepped Harry the Horse Danning.
>
> Bucky was taking no chances. He whisked in two strikes, took aim and fired again. The Horse swung from his heels and the ball sailed through the mild night air into the upper left field balcony.[13]

Danning's walk-off homer gave the Giants a 5–4 victory.

Hershberger, who went hitless that day, blamed himself for the loss. He had called the wrong pitch to Danning, he said, insisting on a fastball even after Walters shook him off. Despite the loss, the Reds maintained a lead in the pennant race of seven and a half games, but Hershberger was despondent. The Reds had three consecutive doubleheaders coming up in Boston against the Bees, and though Ernie Lombardi was almost ready to rejoin the lineup, his understudy was gripped by fear. Hershberger, in his depressed state, had convinced himself that he was blowing the pennant all by himself.

On Friday, August 2, the Reds lost the first game of a doubleheader in Boston by a score of 10–3 with Bill Baker catching. Hershberger caught the second game, and the Reds lost again in 12 innings. Hershberger not only went 0 for 5 at the plate, but he also appeared to be losing his concentration. When Boston's Max West tapped a ball in front of the plate, Hershberger did not move, forcing pitcher Whitey Moore to make the play. McKechnie confronted Hershberger between innings. "See that piece of sod there, Hershey?" asked the manager. "That's where Whitey had to come and field the ball. Is there anything wrong with you?"

"Yes, plenty," replied the catcher. "I'll tell you all about it after the game."[14]

For several hours that evening, Hershberger tearfully spilled out his problems to McKechnie. "My father took his own life, and so will I," he said at one point. He believed with all his heart that he was dragging the team down, and that the recent losses were all his fault. McKechnie, who was afraid to leave Hershberger alone, tried to convince the troubled catcher otherwise, and kept the conversation going until he was sure that Hershberger's mood had improved. The manager and the catcher then ate dinner, after which Hershberger went off to the lobby with his teammates.

McKechnie may have figured that the pressure on Hershberger would soon abate, as Ernie Lombardi was now ready to return to the lineup. "I'm ready," said Lombardi to the local reporters. "I'm eager to return to action. I did a little running in the outfield today, and it didn't pain me."[15] Lombardi's bat was sorely missed by the Reds, who had lost six of their last eight and had seen their lead over the second-place Dodgers shrink from nine games to six.

When Hershberger, who was slated to catch the second game of that day's doubleheader, awoke on Saturday morning, August 3, he told his roommate Bill Baker that he did not feel well. He was unusually quiet at breakfast, and when Baker offered him a ride to the park, Hershberger said that he would come later. Paul Derringer also asked if Hershberger was going to the park, but the catcher responded, "I'm waiting for a friend, but I'll be out soon."

Hershberger did not appear for batting practice before the first game, so McKechnie asked Gabe Paul, the traveling secretary, to call the catcher. Hershberger told Paul that he was not feeling well but would come to the park and watch the first game from the stands.

Instead, Hershberger remained in his room at the Copley Hotel while the Reds played the Bees in the first game. Ernie Lombardi caught that contest, his first start since July 23. After the game, which the Reds won by a 3–1 score, Hershberger was nowhere to be found. McKechnie, fearing the worst, assigned Bill Baker to take Hershberger's place. The manager then sent Dan Cohen, a Cincinnati businessman and rabid Reds fan who sometimes traveled with the team, to the Copley to look for him.

The Cincinnati manager held a team meeting between games. "We have," McKechnie told the players, "an unusually sick man among us who must be treated differently than we are in the habit of treating one another. We must cease playing jokes on him, and, above all, we must cease asking him how he feels. He is so sick mentally that we must overlook anything he does and try to raise his spirits back to normal."[16]

McKechnie had no idea what was happening back at the hotel.

When Dan Cohen knocked on Hershberger's door, he got no answer. So Cohen found a maid, who unlocked the door.

Willard Hershberger was dead.

The catcher had meticulously coated the floor of the bathroom with towels. He then leaned over the edge of the bathtub and sliced his own throat with Bill Baker's razor. His father's suicide had left blood all over the bathroom at the Hershberger house, and Willard was determined not to leave the same gigantic mess.

Cohen called Gabe Paul, who relayed the news to McKechnie on the bench during the fourth inning. The shaken McKechnie left coach Hank Gowdy in charge and accompanied Paul to the Copley. Perhaps the players sensed that something tragic had happened, but Gowdy had been ordered not to talk about it. After the game, which the Reds lost, McKechnie returned to the clubhouse and called the players together. He said simply, "Willard Hershberger has just destroyed himself."[17]

At a team meeting in McKechnie's hotel room that evening, the manager insisted that Hershberger had been in good spirits when they parted after dinner the night before. But, except for his statement that the catcher had threatened to take his own life, McKechnie refused to reveal the details of their conversation. "He told me what his problems were," McKechnie said. "It has nothing to do with anybody on the team. It was something personal. He told it to me in confidence, and I will not utter it to anyone. I will take it with me to my grave."[18] The manager kept his promise. He never told anyone what he and Hershberger discussed on the night of August 2, 1940.

On Sunday, the day after Hershberger's death, the Cincinnati clubhouse was silent before the doubleheader. Most of the players had visited the funeral home to pay their respects that morning, and the somber Reds spoke in hushed tones about their teammate. McKechnie called the players together again and said, "There's nothing we can do, fellows. Let's pitch in a little harder and win this pennant and dedicate it to the gamest little guy who ever hit in a pinch."[19] The Reds also resolved to give a winning World Series share to Hershberger's widowed mother in California. With that, the Reds lost the first game against the Bees and won the second.

Ernie Lombardi never spoke publicly about his teammate's suicide, but the incident affected him deeply. After all, Hershberger was only in the daily lineup because Lombardi was injured, and Hershberger's fragile mental state collapsed under the strain. The reporters said that, in the deathly silence of the Cincinnati clubhouse on the day after the suicide, Ernie distracted himself by reading a newspaper, or tried to. This effort was unsuccessful, as Ernie, like all his teammates, was doing his best to hold back tears.

Still, the Reds had a pennant to win, and the thought of returning to the World Series and giving Hershberger's mother a winning share motivated the grieving Cincinnati players. Other teams might have collapsed under the weight of the tragedy, but the Reds pulled together. They maintained their position during August, in which they won 16 of their 32 games and stayed at least four games ahead of the Dodgers.

Hershberger's death left the Reds with only two catchers—Lombardi and the rookie Bill Baker. So Warren Giles activated coach Jimmie Wilson, who was 40 years old and had hardly played at all during the last several seasons. Still, Ernie caught nearly every game for a month and a half after Hershberger's death. Wilson and Baker filled in, mostly during the second games of doubleheaders, and the Reds rolled on.

The Reds were never in danger after August, and an 11-game winning streak in early September virtually clinched the flag for the Reds. Now, hoped Ernie, a second trip to the World Series would give him a chance to atone for the misfortune of 1939.

But it was not to be.

Ernie's season, and his quest for redemption, came to an end in Brooklyn on September 15. Ernie was riding high that day; he drilled a single in the first inning and caught the Dodgers napping when he beat out a bunt to lead off the third. But in the sixth, with the Reds ahead by an 8–0 score, Joe Gallagher lifted a foul pop near the first-base stands. Ernie raced over, slipped on the concrete curb of the gutter that ran along the edge of the grandstand, and caught his spikes in a board that covered the gutter. As he fell, his weight twisted his right ankle so severely that McKechnie sent him to a Brooklyn hospital for X-rays.

The ankle was sprained, not broken, and Ernie returned to the park on crutches to cheer on his teammates in the second game of the doubleheader. However, the injury was painful enough to keep Ernie off his feet for the next few weeks. Unable to run, the big catcher fell out of shape quickly, and his availability for the upcoming World Series was suddenly a question mark.

To replace Ernie, the Reds turned the job over the Jimmie Wilson, who had played in only eight games that year, and had batted only six times in 1938 and 1939 combined. Wilson, despite his age, teamed with rookies Dick West and Bill Baker to keep the Reds on track. Cincinnati clinched the pennant on September 18 with a 4–3, 13-inning win over the Phillies. Two weeks later, they ended the season a comfortable 12 and a half games ahead of the resurgent Brooklyn Dodgers.

Cincinnati prepared for another World Series, and at least the Reds would not be required to face the Yankee juggernaut again. The Detroit Tigers prevailed in a tight American League race against the Yankees and Cleveland Indians, largely due to the power hitting of Rudy York (33 homers, 134 runs batted in) and Hank Greenberg (41 homers, 150 runs batted in), the Most Valuable Player Award winner. The Reds needed all the power hitting they could muster, so the Cincinnati fans hoped and prayed for Ernie's recovery.

Unfortunately, Ernie's ankle healed slowly, and remained painful during the last two weeks of the season. Fitted with a special shoe, he worked hard to get ready for the Series by walking up and down steps and taking whirlpool treatments at a local hospital twice a day. Yet, though the swelling went down, the pain remained, and he could not walk without a limp. On October 1, the day before the first game of the Series, Ernie worked out with his teammates, but the ankle showed no improvement. Reluctantly, Bill McKechnie assigned Jimmie Wilson to catch the first game of the Series at Crosley Field, and, because Wilson's sore legs required extensive taping before each game, the manager resolved to evaluate Lombardi's condition day by day.

Of course, some reporters could not keep from recalling Ernie's most painful memory of the year before. As Harvey McLemore of the *Cincinnati Post* wrote before the opening game,

> Ernie Lombardi, titanic Reds catcher, has a sprained ankle that is hurting him something terrible. It is hurting him so badly that he has found it impossible to get a wink of sleep, and I figure this as the best thing that could have happened to the Reds.
>
> Because a wide awake Lombardi, one unable to take a snooze at home plate, gives the Reds a big edge. Had Lombardi been unable to sleep last year the Reds might well have won the series from the Yankees.
>
> This year an aching ankle will serve as an alarm clock and keep Ernie in action.[20]

Lombardi was not the only Cincinnati starter in danger of missing the Series. During the last week of the season, shortstop Billy Myers suddenly left the team and went home to Columbus, Ohio. Myers, who batted only .202 and fought injuries all year, was known to be a nervous sort, the kind of shortstop who might boot a routine play and follow it up with a sensational one. Warren Giles tracked Myers down and threatened him by phone. According to historian Lee Allen, Giles told Myers, "If you don't come back and play in the World Series, I'll fine you what salary you have coming and see that you aren't cut into the Series, and you'll never play another game."

Myers replied, "I don't care. I have personal problems and I don't care if I ever play again. And I don't want any money."[21] After a few more phone calls, Giles convinced Myers to rejoin the club, but the shortstop's mental state was a concern. Also, second baseman Lonny Frey was injured and unable to play the field and would see action in the Series only as a pinch-hitter and pinch-runner. Eddie Joost took Frey's place at second, breaking up the Jungle Cats infield at the most crucial time.

11. Tragedy and Triumph

In Game One, played before an enthusiastic sellout crowd at Crosley Field, Paul Derringer faced off against Detroit's 21-game winner Bobo Newsom. Derringer had not yet won a postseason game, losing his two starts in 1931 for the Cardinals and losing one more for the Reds in 1939. Derringer's bad luck in World Series play continued as the Tigers scored five runs in the second inning on five singles, a walk, and a throwing error by third baseman Bill Werber. Whitey Moore relieved Derringer and got the last two outs in the second, but the game was already out of reach. With Ernie on the sidelines, the only Cincinnati offensive threat was Frank McCormick, who went hitless as Newsom breezed to a 7–2 win.

The crowd was a little smaller for Game Two, in which Bucky Walters got off to a bad start. He walked the first two batters, and a single by Charlie Gehringer brought home a run. Hank Greenberg hit into a double play that plated another tally and the Tigers led 2–0. In the second, the Cincinnati bats came to life, as four singles brought in two runs and tied the score. Jimmy Ripple's two-run homer in the third gave the Reds their first lead of the series, and consecutive doubles by Walters and Bill Werber scored another run in the fourth. Walters held the Tigers in check the rest of the way, and the Reds won the game by a 5–3 score. It was Cincinnati's first win in a World Series game since the clinching contest in 1919.

On the train to Detroit that evening, Ernie sat by himself in a car away from his teammates. He had his leg propped up on a seat across from him, and he brooded about his situation. The Reds did not have the hitting to match the powerful Detroit sluggers like Gehringer, Greenberg, York, and others. The Reds were a team of singles hitters, and Ernie's bat was needed to protect Frank McCormick, who batted just before him in the lineup. Perhaps Ernie's mood brightened on the morning of Game Three, when Bill McKechnie reached the same conclusion. The manager named Ernie to start against the Tigers.

Detroit's starting pitcher, Tommy Bridges, was an 11-year veteran who was expected to make only one Series start. He was opposed by Cincinnati's Jim Turner, a 36-year-old right-hander who won 14 games in 1940. The Reds struck first, scoring in the first on a double by Werber and a single by Ival Goodman. In the second Ernie drilled a liner down the right field line. Noticeably limping, he nonetheless made it to second for a double, though he was stranded there as Bridges retired the next three Reds.

Ernie's ankle problem was no secret to anyone, especially the Tigers. In the fourth, when Ernie hit a grounder to Mike Higgins at third, Tiger shortstop Dick Bartell called to Higgins, "Take your time."

Turner and Bridges battled for the first six innings, but the Tigers broke it open in the seventh when a pair of two-run homers by Rudy York and Mike Higgins drove Turner from the game. In the eighth, with the

Reds behind by three runs, McKechnie pulled Ernie and replaced him with Bill Baker. Bridges completed a 7–4 win and the Tigers now held a lead in the Series, two games to one.

McKechnie was terse after the game. "You guys saw what happened out there today," he said. "That's the way it is in baseball." At least Ernie was able to play and contributed a hit. "I was glad Lombardi was able to get in there, but I don't know whether we'll be able to use him again except for pinch-hitting. His right ankle is swollen and sore right now."[22]

Ernie did not appear again in the Series until Game Seven. He wanted to play, but his ankle was still swollen, and he still walked with a pronounced limp. Besides, many of the Reds had come to regard Jimmie Wilson as something of a good luck charm. Wilson, despite playing in a fair amount of pain on his 40-year-old legs, belted two singles in Game Two and held his own behind the plate. In Game One he saved a run by expertly blocking and tagging Detroit's Bruce Campbell at home, though the Reds lost the game anyway.

With Lombardi on the bench, Paul Derringer finally gained his first World Series win in Game Four, allowing only five hits (though he walked six Tigers) in a 5–2 win that the Reds desperately needed. The next day, the Tigers struck back, driving Reds starter Junior Thompson out of the box with three runs in the third and four in the fourth. Bobo Newsom, only two days after his father's death, pitched the game of his life for Detroit, allowing only two hits in an 8–0 shutout.

Now the Reds, down three games to two, needed to win both Games Six and Seven in Cincinnati to clinch the title. In Game Six, Bucky Walters pitched his best game of the season, shutting down Greenberg and Gehringer and scattering five hits in a 4–0 win. Walters helped his own cause when he belted a home run in the eighth inning. This win tied the Series and brought on a deciding Game Seven, with Bobo Newsom facing Paul Derringer.

Game Six also added to the legend of Jimmie Wilson. In the sixth inning, with the bases loaded with Reds and Wilson on third, Bucky Walters hit a slow roller to Detroit third baseman Mike Higgins. Wilson, despite his aching legs, was determined to score, and the *Detroit Free Press* described the play: "With the crack of the bat, Wilson gave his ageing joints a stern talking to, called on them to do or die, and started off in low gear. Ten steps and he was in second gear, doing a furious three MPH. Five yards from home he slipped into high, roared across the plate at between five and six MPH. He beat Higgins' throw by an inch, and the crowd saluted him as if he had performed a miracle, which was exactly what he had done."[23]

In Game Seven, the Tigers reached Derringer for a run in the third on a single by Billy Sullivan, a sacrifice by Newsom, and a single by Gehringer,

11. Tragedy and Triumph

but otherwise neither team scored during the first six innings. Meanwhile, Jimmie Wilson belted two singles and caught the Tiger infield napping when he stole second base in the second inning.

The Reds finally broke through against Newsom in the seventh. Frank McCormick pounded a double off the left field fence, and Jimmy Ripple followed with another liner off the screen in right to score McCormick and tie the game. Wilson sacrificed Ripple to third, and McKechnie sent Ernie Lombardi up to pinch-hit for Eddie Joost.

Ernie never took the bat off his shoulder, as Tiger manager Del Baker (a teammate of Lombardi's on the Oakland club in 1926) ordered an intentional walk, leaving runners on first and third with one out. Lonny Frey pinch-ran for Lombardi, and with that, Ernie's World Series was finished. He limped back to the bench to the cheers of the hometown fans. Billy Myers then belted a long fly ball to Barney McCosky in center, scoring Ripple with the go-ahead run.

That was all Paul Derringer needed. Charlie Gehringer singled to lead off the eighth but never moved from first as Greenberg, York, and Bruce Campbell went out. In the ninth, three ground balls by Higgins, Sullivan, and pinch-hitter Earl Averill game the Reds their first World Championship since the tainted title of 1919.

Tiger shortstop Dick Bartell was not convinced that the Reds won the Series fairly. He complained that Derringer threw spitballs in Game Seven. Even so, Bartell admitted that Cincinnati's superior starting pitching kept the powerful Tiger hitters in check, as Derringer and Walters each won two games. "We lost the Series because we didn't hit,"[24] he said.

Jimmie Wilson, who batted .353 and stole the only base by either team, was the star of the Series, with Ernie Lombardi relegated to the background. As Dan Daniel wrote in *Baseball Magazine*:

> Well, the biggest break the Reds got came when Lombardi hurt his ankle. In place of "Schnozz," the Reds got the greatest catcher for those six games. Crafty, wise, calculating, instilling marvelous confidence in his pitchers, calling the turn on the Tigers hitters in many vital spots—he, James Wilson, was the true hero. Every day he went from the game to an Epsom salt bath. Every day he had to be pasted together with bandages and adhesive, so he could go out and catch that game. The spirit of the Reds was this grand fellow named Wilson. The very spirit of the World's Series.[25]

Ernie played the good sport. "We're going to be all right for catchers next year," he quipped to the *Cincinnati Enquirer*. "With enough spring training under his belt, that Wilson ought to be quite a catcher."[26] But Wilson was not interested in playing another season at the age of 41. He told the fans that they had seen him play his last game.

Still, the 1940 World Series was a bittersweet one for Ernie Lombardi.

An outstanding performance on baseball's biggest stage would have gone a long way toward putting his infamous "snooze" of the year before behind him, but his ankle injury prevented that from happening. Yes, he was a world champion for the only time in his career, taking home a winning share of $5,803.62, but he was more a spectator than a participant. Ernie, the longest-tenured and most popular Red, was an afterthought, while Jimmie Wilson walked off with the laurels.

After the Series, Ernie packed up his car and made the long drive back to Oakland. He was invited to play in two charity all-star games between Bay Area major and minor leaguers, but he declined, citing his painful ankle. Perhaps the major leaguers could have used him; in a game to benefit the Elks Club charities in Oakland on October 18, the minor leaguers defeated Joe and Dom DiMaggio, Babe Dahlgren, Eddie Joost and other big leaguers by a score of 11 to 6. A few days later in San Francisco, despite a long homer by Joe DiMaggio, the minor leaguers prevailed again 11 to 7.

Vince Monzo, Ernie's brother-in-law, caught for the minor league squad in the first game. Monzo, who happily took lessons from Ernie in both catching and hitting, played with the San Francisco Seals of the Pacific Coast League for four seasons and the Hollywood Stars for two. He was once considered a prospect, but an arm injury drove him out of the game by 1942. Monzo then opened a café in Oakland.

Monzo's career ended due to his injuries, but now the question was, what about Ernie? The sprained ankle was the most serious injury of his career, and the pain and swelling remained through the late fall and early winter. In late November Ernie turned down another Oakland charity game because his ankle still hurt. He had three months to rehabilitate his injury before the Reds were scheduled to report for spring training in Tampa.

12

Letdown

> "This is the only time of year Ernie Lombardi ever speaks for publication.... It's the usual four-word statement: 'I want more money!'"[1]
> —*Cincinnati Post*, January 1941

The Lombardi family of Oakland, California, was an unusually close-knit clan. Despite his success in professional baseball, Ernie still lived in the same house, at 1411 13th Street, that he grew up in and that Dominic Lombardi had bought not long after his arrival in America. Dominic, still the head of the household, was in his early sixties, though his health was poor and he no longer operated his grocery store. All four of Dominic's children still lived in the house, including Ernie's single sister Rose; his divorced sister Rena and her two children; and his married sister Stella and her husband, minor league catcher Vince Monzo. Ernie's salary helped support his father and the rest of the family as well.

The four Lombardi siblings were always close. When Stella married Vince Monzo in 1935, they postponed the ceremony until the late fall of the year so Ernie, the best man, could be present. Rose Lombardi never married, and for the longest time, it looked as if Ernie would never do so either. He played ball, took care of his family, and appeared to have little interest in creating a family of his own.

The women in Cincinnati were interested in him, though. In early 1940 a Cincinnati radio station took a poll of female fans to identify the most popular Red. Ernie finished first (with Willard Hershberger in second place). "The big fella gets more mash notes from starry-eyed twists than another other single guy lucratively engaged in the glorified game of rounders," wrote Frank Grayson of the *Times-Star*. "They are all perfumed missives, and the dear little writers would not feel highly complimented if they could but see the object of their misdirected affections pick up the monogrammed envelopes by their corners and deposit them in the nearest ash can."[2] Still, there is evidence that Ernie dated, on occasion, in Cincinnati, though none of his relationships ever became serious.

However, he did have a girlfriend in Oakland. Hardly anyone knew anything about her, or even knew her name, which is the way Ernie liked it. "Botch has been going around with her three or four years," said the *Oakland Tribune*, "but there's no talk of marriage. His invalid father and his sister are his first loves. He supports them."[3]

Ernie guarded his privacy as closely as possible. He was always a shy, bashful sort; as Oakland sportswriter Art Cohn wrote of him, "There is a childlike quality about Lombardi. Compared to him [Lou] Gehrig was an egomaniac."[4] The writers in the Eastern cities saw Lombardi as grumpy and surly, giving one-word answers to their questions, but the big catcher simply didn't trust those outside his circle. During the summer, his team was his protective cocoon; in the winter, he found his comfort zone in his close family and neighborhood friends. A glib, talkative sort like a Leo Durocher or a Dizzy Dean could easily give a reporter enough material to fill up a column. Ernie was simply not suited to do that.

He had been burned before. When asked to give a speech at the post-season banquet in Cincinnati in 1938, Ernie had made a mess of it, poisoning his relationship with team management. And he still carried the burden of the worst moment of his life, the infamous "snooze" in the 1939 World Series that the papers would never let him forget. The writers back East could not care less about Ernie as a person. They would rather make fun of his nose and his lack of speed.

Other players sought publicity, appearing on radio shows, advertising products in magazines, and getting their names in the gossip columns. Ernie Lombardi had no use for it. Unlike Joe DiMaggio, who dated starlets and made the rounds of New York nightclubs, Ernie was perfectly happy in his old neighborhood. People in West Oakland didn't call him "Schnozz." To them, he was "Botch," the nickname he had carried since his teenage years on the sandlots at Bay View Park.

Despite his status as a nationally-known All-Star ballplayer, Ernie's life in Oakland during the off-season was an uncomplicated one, as the Oakland paper explained:

He's a simple man. There are only two kinds of days in his life. The days he plays baseball and the days he doesn't. For the five months he's home one day is like the next, year after year....

He gets up about 10:30 each morning, eats breakfast, visits an old crony or two and then goes to Mike Kreeg's service station on Fourteenth Street. Mike is an old friend of his. Lombardi likes to sit there by the hour, watching Mike pump gas and change the oil and pump more gas.

Along about 4:30 he rouses himself, drops in at Mickey's Inn for a beer and then goes home to eat. After dinner he goes back to Mickey's for a couple beers and maybe visits his girl.[5]

12. Letdown

With so many people to support, perhaps it was inevitable that Ernie Lombardi would hold out once again in the early months of 1941. Though he participated but little in the World Series, the Reds were now the reigning World Champions, and Ernie was one of the team's major contributors before his September injury. He batted .319, the second highest average in the league, in 1940, and took on a heavy load in the catching department after the untimely death of Willard Hershberger.

Besides, many people, especially in Cincinnati, believed that Ernie should have won his second batting title in 1940. The winner was the oddly-named Pittsburgh utility man Debs Garms, who batted only 358 times in 103 games (83 of them in the field) and compiled an average of .355. Ernie, at .319, batted 376 times, only 18 times more than Garms, but spent 101 of his 109 games in the field. The National League rule at the time stated that a player must appear in 100 games to qualify for the batting crown, but most people assumed that it meant 100 games in the field. But league president Ford Frick refused to make the distinction and declared Garms the champion, with Ernie in second place.

Reports from Oakland said that Ernie wanted some or all of the $6,000 pay cut that he took the year before restored. So it was no surprise to anyone that Ernie sent his first contract offer back unsigned. "I don't expect any trouble getting together with Warren Giles," said Ernie. "Last spring I got three contracts from him before agreeing on a salary. This one is only the first, and I'm sure we'll settle our differences in time for me to start training in Tampa February 24."[6]

For once, Lombardi dealt from a position of strength. Willard Hershberger was gone, and Jimmie Wilson, the hero of the World Series, was hired to manage the Chicago Cubs. The only catchers left on the major league roster were Bill Baker and Dick West, neither of whom looked ready to replace the veteran Lombardi. So Ernie remained in Oakland and waited for Giles to make an acceptable offer. When Giles sent his first contract offer, Ernie told the *Oakland Tribune* that he ignored it. "I didn't answer it," he said, "because it failed to mention an offer of more money."[7]

As usual, he missed the start of training camp in Florida. He worked out at Bay View Park in Oakland with Neil Clifford, a local catching prospect who had recently been signed by the Reds. But Warren Giles had no way of knowing the Ernie's "workout" consisted of leg-stretching exercises and playing catch.

The Reds were eager to get Ernie into camp and see if his ankle injury had healed, so Giles made a special effort to find a salary figure that both the catcher and the team could live with. The effort was successful, and on March 7 Ernie agreed to terms and headed for Florida. The papers said that Ernie was given a $3,000 raise, restoring his base salary to its 1939 level of

$17,000. When he arrived in Tampa on March 11, Ernie told the papers that the Reds had nothing to worry about. "I'm only a couple of pounds overweight," he insisted, "and believe I'll be able to get into good condition soon. My ankle, sprained last September, again is sound."[8]

However, that statement was simply not true. Ernie's ankle was still painfully sore, and he could not run without a limp. The team physician, Dr. Richard Rohde, treated the ankle with heat baths and stretching, but the Reds were concerned. If Ernie's ankle was still hurting after five months of winter, they reasoned, how could it be healed when the season started in a few weeks? Though the catcher tried to downplay the situation—"I know Doc Rohde will do the job okay with all those machines he has,"[9] he said—by March 24, 13 days after his arrival, Ernie had not yet batted or run the bases. On that same day, the *Cincinnati Post* asked in a headline, "Is Ernie Lombardi at the End of the Line?"

Slowly but surely, Ernie rounded into playing condition, though he was noticeably slower than before the injury. He could still hit, though. He launched some impressive home runs over the left field fence in Tampa, and his line drives were as sharp as ever. In Louisville, in an exhibition game against the Red Sox, Ernie's liner injured Boston second baseman Bobby Doerr's thumb. The liner tore Doerr's glove off his hand, and for a while, Doerr thought his thumb was broken, though it was merely severely bruised.

It was in Louisville that Ernie was robbed of $300 from his hotel room. His roommate had left early in the morning and forgot to wake up Ernie to lock the door from the inside. While Ernie slept, a thief walked in, took the money from the catcher's wallet, and left. The thief was never found, and the robbery weighed on Ernie's mind as the season began.

The Reds made a few changes after their World Series win. Eddie Joost was ready to take over at shortstop, so the team traded Billy Myers to the Cubs for outfielder Jim Gleeson and infielder Bobby Mattick. Gleeson was expected to solidify left field, where several different men split time in 1940. The club also made a trade with the Yankees for Monte Pearson, the right-hander who throttled the Reds in the 1939 World Series. Otherwise, the Reds entered 1941 with mostly the same roster as the year before.

As usual, Ernie started nearly every game for the Reds in the early months of the season, but for once the big catcher could not get started with the bat. On May 3, after four hitless games in a row, Ernie's average stood at .125, with only six hits and one run batted in in 48 times at bat. That RBI came on a foul fly. His two solo homers in the next two games gave the Reds cause for optimism, and his first-inning grand slam on May 22 against the Giants, and a four-hit game against the Cubs the next day, lifted his average to .240.

12. Letdown

Lombardi was not the only Red in a slump. Frank McCormick, the Most Valuable Player Award winner in 1940, never got his bat going in 1941, and Bill Werber hit poorly all season. Jim Gleeson failed to fill the hole in left field, as did Lloyd Waner, the veteran star imported from Boston in mid-season. Right fielder Ival Goodman was injured and played in only 44 games, and catcher Bill Baker was sold to Pittsburgh in May, leaving the light-hitting Dick West as Lombardi's backup. The defending champions played sub-.500 ball in April and May and began June in fourth place, 12 games out of the lead.

Though Paul Derringer won only four of his first 11 decisions, Johnny Vander Meer made a fine comeback after two years of fighting his control problems. On April 22, with Ernie catching, Vander Meer dominated the Cubs with a 4-hit, 1–0 shutout in which he struck out 12 batters. "I never before had as much on the ball in my life," said Vander Meer after the game, and Ernie concurred. "Johnny pitched better in this game than he did in either of his successive no-hit games in 1938," claimed Ernie, "because he had more stuff and also better control. His fast ball missed the plate some, but his curve hardly ever got out of the strike zone."[10]

Jimmie Wilson, the former Red now managing the Cubs, was amazed at what he saw that day. "My players just couldn't see the balls Vander Meer was pitching," he said. "It was on them before they could start their swings."[11] Ernie had always been one of the young pitcher's biggest supporters (though rumor had it that the other Reds, upset with Vander Meer's poor performance in 1939, voted him only half a share of the World Series money that year), and Vander Meer always gave his veteran catcher a large amount of credit for his success. Vander Meer loved pitching to Ernie, and on June 6, at Philadelphia, with Ernie catching, Vander Meer nearly threw his third no-hitter, allowing one hit and one walk and striking out 12.

Another surprise in 1941 was the emergence of right-hander Elmer Riddle. McKechnie believed in bringing pitchers along slowly, so he used Riddle, a 26-year-old Georgian, in one game in 1939 and 15 more in 1940 before letting him throw one inning in the 1940 World Series. Riddle remained in the bullpen in 1941 until McKechnie decided that he was ready to join the rotation. The result was an 11-game personal winning streak in June and July and, at season's end, a 19–4 record. But the Reds were fading, and Riddle did not draw the publicity that Vander Meer received three years before. As one writer put it, "This time a year ago, when the Cincinnati Reds were sailing along to their second straight National League pennant, Elmer Riddle would have been a baseball sensation. But Elmer was a year late."[12]

Paul Derringer took a big step backward after three 20-win seasons, with 12 wins and 14 losses, while neither Whitey Moore nor Junior Thompson could match their 1940 performances. Monte Pearson was a washout,

The slugging core of the Cincinnati lineup: (from left) Ernie Lombardi, Ival Goodman, Frank McCormick, Wally Berger, and Harry Craft (author's collection).

winning only one game before being sold to the Pacific Coast League in August. Cincinnati's pitching, other than the top three of Walters, Vander Meer, and Riddle, was suddenly a weak point. McKechnie rearranged his lineup several times during the season, trying to light a fire under his team, but too many Reds had bad seasons all at once.

Perhaps no Cincinnati player fell as far as Ernie Lombardi, whose batting average remained under the .200 mark until the middle of May. The big catcher showed flashes of his old form, as when he belted two doubles and drove in three runs in Vander Meer's one-hitter against the Phillies. This set him on a hot streak in which he drove in nine runs in four games. But too many 0 for 4 games surrounded that brief streak, and both his batting and slugging averages were the lowest of his career.

The entire Cincinnati team, not just Ernie, fell into an offensive funk. The Reds had won two pennants on the strength of pitching and defense, with just enough hitting to win. In 1940, the world champion Reds scored only 29 more runs than the league average. But in 1941, McKechnie's crew scored 42 runs below the league average. With mediocre pitching, they simply did not score enough runs to win consistently.

As the manager of the defending National League champions, McKechnie was charged with assembling the National League All-Star team for 1941. He chose Brooklyn's Mickey Owen, Pittsburgh's Al Lopez, and New York's Harry Danning as his catchers, leaving Ernie off the team for the first time in five years. But when Owen was injured, McKechnie offered to put Ernie on the All-Star roster. Lombardi, a proud man, declined the honor. He told his manager that he was "so tired" and "so disappointed" with his season so far and elaborated for the papers. "I have been having a poor season," he said, "and I'm sure the three-day rest will do me more good than competing in the All-Star game."[13]

Owen recovered and played anyway while Ernie rested in Cincinnati, missing a memorable All-Star Game in Detroit which ended with Ted Williams' walk-off homer in the bottom of the ninth inning.

The rest did little good, and on July 11, after Ernie went hitless in 15 times at bat during the previous week, McKechnie benched the popular catcher for eight games, promoting Dick West to the starting position. Except for one failed pinch-hitting appearance, Ernie remained on the bench for the next week and a half. Many believed that Ernie's season-long slump affected the rest of the team. As Bob Considine put it in the *Cincinnati Enquirer*, "[Ernie] had a way of softening enemy pitchers for the rest of the mob, but this year he couldn't soften a marshmallow with a fifty-four ounce bat."[14]

However, McKechnie kept Ernie busy during his layoff. One day, during pre-game fielding practice, coach Jewel Ens drove Ernie and Paul Derringer all around the infield, catching pop-ups from a fungo bat. On another day, McKechnie assigned Ernie to pitch a few minutes of batting practice. The manager did not want Ernie to fall out of shape, and he made sure that the big catcher's time off was not a vacation.

Ernie's loss of speed was never better illustrated than on July 30 against the Giants. In the seventh inning, with Ernie on second and Harry Craft on first, Eddie Joost belted a long fly ball that hit the base of the center field wall. Ernie hesitated to make sure the ball was not caught and got such a slow start from second that McKechnie, coaching at third, threw up the stop sign. Ernie stopped at third, only to see Craft arrive at the base at the same time. After a mad scramble, Giants shortstop Dick Bartell tagged Craft out, while Joost scampered back to first.

Thoroughly embarrassed, Ernie looked to atone for the basepath fiasco, and when catcher Harry Danning let a passed ball get about 15 feet away from him, Lombardi roared down the baseline and scored. His run didn't really matter, as the Reds won the game by a score of 9 to 0, but at least Ernie gained some bit of redemption.

By this time he was starting, finally, to show signs of life with the bat. He drove in three of the nine Cincinnati runs that day with two well-placed singles, and by the end of July he brought his average up to

.248, though he had not hit a home run since June 7. Unfortunately, it was too little, too late. The end of July saw the Reds in third place, nine games behind the league-leading Dodgers and seven behind the second-place Cardinals. Those two teams ran away with the race, and the Reds were never able to make up ground. Even an 11–1 stretch by the Reds in August failed to lift them out of third position.

On August 5, after the Reds scored only two runs in losing three games to Boston and one to Pittsburgh, all at home, McKechnie shook up the entire lineup. He benched Ernie again, replacing him with Dick West, and also moved Eddie Joost from short to second, inserting Bobby Mattick at short, and benching veteran second baseman Lonny Frey. The manager also replaced Bill Werber at third with another rookie, Chuck Aleno, and benched center fielder Harry Craft, inserting Ernie Koy into the outfield.

Most of these players made their way back into the lineup, but when Ernie returned on August 9, McKechnie dropped him to the eighth spot in the batting order. He remained in the seventh or eighth position for most of August, a real comedown for the former Most Valuable Player. Even worse, the fans in Cincinnati now booed the struggling catcher on a regular basis. They vented their displeasure against manager McKechnie and other Reds, but Ernie, once so popular in Cincinnati, bore the brunt of the booing.

Perhaps the fans were jaded by the team's success. Only a few years before, the Cincinnati franchise was the weakest in the National League. During the early 1930s the Reds finished last four years in a row and would have either moved or folded had Powel Crosley not bought the club. Warren Giles and Bill McKechnie had brought the city two pennants and a World Series title, and three Most Valuable Player Award winners in a row (Ernie, Bucky Walters, and Frank McCormick). But to the Queen City fans, all that was in the past. They were now used to success and demanded a winner, but the team's moment had passed. McKechnie tried everything, but the 1941 Reds were too far behind to challenge for their third pennant in a row.

Perhaps the only fun Ernie had in 1941 came on August 27 when he stole second base against the Dodgers. It was Ernie's first steal in four years and caught the Dodger infield totally by surprise. But Ernie was stranded on second, and the Reds lost the game, missing their last faint chance to make up ground on the leaders. The Reds never rose above third place, a position that would have been a cause for rejoicing a decade before but was now a bitter disappointment for the fans at Crosley Field. On August 30, Cubs pitcher Lon Warneke held the Reds without a hit, the only no-hitter by any major league pitcher in 1941.

With the Reds out of the pennant race, attendance fell sharply. The club had led the National League in attendance in 1939 and 1940, but in 1941 the Reds were hard-pressed to top the 650,000 mark. In response, team management let it be known that some of the high-priced veterans would receive their walking papers at season's end. The successful, exciting run of McKechnie's two-time National League champions and 1940 World Series winners was now over.

Ernie's 1941 season was the worst of his career. He was never really healthy, and his ankle bothered him all year. He brought his batting average up to .264 by season's end, but his power was gone. He hit only 12 doubles and 10 home runs while scoring a paltry 33 runs. After ten seasons in Cincinnati, it looked as if Ernie's nagging injuries and increasing weight spelled the imminent end of his career.

The Reds closed the 1941 campaign in Pittsburgh, but Ernie Lombardi was not there. McKechnie gave Ernie, Paul Derringer, and Bill Werber permission to skip the series against the Pirates and go home a few days early. Derringer hurried home to Florida to see his newborn son, but for Lombardi and Werber, this decision seemed to indicate that both men were finished with the Reds.

Ernie drove home to Oakland with his future uncertain. While he played in the local all-star charity games as usual, the rumor mill spun wildly in the nation's newspapers. Various reports had him going to the Giants, the Cubs, and even Larry MacPhail's Dodgers. But it was almost certain that Ernie would be leaving the Reds. As Warren Giles told the team's annual stockholders' meeting in November, "Some of the older players on the club have reached the peak of their effectiveness and should be replaced."[15] It didn't take much imagination to figure that the 33-year-old Ernie, among others, would wear a new uniform in 1942.

Tragically, 1941 was not finished with Ernie Lombardi. During the season, Ernie lived with Eddie Joost; Joost's wife; and their two-year-old son, also named Eddie. Ernie loved kids, and he and little Eddie became great friends. But in October, after the Joost family returned to their home in San Francisco, little Eddie fell ill with a blood infection. The child died in early November, and his loss devastated the big catcher. Ernie also learned that his father Dominic's health was fading, slowly but inevitably. So Ernie's off-season was filled not only with uncertainty, but also with grief and worry.

13

Boston

"So the Reds are going to tie the can to Ernie Lombardi. Wonder if there is any chance of big Botchy returning to Brooklyn after all these years. Probably not, but in spite of his cumbersome slowness, he'd have looked pretty good up at the dish last summer when the enemy was throwing so many lefthanded pitchers at the Dodgers."[1]
—*Brooklyn Eagle*, November 1941

Bill McKechnie liked Ernie personally, but the manager could not ignore the unmistakable signs of the big catcher's decline. Ernie batted only .264 in 1941, was overweight and injury-prone, and had passed his 33rd birthday. Less than one third of his hits went for extra bases, and he scored only 33 runs in the 117 games he played. Both McKechnie and Warren Giles believed that Ernie was going downhill fast, so they purchased Rollie Hemsley, a four-time All-Star in the American League, from Cleveland to do battle for the starting position.

Hemsley had failed to dislodge Ernie from the starting catcher's job in Cincinnati eight years before. The Reds acquired Hemsley from the Cubs in 1933 to share the position with Ernie, but Hemsley batted only .190 before the Reds traded him to the St. Louis Browns in August of that year. Hemsley built a good defensive reputation in St. Louis and Cleveland, though his alcohol-fueled exploits earned him the nickname "Rollicking Rollie." His self-destructive fondness for booze was the talk of baseball—he was traded several times because of it—but he joined a new organization called Alcoholics Anonymous in 1939 and appeared to have a handle on his drinking.

In fact, Hemsley, who revealed his membership in Alcoholics Anonymous after catching Bob Feller's Opening Day no-hitter in 1940, was the first member of AA to publicly break his pledge of anonymity, resulting in a massive wave of publicity for the fledgling organization. Before the deal was completed, Hemsley told Giles, McKechnie, and the local press that he had not had a drink since April 13, 1939. "And when I take another one, I'll be out of baseball," he promised.

"I'll say you will,"[2] replied McKechnie.

In an interview with Tom Swope of the *Cincinnati Post*, McKechnie sounded as if Hemsley had already won the competition. He compared his new catcher to the late Willard Hershberger, "a rip-snorter ... who dashes all over the place, backing up first and third, knocking down the grandstand to get foul flies and injecting pepper into the rest of his team."

And what about the incumbent? "Lombardi has been a great man for this club—a great man," he said. "He's a different type than Hemsley but he's been valuable. He's just different by nature. He's battled hard and earnestly but never gave the appearance of hustling as much as do catchers of the Hemsley type."[3] It appeared that McKechnie, a defense-first manager, had finally found his ideal catcher, and that catcher's name was not Ernie Lombardi.

Ernie knew that his career was on the line, so he worked much harder during the off-season. "I'm kinda expecting a cut," he said, "but I'm going to be in great shape when the spring training season opens."[4] He told the *Oakland Tribune* that he spent the winter cutting wood to toughen his hands and walking around Lake Merritt every morning to strengthen his ankles. He also, for once, paid attention to his diet. He claimed that he had not touched spaghetti in more than three months. Privately, though, Ernie resigned himself to a trade, and told his friends that he hoped to be dealt to the Giants.

With the newly-sober Hemsley on board, Ernie's tenure in Cincinnati was finished, and on February 7, 1942, the Reds sold Ernie to the Boston Braves for an undisclosed sum. Warren Giles explained to the newspapers, "This was not a big deal.... The only reason for the deal was that we thought we could not use both Hemsley and Lombardi and we think Hemsley is the better catcher, notwithstanding that we believe that Lombardi will have a better hitting season than his .264 of last year."[5]

McKechnie agreed. "Hemsley is going to permit us to play a different type of defense," he said. "Hemsley won't hit the long ball like Lombardi did occasionally, but he'll do everything else better. He can bunt, steal bases, and throw with any catcher in the business. We'll also be able to play more hit-and-run with Hemsley in the lineup." Hemsley was one year older than Ernie and had batted only .240 for the Indians in 1941, but he was faster and more nimble than Lombardi. Hemsley was available because he hoped to be named manager of the Cleveland club after the 1941 season, but Lou Boudreau got the job instead.

The Braves desperately needed hitting, and general manager Bob Quinn and field manager Casey Stengel had tried to pry Ernie loose from the Reds for more than a year. In May of 1941 the Reds and Braves were close to a deal for Ernie, but on May 23, the very day that the trade was supposed to close, Ernie belted four singles and drove in two runs in an 8–4 win at Chicago. This performance gave McKechnie the idea that Lombardi, who carried a .212 average into the game, had finally broken out of his slump, so the Cincinnati manager called off the deal.

The Braves left a lot of runners on base in 1941 on their way to 92 losses and a seventh-place finish, so at the winter meetings in December Quinn and Stengel did their best to improve the Boston offense. They fixed their sights on Johnny Mize, the slugging 30-year-old first baseman of the St. Louis Cardinals, but lost interest after learning of Mize's list of nagging injuries. The Cardinals sold Mize to the Giants for three players and $50,000 in cash. The Braves then made a play for Dolph Camilli, the Brooklyn first sacker who won the Most Valuable Player award for the pennant-winning Dodgers. Quinn offered a large sum of cash, while the New York Yankees reportedly offered both cash and players, but the Brooklyn club decided to keep the popular Camilli. Only when the Mize and Camilli deals fell apart did the Braves make the deal for Lombardi.

Ernie's new manager, Charles Dillon Stengel, was a baseball lifer who had found success in the minor leagues, but not yet on the major league level. An outfielder from Kansas City, Stengel joined the Brooklyn Dodgers in 1912 and helped Wilbert Robinson win the pennant in 1916. He then bounced around, from the Pirates to the Phillies to the Giants, where he met John McGraw and set his sights on a career as a manager. By 1942, Stengel was best known for two things—his two home runs against the Yankees in the 1923 World Series, and his clownish behavior. He once trapped a bird on the field, put it under his hat, and shocked the fans when he tipped his cap and the bird flew out. He celebrated one of his World Series homers

Casey Stengel, Ernie's manager in Boston and, six years later, with the Oakland Oaks (National Baseball Hall of Fame Library, Cooperstown, New York).

by thumbing his nose at the Yankee bench on his way around the bases. That earned him a letter of reprimand from the commissioner, Judge Landis.

In 1927 Stengel signed on as playing manager of the Toledo Mud Hens of the American Association and won the Little (minor league) World Series in his first year at the helm. When his Toledo gig ended, he coached in Brooklyn for Max Carey for two years, then succeeded Carey as manager in 1934. Released by the Dodgers after four mediocre seasons, he replaced Bill McKechnie in Boston in 1938. Stengel led the team to a winning record, but just barely, in his first season, but followed it up with three straight seventh-place showings, with only the hopeless Phillies keeping them out of the cellar of the National League.

For once, Ernie reported to spring camp on time. He was unhappy with his contract, which reportedly called for a salary of $9,000, a real comedown from the $17,000 he earned in Cincinnati. But the Braves had all the leverage due to Lombardi's poor 1941 season and his advancing age. So Ernie agreed to terms, then drove from Oakland to the Braves camp at Sanford, Florida, in late February. Said general manager Bob Quinn, "Lombardi is capable of making himself of much value to us and says he is already in good shape. He talks like a hustler and I hope it will turn out that way."[6] Indeed, the papers reported that Ernie arrived in camp at 219 pounds, fit and ready to go.

One promising prospect at the spring training camp was a 21-year-old left-handed pitcher named Warren Spahn, who won 19 games at Evansville of the Three-I League. Spahn had appeared at the spring camp the year before, but an errant throw by a teammate struck him in the face and broke his nose. Still, he performed well enough to impress Stengel, who told the press, "He's only 20 years old and needs work. But mark my words, if nothing happens to the kid, he can be a great one. Someday he's going to be one of the best left-handers in the league."[7] His outstanding season at Evansville made Spahn the top pitching prospect in the Braves' organization.

Spahn still needed to impress Ernie Lombardi, the very definition of the "grizzled veteran." Spahn recalled years later that during a practice session, "I threw a pitch that was way outside to a right-hand hitter. Lombardi just reached out with his bare hand and grabbed it," said Spahn. "And I thought I was throwing hard. When he goes to throw the ball back, he sends it back twice as hard as I'd thrown it."[8] Spahn thought to himself, "The major league is going to be impossible," but he performed well enough to open the 1942 season with the team.

However, the Braves and the other 15 major league teams could not ignore the onset of World War II, which the nation entered after the Japanese attack on Pearl Harbor on December 7, 1941. Congress declared war on

Japan on December 8 and on Germany on December 11, and on December 20 an amendment to the Selective Service Act required all men between the ages of 18 and 64 to register for the draft and declared all men between the ages of 20 to 44 as liable for military service. This included virtually every major league baseball player, though men in their thirties and those with families could expect to be deferred for some period of time.

With that in mind, the Braves signed several older veterans. Paul Waner, 39, the longtime star of Pittsburgh's outfield, signed with Boston and hoped to gain the 44 hits he needed to pass the 3,000 mark for his career. Ernie Lombardi, at 34, was expected to do most of the catching, while Tony Cuccinello, also 34, came out of retirement to serve as a player-coach. Most of the other Braves were married men in their late 20s and early 30s, and though several major league stars—Hank Greenberg and Bob Feller among them—had already joined the military, most of the Braves appeared safe from the draft.

Casey Stengel was a realist. He cheerfully told the Boston papers that he did not expect his Braves to challenge for the pennant, or even for a spot for the first division, but he was satisfied that most of his men would not be drafted, at least for a while. "I've got what you might call a well-seasoned club," he said. "They're settled family men for the most part and right in their baseball prime, though [Johnny] Cooney probably isn't quite as good as he should be in another four or five years at the rate he's developing."[9] Cooney was a 41-year-old pitcher-turned-outfielder who first played for the Braves in 1921.

Stengel was also happy with his new catcher. As the *Boston Globe* reported, "The big man must have been jolted by his sale to the Braves, for he is some 20 pounds lighter than ever before in his major league career. He practically looks like a race horse and is playing his head off." When the Braves played the Reds in late March, his ex-teammates noticed his newfound fitness too. Complained one Red, "If he had been in this kind of shape a year ago we would have won the pennant without working up a sweat."[10]

Ernie quickly discovered that Stengel ran a loose camp. In one game between the rookies and the veterans, the manager had several pitchers playing the outfield and, just for fun, put Ernie in center field for the last few innings. Stengel did not even get upset when Ernie made an embarrassing misplay in a game against his former team, the Reds. Rollie Hemsley belted a double that scored two runs, and while Ernie argued a safe call at the plate with umpire Al Barlick, Hemsley stole third while Ernie's back was turned. Ernie did not hit well in the spring, with only one home run to his credit, but appeared determined to put 1941 behind him and reclaim his reputation as a hitter and catcher.

Ernie caught Warren Spahn in game action only once. On April 20, in the seventh game of the season, the young lefthander entered the contest in the fourth inning of a depressing blowout against the defending league champion Dodgers. Spahn retired the Dodgers in the fourth but allowed two runs in the fifth to put the Braves behind 7 to 0. In the sixth, Stengel ordered Spahn to brush back leadoff batter Pee Wee Reese, the Dodger shortstop. Spahn, with Lombardi providing the target, threw three inside pitches, but not aggressively enough for the manager's taste. At the end of the inning, Stengel blew up at the young pitcher. "Young man, you've got no guts," he yelled. "Go pick up your railroad ticket to Hartford."[11]

Spahn rode the train to Hartford of the Eastern League that evening. He returned to pitch two games in September, then spent the next three years in the United States Army. He fought in Europe with the 9th Armored Division and earned a Purple Heart, a Bronze Star, and a Presidential Citation, and was the only major league player to receive a battlefield commission. Years later, Stengel admitted his mistake. "Yes, I said 'no guts' to a kid who wound up being a war hero and one of the best pitchers anybody ever saw. You can't say I don't miss 'em when I miss 'em."[12]

Ernie got off to a slow start in 1942, as he often did, but his bat heated up with the weather. In mid–May he belted home runs on three consecutive days, and on May 19 a 5 for 5 day in a 10–7 win over the Phillies shot Ernie's average up to a league-leading .346. Though the Braves fell to sixth place and stayed there, Ernie looked like the Lombardi of old, at least in the batter's box.

He was 34 years old now, and the aches, pains, and minor injuries drove him from the lineup several times. On May 13 a knuckleball from teammate Jim Tobin split one of Ernie's fingernails and kept him out of action for three games, and on June 15 a foul tip off Hiram Bithorn's bat in Chicago split Ernie's index finger and nail, forcing him to the sidelines for four more games.

In Boston, Ernie boarded with Jim Tobin and his family. The pitcher called Ernie "the man who came to dinner and stayed," but Ernie was a welcome houseguest for Tobin, his wife, and their two-year-old daughter. Tobin, who was born in Oakland, was a longtime friend and acquaintance who pitched for the Oakland Oaks for several years after Ernie left. On the day that Tobin's knuckler split Lombardi's finger, the pitcher belted three home runs, the only pitcher in the post–1900 era to perform the feat. Ernie's injury happened, said Tobin, because Ernie "reached for the ball as though he was spearing a steak out at our house."[13]

Ernie stole his only base of the season on May 9 against the last-place Phillies. With the Braves holding a 5–2 lead, Lombardi walked to lead off the eighth inning. Stengel noticed that the Phillies were paying no attention to the big catcher at first base; the pitcher was reading the signs, the shortstop and second baseman were totally oblivious, and the first baseman was not holding Lombardi on the bag. As the pitcher delivered the ball, Stengel called out, "Steal it, Lom!" Ernie rose to the challenge and set out for second. Neither the shortstop nor the second baseman moved to cover the bag, and the catcher's throw sailed into center field. When the outfielder made a wild throw back to the infield, Ernie came all the way around to score with a big smile on his face.[14]

This stolen base was the next to last of Ernie's career. He simply could not run anymore; as Bill James described him, "As he got older he acquired a huge belly, which he lugged around with great effort.... His knees were too low to the ground, and his center of gravity was four feet behind him." The Ernie Lombardi who hit nine triples for the Reds in 1932 was long gone; he had no triples for the Braves in 1942 and hit only two more during the last five seasons of his career. James called Ernie "surely the slowest player ever to play major league baseball well."[15]

Despite his lumbering nature, Ernie still amazed teammates and opponents with his hitting skills. As his Braves teammate Sibby Sisti, a 21-year-old infielder, said,

> Ernie Lombardi was a tremendous hitter, a guy who couldn't run a lick. I always felt sorry for him because when I—or any infielder—played against him they would play deep on the grass, in the outfield, 'cause poor Ernie couldn't run worth a lick. And then in '42 when he came to play with the Braves I saw the same thing that I had seen three years previous, that the opposition would always play him deep. The poor guy—he hit around .300, and with ordinary speed it would have been around .350.[16]

The Braves discovered that Ernie was a great teammate. Tommy Holmes, a rookie infielder with the Braves, always remembered Ernie's kindness to young players:

> We had a few rookies on the team and in those days they weren't making much money, maybe six hundred a month. They were pretty excited about making their first Western trip. Lombardi—bless him, I'll always remember him for this—went around to all the kids and said, "Hey, kid, got enough money?" And without waiting for an answer he'd push a twenty on them. Just wanted to make sure they had a few extra, to tip porters and waitresses, or buy themselves a beer, and so on. He wanted them to be able to feel like big leaguers.[17]

Despite all the injuries, Ernie hit much better in 1942 than he had the year before, and by mid-season his name appeared at the top of the National League batting listings. Perhaps the Reds regretted letting him go, as Rollie Hemsley flamed out spectacularly, hitting only .113 before the

Reds released him in July. As Hemsley's replacement Ray Lamanno, like Ernie a native of Oakland, told him at mid-season, "Man, you're driving McKechnie crazy with the way you're hitting. He's pulling his hair out."[18]

Ernie's explanation of his resurgence was a simple one. He stated that he was healthy again. "In 1941 I never got in shape," he said.

> I wasn't able to chop wood during the winter. I had that bad ankle, something wrong with my back and some kidney trouble.
>
> Between all of them, I never was able to get my weight down. I didn't get any spring training and stayed around 240 [pounds] all year. That was too heavy. My best playing weight is around 230 pounds.
>
> [In 1942] all my ailments cleared up. My ankle was strong again, and I got back into stride. I guess that's about it.[19]

As the season wore on, Ernie was the only Brave producing at the bat. Outfielder Max West led the team in homers with 16, though he batted only .254, and except for Ernie, no Boston regular batted higher than Tommy Holmes' .278. Paul Waner gained the 3,000th hit of his career on June 19, but the 39-year-old Waner, a three-time batting champion, was not the hitter he once was. No Brave batted in more than 56 runs, and due to poor hitting support, pitching workhorse Jim Tobin lost 21 games. Ernie's bat and Casey Stengel's wit were the only attractions for the fans as the Braves sank in the standings.

Ernie kept hitting, though he had to work his way around injuries all season long, and his performance landed him on the National League All-Star team as a reserve. The game was played at the Polo Grounds in New York on July 6, and Ernie took over at catcher in the seventh inning, replacing the starter, Walker Cooper of the Cardinals. He walked in the seventh but failed to score, and, after catching his old Cincinnati teammate Bucky Walters in the ninth, ended the game with a groundout. (He just missed catching Johnny Vander Meer, who pitched the middle three innings.) The American League won by a score of 3 to 1, but Ernie was an All-Star once again.

The Braves were going nowhere on their way to a seventh-place finish, but Ernie Lombardi's quest for the batting title provided the Boston fans—what few there were—with a focus of interest during the campaign's final two months. On August 1 Ernie stood in second place in the batting race with a .336 mark, seven points behind Brooklyn's Pete Reiser, the 1941 champion. But Ernie batted only .197 in August, and his hopes for a second batting title took a hit on August 12 when he suffered a severe sprain of a finger on his throwing hand. This put him out of action for 12 games, and when he returned, it took him a few games to find a comfortable grip on the bat. By the end of August his average had fallen to .313, and because he had accumulated only 246 at bats, the National League statistician dropped his name from the official listings.

But Ernie was healthy in September, starting all but four games in the month, and he went on a tear at the bat. Twelve hits in six games around Labor Day raised his average into the .330s, and he emerged as a threat for the title once again. On the morning of September 12, Ernie's average stood at .333 with Pete Reiser and Cardinal outfielder Enos Slaughter well behind at .319. However, Ernie's total of 267 times at bat was less than half of Slaughter's 536. The question was, could Ernie be considered for the batting title, given that he missed so many games during the season?

Perhaps Lombardi's popularity helped him in this regard, because on September 15 National League president Ford Frick ordered Ernie's name restored as the official leader in the batting race. League rules stated that a player qualified for the batting title by playing in 100 games or more, and if Ernie remained healthy for the rest of the season, he would clear that requirement no matter how many times at bat he might accumulate.

The league batting championship no longer carries as much cachet in the 21st century as it once did, but during the 19th and 20th centuries the batting title was a highly coveted honor. In many years, the race was hotly contested, with batters sitting out the last game of the year to protect their averages, and runners-up furiously trying to accumulate hits to pass the leader. The winner of the batting crown received a silver bat as "the champion batsman of the league," and reference books listed the annual winners. Ernie's title in 1938 had raised his profile considerably, and a second one would show, once and for all, that the big catcher was once again one of the top hitters in the National League.

But even if he cleared the 100-game threshold, his limited number of times at bat posed a problem. Ernie not only missed games with injuries, but also came out of games for pinch runners in the late innings. He pinch-hit 24 times in 1942 and played only 85 games in the field, barely more than half of the contests on the schedule. Ernie could not be called a part-time player, but neither was he in the lineup every day, accumulating four or five times at bat in every game like Reiser or Slaughter.

Four years earlier, the American League had faced a similar situation. Boston's Jimmie Foxx enjoyed an incredible season, with 50 home runs, 164 runs batted in, and a batting average of .349 with 197 hits in 565 official at bats. However, Taft Wright, a part-time outfielder and pinch-hitter for the Washington Senators, appeared in exactly 100 games and, with 92 hits only 263 at bats, eked out a slightly higher average at .350. Wright, though he compiled fewer than half the number of hits and times at bat as Foxx, nonetheless qualified for the title under the rules in place at the time. Should Wright, therefore, have been recognized as the league batting champion for 1938?

The answer, supplied by American League president Will Harridge, was an emphatic no. Harridge, applying common sense in contrast to a slavish adherence to the rules, decided that Foxx deserved the batting title more than Wright. Harridge awarded the crown to Foxx to the general approval of fans and writers nationwide. Though writer George Vass complained in 2005 that Harridge's decision proceeded to "hand Foxx a phony batting title that has defiled the record books for almost 70 years,"[20] most observers, then and now, agreed that Foxx, not Wright, deserved the crown.

Furthermore, Harridge decreed that, beginning in 1939, American League hitters would be required to amass at least 2.6 at bats per scheduled game (400 at bats in a 154-game season) to qualify for the batting title. This, the league president hoped, would keep the title from being awarded to a mere part-time player.

On the other hand, the National League saw no need to change its eligibility rules and kept the 100-game standard. In 1940 Pittsburgh's Debs Garms, who played in 103 games and batted only 358 times, ended the season with a .355 average. National League president Ford Frick ignored the controversy in the junior circuit of two years before and declared Garms the champion. In second place was none other than Ernie Lombardi at .319 (though Lom batted only 376 times himself) with Chicago third baseman Stan Hack in third place at .317.

Now, as the 1942 season ground to a close, Ernie Lombardi's average outpaced his closest challengers, the Cardinal duo of Enos Slaughter and rookie Stan Musial, but Lom had missed part of the campaign with one injury after another. He crossed the 100-game threshold with five games to spare, but his total of 305 at bats was more than 50 fewer than Garms had amassed in 1940. Did Lombardi, with only 102 hits, do enough to win the title?

Yes, said Ford Frick. Ernie had met the standard of games played, and therefore was the winner without much controversy. Besides, the league president believed that catchers, who played the most physically taxing and injury-prone position on the field, should be afforded some measure of consideration. On September 26, the last day of the season, Ernie belted a single and a homer off New York's Carl Hubbell in the first game of a Saturday doubleheader to bring his average to .330. Slaughter closed the year at .318, so the league recognized Ernie as the 1942 batting champ (though some Cardinal rooters grumbled, to no effect). Lom's .330 average was the lowest to win the title in either league since 1919, when Edd Roush of Cincinnati posted a .321 mark.

With the batting crown secure, Ernie sat out the last game of the season, the second game of the season-ending doubleheader, which ended in unusual fashion. With Clyde Kluttz catching and rookie Warren Spahn (who had returned to Boston in September) on the mound, the Braves trailed the Giants by a score of 5 to 2 in the eighth inning. The Giants let kids into the Polo Grounds that day for free as part of a scrap metal drive for the war effort, and when the Giants came to bat in the bottom of the eighth, the young fans could no longer hold their behavior in check. They surged out of the stands and swarmed the field, and when they ignored calls to return to their seats, the umpires stopped the game and forfeited the contest to the Braves.

Ernie was back on top again, after the World Series debacle of 1939 and his poor season for the Reds in 1941, and he enjoyed every minute of the attention that came his way. Asked about his resurgence at the bat, he explained that he made a special effort to lose weight during the previous winter months. "It was diet that did it," said a gleeful Ernie.

> I chopped off those pounds by chopping wood, and chopping potatoes and starchy foods out of my diet.... I knew I had a few more good years left, so I made up my mind that I'd take off some weight and prove that I could still do a major league job....
>
> The bigger the size of the woodpile, the bigger the batting average.[21]

The batting title was not Ernie's only contribution to the Braves in 1942. He made an impression on Warren Spahn, who eventually won more games than any left-handed pitcher in baseball history, and he also gave advice to a right-handed rookie named Johnny Sain. Sain, a finesse pitcher with an unimpressive fastball, had spent six years in the minors before making his major league debut in relief on April 17 with Ernie as his catcher. Under Lombardi's guidance, Sain pitched two and a third shutout innings that day to earn the save.

At season's end, Sain enlisted in the naval air corps and spent the next three years away from baseball, but he fondly remembered Ernie Lombardi. Ernie gave his address to Sain and told him, "When you find out where you're stationed, give me your address. I'll send you cigarettes, candy, anything you want. Just tell me where you are."[22] Both Warren Spahn and Johnny Sain became stars, and in 1948, long after Ernie left the Braves, Spahn and Sain pitched the Boston club to the National League pennant.

14

New York

"How does it feel to be batting champion? Well, I guess it proves that 'Lom' ain't quite washed up yet."[1]
—Ernie Lombardi, October 1942

After his remarkable comeback performance in 1942, Ernie expected a salary boost for 1943. He had suffered an $8,000 cut after his injury-filled final campaign in Cincinnati, and the Braves, who paid him $9,000 in 1942, received a batting title and a .330 average at a bargain price. Now Ernie, as he neared his 35th birthday, wanted to move back up the salary ladder. He demanded $15,000 to play in 1943.

The problem was that the Boston club could not raise his salary that high. With World War II raging, and inflation running at a high level, Congress passed the Stabilization Act of 1942. This act put a freeze on the salaries that companies were allowed to pay their employees, and effectively imposed a salary cap for every major league team. Because no Brave earned more than $12,500 in 1942, the team could not legally pay any player more than that.

The *New York Post* explained the issue. "The Braves' ceiling is $12,500, the salary paid Eddie Miller, the shortstop traded to the Cincinnati Reds," said the *Post*. "As the league's best hitter last year, Lombardi figured he was worth $15,000 for the '43 campaign. President Bob Quinn of the Braves agreed with him."[2] The Braves might pay Ernie $12,500, but not $15,000.

The big catcher had options. He could return to the Braves for $12,500 or demand a trade to another team that had more to give. Or he could simply remain in California. In late 1942 Ernie went to work in a war materials factory as a sheet metal artisan. This job was his contribution to the war effort, and while it certainly paid much less than $10,000 a year, it allowed him to be at home with his family. In early 1943 Ernie declared that he would not return to Boston for the 1943 season. He demanded a trade to a team that would pay him $15,000 a year.

Meanwhile, the New York Giants, who finished in third place in 1942, needed a jolt of power after their best hitter, first baseman Johnny

Mize, entered the Navy and left a hole in the Giants' lineup. The Giants, who paid higher salaries than the Braves, had room under the cap, and needed another strong hitter. Their main catcher, the four-time All-Star Harry Danning, was set to be drafted into the Army, and the New York team needed to replace him.

Besides, the Giants had long coveted Lombardi. Bill Terry, who had tried to obtain Lombardi for years, had been promoted to the general manager position in 1941, and star outfielder Mel Ott, still a dangerous hitter, was now the playing manager of the team. Both Terry and Ott lobbied team owner Horace Stoneham to trade for Lombardi after Ernie's disappointing 1941 season in Cincinnati. Terry left the Giants to go into private business in 1942, but Ott and Stoneham were still interested in Ernie.

With wartime travel restrictions in place, the Braves opened their spring training camp in Wallingford, Connecticut, in March. Bob Quinn sent Ernie a contract, probably for the maximum value of $12,500, but Ernie returned it unsigned. He remained in Oakland, waiting for a trade. "I guess there is quite a difference from what may be the club's best offer and what I'm asking,"[3] he said.

Also, Ernie had more than baseball on his mind. Dominic Lombardi was 66 years old, and his health had been failing for several years. He could no longer work and remained in the house at 1114 13th Street in the care of his family. Ernie was now the sole financial support not only of his father, but also of his sister Rose, who cared for Dominic. Because of that, he applied for, and received, a draft classification of 3-A (family hardship deferment) from Selective Service. However, if the military needed more soldiers, Selective Service could tighten the family hardship rules and the men in 3-A could quickly be reclassified. Ernie, who was single and childless, might yet be eligible for the military draft.

Ernie sat out all of spring training, but on April 19, five days before the start of the 1943 season, Ernie came to terms with the Braves and boarded a cross-country train to Boston. He arrived on the 23rd as the Braves prepared to open the campaign against the Giants. The Braves announced that Ernie would not see action right away, as he was not yet in playing condition, but no doubt the team held him out of action while trade negotiations proceeded. The Boston club was set to play its first five games against the Giants—two in Boston followed by three in New York— and the two clubs haggled over Ernie's future.

On April 27, 1943, the Braves and Giants reached a deal. The Braves sent Ernie to the Giants for two players, catcher Hugh Poland and infielder Connie Ryan. Poland was a defense-first catcher who had failed to hit for the New York club, while Ryan was a highly regarded prospect who had performed poorly for the Giants in 1942. Rumor had it that the Giants also sent a large amount of cash, perhaps as much as $30,000, to the Braves, but that story was roundly denied by all involved. As one reporter put it, Boston's acquisition of Poland and Ryan was a fair exchange for "a bachelor who might be called to war any day."[4]

Ernie was delighted. "To say that I'm highly pleased to become a Giant doesn't adequately express my feelings," said Lombardi. "I've had my eye on that left-field scoreboard in the Polo Grounds for a long time. Now, I'm going to see what can be done about it as a home-field target."[5] Lom had never played in a home ballpark that suited his hitting style, and the Polo Grounds were made for a right-handed pull hitter.

The Giants had won three National League pennants during the 1930s under manager Bill Terry, but while Cincinnati dominated the league in 1939 and 1940, the New Yorkers dropped to fifth and sixth place. After the 1941 season Terry moved up to the general manager spot. His replacement was outfielder Mel Ott, the popular slugger who had joined the Giants in 1926 at age 17 without ever playing a game in the minor leagues. Ott's first season as manager was a positive one; while the Cardinals and Dodgers ran away from the rest of the league, Ott's Giants finished a solid third, with the manager himself leading the league in home runs (30), runs scored (118), and walks (109), finishing third in the Most Valuable Player balloting.

It wasn't an easy transition for Ott. He was the first playing manager to direct his team from the outfield since Ty Cobb and Tris Speaker two decades earlier, and it was difficult to call plays and visit the mound from so far away. But he learned to handle his dual role and remained the team's top slugger.

Now, the Giants had plenty of holes to fill, mostly due to the military draft. Harry Danning was gone, as was Johnny Mize, half of a fearsome slugging tandem with Ott. Pitching star Carl Hubbell's career wound down at age 40, third baseman Bill Werber (the former Cincinnati Red) retired, and key starters Bob Carpenter and Hal Schumacher joined the war effort. Like every other major league team, the Giants were now required to piece together a team with youngsters, older men, and the draft exempt.

Danning's departure left a huge void at the catching position, as the two backups, Gus Mancuso and Ray Berres, hit .193 and .188 respectively in 1942. Mel Ott believed in a strong defense, but he also needed hitting in his lineup, so he brought in Ernie Lombardi to share the starting job with Mancuso. Mancuso, a 14-year veteran, was no longer an effective hitter, but owned a reputation as a good handler of pitchers. He was, however, generally considered to be the slowest major league player aside from Ernie Lombardi, giving the Giants the oldest, and by far the slowest, catching tandem in baseball. John Drebinger of *The New York Times* once wrote that Mancuso "always looks to be running in a sand pile."⁶

Ernie's New York debut did not go well. On April 28, Ernie watched from the bench as his new team carried a 2–0 lead into the ninth inning. The Braves put two men on base in the top of the ninth, then sent Connie Ryan, their newly acquired infielder, up as a pinch-hitter. Ryan promptly blasted a three-run homer to give Boston a 3–2 lead. In the bottom of the ninth, Mel Ott sent Ernie up to hit for starting catcher Gus Mancuso. He grounded into a double play to end the game.

Though Ernie had been a popular player in Brooklyn, Cincinnati, and Boston, the New York fans held him at arm's length, at least at first. Both the Giants and their new catcher started the 1943 season poorly. Ott's team lost seven of its first nine games and dropped quickly into the second division, while Lombardi went hitless in his first 10 trips to the plate. He started the season as a pinch-hitter, and when he drew his first starting assignment on May 1 against Brooklyn, the results were disastrous. In a 9–2 Dodger win at the Polo Grounds, Ernie not only went 0 for 4 at the plate but allowed three stolen bases. Ernie did not gain his first hit of the season until May 13, when he whacked three singles against the Cubs to raise his average to .214.

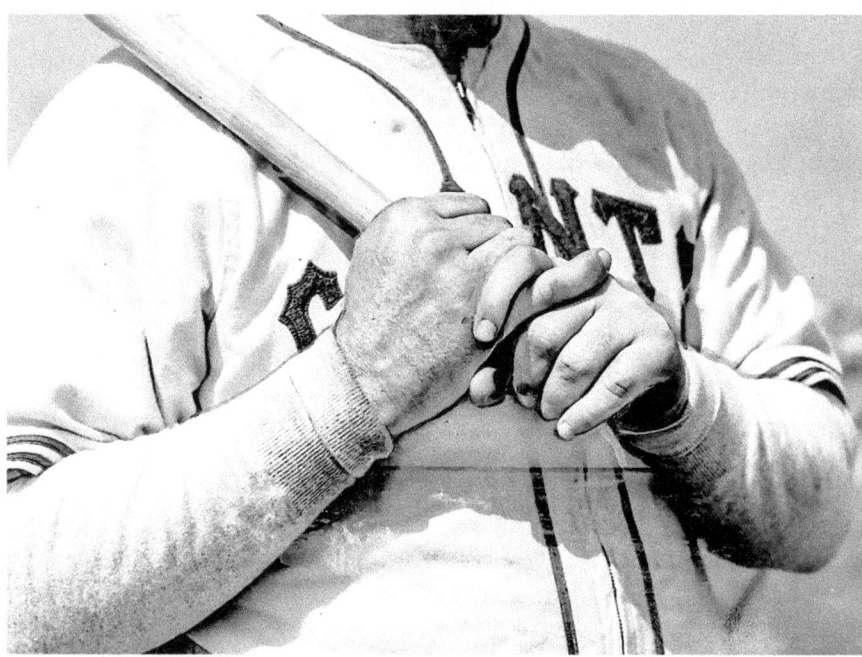

In the later years of his career, Ernie still used the golf grip on his bat (National Baseball Hall of Fame Library, Cooperstown, New York).

While Ernie struggled with his new team, Dominic Lombardi's health took a turn for the worse. He suffered two strokes in quick succession, and on May 19, after Ernie went hitless in a 3–2 win over Cincinnati, the big catcher received a call from Oakland. Dominic Lombardi had died that afternoon at the age of 66. Ernie immediately left the team and headed home to Oakland. Dominic Lombardi, the immigrant who came to America as an unskilled laborer and built his own grocery business, was buried next to his wife Maria, who had passed on 22 years before. In a final nod to his Italian heritage, Dominic's tombstone bore his birth name, Domenico.

Dominic's death put Ernie's draft status in jeopardy. He could no longer claim his widowed father as his dependent, and because he was single and childless, the catcher could easily be reclassified as 1-A and be on his way to Europe or the Pacific. Selective Service scheduled Ernie for a preliminary exam on July 13, but because the All-Star Game in Philadelphia was set for that afternoon, National League President Ford Frick asked that Lombardi's exam be moved up a day. Selective Service agreed, and Ernie took his initial screening on Monday, July 12.

By this time, Ernie's bat had come alive. Though the Giants fell into last place and stayed there for the rest of the season, Lombardi batted .364 in June to lift his average into the .280s. His performance was one of the few bright spots in a disastrous year for the Giants, and the New York sportswriters began to give him some positive press. After Ernie banged a walk-off homer against his old Cincinnati teammate Paul Derringer in a win over the Cubs, the oft-acerbic writer Dick Young of the *Daily News* made an appeal to the Selective Service:

> Memo to Ernie Lombardi's local draft board. Listen, fellows: Schnozzola has flat feet. He can't hike. He couldn't possibly help you. Besides, he hits such nice timely homers. Like the one he plastered into the upper left field tier against Chicago's Paul Derringer with two out in the 10th frame of yesterday's opener to give the Giants a 4–3 triumph, before some 25,000 fans who'll gladly sign this petition.[7]

Ernie's impressive comeback led Cardinals manager Billy Southworth to give the big catcher a reserve spot on the National League All-Star team. It was his seventh All-Star selection. He entered the All-Star game (the first ever played at night) as a pinch-hitter in the sixth inning and took Walker Cooper's place behind the bat for the rest of the game, which the American League won by a score of 5 to 3. Ernie was the first player in history to represent three different teams in All-Star play.

In June of 1943 Lom used an unexpected burst of speed to end the playing career of his one-time Cincinnati teammate, the slick-fielding, light-hitting shortstop Leo Durocher. At the time, Durocher was, officially, the playing manager of the Brooklyn Dodgers, but preferred to manage from the bench, and had not seen action on the field in nearly two years. However, with regular shortstop Pee Wee Reese in the military and no better options available, Durocher put himself in the lineup. The 38-year-old manager played passably well for about a week before the Brooklyn club met the Giants at the Polo Grounds on June 15. In the first inning of that game, with runners on second and third, Ernie Lombardi tapped a grounder to short.

Leo caught the ball, straightened up, then threw to first as he had done thousands of times in his long career. Lombardi, hustling down the line, stunned the crowd when he beat it out for a single, scoring one runner and advancing the other.

Durocher couldn't believe it. "That settles it," he proclaimed. "When Lom can beat out a hit on me, that means I'm washed up. I'll never play again!" He took himself out for a pinch-hitter a few innings later and, true to his word, never played shortstop again.[8]

But for the most part, Ernie was slower than ever. He hit only seven doubles in 1943 and scored only 19 runs. But he hit over .300 for the ninth time in his career, and his offensive output was not one of the Giants' problems. Mel Ott dropped to .234, Gus Mancuso hit .198, and first baseman Joe Orengo, a Bay Area product of the Pacific Coast League, failed to fill Johnny Mize's shoes, batting .218 with six home runs.

The team needed offense, so Horace Stoneham acquired Joe Medwick, the former slugging star of the Cardinals and 1937 Triple Crown winner, from the Dodgers in June. Medwick was once one of the most dangerous hitters in baseball but had never been the same after a serious beaning in 1941. Stoneham paid only $7,500 for Medwick, who had a reputation for churlishness with fans and reporters, and many writers criticized the move. Wrote Frank Graham of the Consolidated News Features, "The transaction serves merely to indicate how far Medwick has slipped and how desperate Mel Ott has become in his efforts to find someone besides Ernie Lombardi and himself who can hit a ball for more than one base at a time."[9]

The Giants' pitching staff was a disaster area, with journeymen Cliff Melton (9–13), Johnnie Wittig (5–15) and Rube Fischer (5–10) making most of the starts, and Carl Hubbell winning only four games in his final season. Mel Ott needed pitching so badly that he took on Van Mungo, the onetime strikeout king of the Dodgers, as a reclamation project. (Mungo made his debut for Brooklyn in 1931 as a teammate of Ernie Lombardi, though Ernie caught him only once.) Mungo's career had fallen apart due to arm problems and a series of alcohol-fueled escapades, but he won 11 games at Minneapolis in 1942 and claimed to have conquered his demons. Mungo won three games and lost seven for the Giants but appeared to be on the comeback trail.

14. New York

The best pitcher for the Giants in 1943 was reliever Ace Adams. Adams, whose real first name was Ace, pitched in a league-leading 70 games with nine saves and 11 wins. Adams made only three starts, as Ott used him almost exclusively in the late innings with the game on the line, which was a rarity then but much more common in later years. One source calls Adams the "first of the iron-man relievers," not that Ace enjoyed the way he was used. "You couldn't make any money relieving," he complained. "Relieving was the low dog."[10]

Adams reacted very badly to one of Ernie's old tricks. Frustrated that Adams was not throwing harder, Ernie caught an outside pitch from Adams barehanded and fired it back. "I was hot," Adams recalled. "I said, 'What the hell are you trying to do, you big son of a gun, showing me up like that! ... Yeah, he could have at least rubbed and let the fans know I had something."[11]

Adams set a new major league record for relief appearances in 1943, but he and Ernie Lombardi were the only bright spots for the Giants. On September 8, the day Adams set his record, only 1,369 fans paid their way into the Polo Grounds to see the Giants lose to the Phillies, 3 to 2. The two New York runs came on solo homers by Ernie Lombardi and rookie shortstop Buddy Kerr. This loss left the Giants 41 and a half games out of first place. They had long since been mathematically eliminated from the pennant race.

At least Ernie received some good news on September 17. After a physical examination ordered by his draft board, Selective Service rejected the veteran catcher and classified him as 4-F. Rumors abounded that Ernie failed, not for physical reasons, but for mental ones; some reports stated that the military psychologists rejected him because he had a fear of crowds. That claim seemed spurious, as Ernie had performed before tens of thousands of cheering fans for more than a decade. But the big catcher made no comment. He was now out of danger of induction, and his career with the Giants continued uninterrupted.

Ernie also made a good showing in New York's Baseball War Bond League. This was a contest run by the federal Treasury Department in which the fans cast votes for their favorite local players while buying war bonds. When the contest concluded in September, Mel Ott won the poll, with the Dodgers' Dixie Walker in second place and Ernie Lombardi in third. The fans, after a rough start, had accepted him after all.

The season was a disaster for the Giants and ended for Ernie Lombardi with his worst injury of the season. On September 22 in Cincinnati, a foul tip from the bat of Frank McCormick slammed into Ernie's right index finger and forced him to leave the game in the fourth inning. The finger was so badly sprained that Ernie sat out nine games, made one failed pinch-hitting appearance, and then went home to California to recuperate. He ended the year with a .305 average and ten home runs while splitting the starting assignments almost evenly with Gus Mancuso.

The Giants finished last in the National League for the first time since 1915, mainly due to weak pitching and the lack of power in the lineup. Mel Ott led the team with 18 home runs but batted only .234, while Ernie was the only other Giants' player to reach double figures in homers. But Horace Stoneham trusted Ott to lead the Giants back into contention. He signed his manager to a new three-year contract with a modest raise. Stoneham also put Carl Hubbell, the now-retired star pitcher, in charge of an expanded farm system. Though the war drained the Giants, and every other team, of manpower, Stoneham was confident that the Giants would find the talent to compete in the National League.

15

The War Years

> "To me, Schnozz was an old guy, and very quiet. He wouldn't say much, but he'd walk around the locker room singing 'Mairzy Doats and Doezy Doats,' a novelty song that was very popular at the time. Lombardi loved that song. He'd go around singing it all the time. He was quite a character."[1]
>
> —Bobby Thomson, Giants teammate

New York Giants manager Mel Ott and owner Horace Stoneham knew that they had a difficult task before them. After the disastrous last place finish in 1943, and a sharp drop in attendance at the Polo Grounds, Ott and Stoneham worked to rebuild the Giants. But their task was complicated by the war. Military callups decimated the team in 1943, and as the war effort intensified, the 1944 season promised to be every bit as difficult.

At least they didn't have to worry about the catching situation, as all three Giant backstops—Ernie Lombardi, Gus Mancuso, and Ray Berres—were labeled 4-F by the Selective Service. In 1944, a player's draft status was every bit as important as his past statistics, so the Giants looked for talent in the ranks of the ineligible, the young, and the old. During spring training, the Giants expected to open the season with 11 men in the 4-F bracket and three more in 3-A, those exempted due to support of family members.

Among the 4-Fs recruited by the Giants was Phil Weintraub, a 36-year-old first baseman who failed a tryout with the Reds in 1936. Weintraub, one of baseball's few Jewish players, returned to the minors after a stint with the Phillies in 1938, and hit well at Toledo in 1942 and 1943. The Giants drafted him off Toledo's roster and hoped that he would provide the power at first base that they lost when Johnny Mize left for the service. Another was second baseman George Hausmann, a career minor leaguer who was only five feet five inches tall. He impressed Ott in camp and earned a starting spot.

The Giants felt confident that Johnny Allen, a 39-year-old pitcher, and Ott, at age 35, would not be called into the service anytime soon. Neither would pitcher Lou Polli, 42, who played in five games for the St. Louis Browns in 1932 and had bounced around the minors ever since. And Joe Medwick appeared healthy and ready to resume his status as one of the league's top hitters. If the team's power core of Medwick, Ott, and Ernie Lombardi remained intact, the Giants believed that they could challenge for a spot in the first division.

As usual, spring training—this time in Lakewood, New Jersey—started without Ernie Lombardi, though for once his contract did not appear to be an issue. In mid-March, Ernie told the Giants that he had personal business to attend to in Oakland, but that he expected to arrive at camp in a week. The big catcher was tight-lipped about his reasons for remaining at home, but on March 25 he contacted the Giants again and told them that he expected to arrive by April 1, only 17 days before the start of the 1944 season.

Mel Ott was frustrated with the string of delays. "He says he needs that time to wrap up his business in Oakland," said the manager, "and don't ask me what business, because I don't know. Neither, perhaps, does Lombardi." Horace Stoneham did not know either. Said Stoneham, "The salary situation is perfectly all right, despite the fact that he hasn't actually signed his contract."[2]

Though Ernie never told anyone why he remained away from camp for so long, he almost certainly had to deal with the aftermath of his father's death. There was property to divide, a will to process, and accounts to close. March turned to April, and still Ernie was absent from camp. As Ott told the *Daily News*, "An older player seems to require more practice to get his timing right. Therefore, I'd like to have men such as Weintraub, Medwick, Mancuso, Lombardi, and myself out there swinging for a couple of hours every day."[3]

The New York team wasn't getting much work done anyway, as snow and rain fell on Lakewood on a daily basis. Perhaps Ernie, reading the accounts of the stormy East Coast weather in his daily newspaper, wanted to remain in the milder climate of Oakland for as long as possible. Or, suggested the New York papers, since a player did not receive his salary until the start of the season, why slog around in mud and rain until it was absolutely necessary?

Ernie finally rolled into Lakewood on April 6, 12 days before the start of the season. The local writers guessed that he weighed at least 245 pounds, but Ernie, as usual, waxed optimistic, proclaiming that the extra pounds would melt away quickly. Despite Ernie's lack of practice, Ott decided not to split the catching position evenly as in the previous year. Ott plugged Lombardi into the starting position, with Mancuso as the backup.

Ernie, who liked to be the undisputed number one, responded with a hot start. He played in all of the Giants' first 32 games, appearing as the starting catcher 27 times in that stretch. Ernie's best game of the season came on April 30, in the first game of a doubleheader against Brooklyn. The big catcher belted two doubles and a single, driving in seven runs (a career high) in a wild 26–8 win over the Dodgers. Phil Weintraub had an

Lombardi wound down his career with the New York Giants (National Baseball Hall of Fame Library, Cooperstown, New York).

even better afternoon, driving in 11 runs, one short of the major league record, on two doubles, a triple, a homer, and a bases-loaded walk. Babe Ruth, who was at the game that day, congratulated Weintraub. "Kid, that was some performance," said Ruth. "You knocked in enough runs for a month. Some guys don't get that many in a season."[4]

April went well for both Ernie and the Giants, as the team won seven of its first nine games and Ernie ended the month with his batting average well over .300. But Ernie's lack of conditioning began to show, and as his bat faded in May, so did the Giants. The pitching, always a problem area, failed and dragged the Giants down in the standings. At the end of May, with the team in sixth position, Ott decided to give Ernie a rest. He alternated Ernie and Gus Mancuso in the starting spot for a few days. Still, Ott was counting on Ernie. "When Ernie Lombardi starts blasting the ball," said Ott, "I believe the Giants will move as they did at the outset."[5]

In 1944, Ernie finally found his ideal road roommate. Bill Voiselle, a tall, right-handed pitcher from the tiny town of Ninety-Six, South Carolina, played in a few games for the Giants in 1942 and 1943, but blossomed in 1944. Voiselle became the ace of the staff, winning 21 games and leading the league in strikeouts. And he didn't mind Ernie's snoring. Voiselle was hard of hearing, and his hearing loss gave him a 4-F rating and kept him out of the military.

Ernie suffered his first major injury of the season against the Pirates on June 4, when Jim Russell slid into him at the plate and cut a gash in the catcher's forehead with his spikes. Ernie left the game, and with two off days in the schedule coming up immediately afterward, the Giants expected their catcher to get some rest and give his injury a chance to heal.

But Ernie did not plan to simply put his feet up and take it easy. On June 6, he sprung a surprise on the entire baseball world.

He got married.

His new wife was Berice Marie Ayers, a 43-year-old woman from Oakland who

- was seven years older than Ernie,
- was not of Italian descent, and
- was married and divorced three times before.

Berice Ayers had worked as a telephone operator and as a dressmaker in the past. Though married three times, she had no children. She rode a train from Oakland to be present during Ernie's two off days, and they were married by a probate judge in New Canaan, Connecticut.

Soon, Berice and Ernie moved into their own place in Oakland. Ernie, for the first 36 years of his life, lived in the Lombardi family home on 13th Street in Oakland, partly because his family was so close, and partly because it made no sense, in Ernie's perspective, to maintain a permanent home in Oakland when he was playing ball on the other end of the country from March to October every year. Now, finally, Ernie would make a home of his own.

Every major league baseball team did its part for the war effort, often playing exhibition games to raise money for veterans or to sell war bonds. But on June 26 at Yankee Stadium, some 50,000 fans were treated to perhaps the strangest game in major league history—a game with three teams. The Yankees, Dodgers, and Giants played a three-team game in which the Dodgers faced the Yankees in the first inning, the Dodgers faced the Giants in the second, the Yankees opposed the Giants in the third, and so on. The final score was Dodgers 5, Yankees 1, Giants 0.

The Giants fought to stay in the first division as the summer of 1944 wore on, but a disastrous 14-game losing streak brought the team crashing to earth in August. They fought their way back to fourth position in September, only to suffer through a nine-game skid and fall back to fifth. They ended the season there with a 67–87 record.

Double plays were a huge problem for the New York offense. With 42 twin killings in their first 29 games, the lack of team speed killed rallies. Ernie was the main culprit, grounding into 13 double plays before the end of May. He wound up leading the National League (for the fourth time) by hitting into 23 double plays. Ernie, who held his own during the middle months of the campaign, totally ran out of gas in September, batting .203 for the month. He was 36 years old and looked every year of his age.

Gus Mancuso and Ernie Lombardi were the two slowest players in baseball, and on September 1, 1944, Brooklyn manager Leo Durocher found a way to take advantage of that fact. In a game at Ebbets Field, with Ernie on deck, Dodger pitcher Art Herring hit Joe Medwick on the elbow. As Medwick writhed in pain, Durocher called Mel Ott onto the field. The rules then allowed a manager to put in a temporary pinch runner for an injured player, who would be permitted to stay in the game afterward. "Put in a runner for him, Mel," said Durocher. "And if Medwick can play the outfield it's all right with me if you want to put him back in the game."[6]

Ott agreed, though he surely knew that the rules also allowed the opposing manager to choose the pinch-runner. Durocher chose Mancuso. To no one's surprise, Ernie then bounced into what Harold C. Burr in the *Brooklyn Eagle* called "the season's easiest double play.... It was a study in slow motion, with two pairs of legs pumping away on a treadmill." To make things worse, Medwick's elbow was so badly bruised that he never returned to the game. The injury put him on the sidelines for more than a week.

A few days later, umpire Bill Stewart made an embarrassing mistake in a game between the Giants and the Braves. With the Braves at bat and a runner on first, a wild pitch got away from Ernie. Stewart, who forgot that there was a man on base, absent-mindedly flagged down the ball and flipped it to Lombardi. This kept the runner from advancing. "Maybe that's what Ernie's longed for all along," noted one writer, "an umpire-retriever."[7]

The Giants were well out the race by this time, as the St. Louis Cardinals ran away with the pennant for the third year in a row. Ernie, hampered by his lack of spring training and his usual rash of nagging injuries, posted a batting average of .255, the lowest of his career ("close to his weight," as Dick Young wrote in the *Daily News*). After banging a homer, his tenth of the season, and driving in four runs in a 12–1 win over the Phillies on September 14 (giving Bill Voiselle his 20th win), Lombardi closed the 1944 campaign in a 5 for 32 skid. After September 24, when he split a finger and left a game against the Pirates in the first inning, Mel Ott used him only as a pinch hitter during the last week of the season.

Ernie, once again, was at a career crossroads. The 1944 campaign was the worst of his career, and if he wanted to continue playing the game he loved, he needed to rededicate himself to fitness and health. Someday, hopefully soon, the war would end and all the top-shelf players would return to the major leagues and restore the level of competition to what it had been. If the aging catcher did not want to be left behind, he would have to raise his game.

Ernie turned 37 in April of 1945, and was determined to avoid the physical problems that dogged him the year before. He signed his contract and reported to the Giants' camp at Lakewood, New Jersey, in early March, and told the papers that his abbreviated spring training in 1944 hindered him all year. "I figure that I could have played a lot more games last year and would have done a lot more hitting if I'd been able to get more spring training under my belt," the catcher told the *Daily News*. "This year I'm going to be ready for the opening game—and the ones that follow."

So Ernie kept his weight down during the off-season, signed his contract on March 7 (which was, for him, earlier than usual), and arrived at camp in good playing condition. One test came early, when the Giants took on a team from Bainbridge Naval Training Base in Connecticut. This service team had Stan Musial in center field, Eddie Miksis of the Dodgers at short, and Dick Sisler of the Cardinals at first base, among other players with professional experience, so it was no pushover. The Giants made quick work of them, scoring six runs in the first inning with a grand slam by Ernie Lombardi on their way to an 8–3 win. Ernie added two singles later in the game. Three days later, Ernie belted another homer against the Curtis Bay Coast Guard team in Baltimore.

Mel Ott was counting on Ernie to make a comeback. Gus Mancuso, who shared the starting spot with Lom in 1944, was now with the Phillies, leaving Ray Berres and rookie Johnny Toncoff as his backups. With more players in the military than ever, the Giants expected Lombardi to be a workhorse again.

For once, the St. Louis Cardinals were not expected to run away with the pennant in 1945. The two St. Louis teams, the Cardinals and the Browns, were less affected by the draft than most other clubs, and some claimed that the local draft board in the Mound City must have been composed of baseball fans. The Cardinals and Browns kept enough of their talent to win the two league titles in 1944. But when the Cardinals lost several All-Stars, including outfielder Stan Musial and catcher Walker Cooper, to the service and traded pitching star Mort Cooper to the Braves in a contract dispute, the defending champions looked vulnerable.

Despite his aging roster, Mel Ott decided to turn the Giants into a running team, ramping up the aggression on the basepaths. That included Ernie Lombardi, who made national headlines on April 27 when he bunted for a hit against the Dodgers. The sight of Ernie laying down a bunt and beating it out was the highlight of the game, according to Hy Turkin of the *New York Daily News*. Turkin's article exclaimed that Lombardi, "the leaden-legged Giant who navigates with the speed of lava, beat out a bunt ... yes, BEAT OUT A BUNT!" The headline on the article was "Lombardi Beats Out Bunt! Voiselle Blanks Flock, 5–0."[8] The paper even showed a photograph of Lombardi crossing first base ahead of the throw, with the caption, "Seeing Is Believing."

But Ernie, whom writer John Lardner described as "the world's most stationary human," was sensitive about his lack of speed. He said in 1945,

> Last summer, the Boston third baseman moved out to left field when I came up. That burned me up, so I tapped one down to third base and ran like all get-out. Jim Tobin, the pitcher, just stood there for a few seconds and looked at me, surprised-like. Then he called out, asking what I was doing.
>
> Finally he walked over to third, picked up the ball, and threw me out by three steps. I was never more humiliated in my life.[9]

And he hated the fact that infielders played him so far back. "That [ex-Cardinal manager] Frank Frisch—it was his idea. I suppose he thinks he's funny!"[10]

The Giants got off to a great start in 1945, not because of their baserunning, but because of their power. On May 26 the Giants, with a 25–7 record, led the National League by six and a half games. They were bashing home runs at a furious pace, and at the end of May Ernie led the league with 12 homers. Ott had seven homers and a .385 average, and Phil Weintraub had eight homers. Ott's team was also getting good pitching, led by the resurgent Van Mungo, who spent 1944 in the military. Mungo stayed sober in 1945 and, after a rough April, won six decisions in a row in May and June.

It was nice while it lasted, but the Giants faded, as usual, in June. A 3–14 skid dropped them out of the lead by June 13, and another losing streak knocked them all the way down to fifth by the end of the month. Joe Medwick, battling injuries, was traded to the Braves in June for Clyde Kluttz, a catcher acquired to back up Ernie as the summer heated up. Also, Ott's new penchant for aggressive baserunning backfired more often than it succeeded, as more Giant runners were thrown out on the bases than ever. Some of their efforts were almost comically ill-advised, as when Ernie tried to score from second against the Cardinals on a short blooper to the outfield on July 12. He was thrown out easily at home by Red Schoendienst.

As the Giants retreated, the Chicago Cubs moved to fill the void. In May they trailed the Giants by as much as nine games, but a 16–1 streak vaulted them into the league lead in July, and from then on, the Cubs and Cardinals made a two-team race of it. The deciding factor for the Cubs was the acquisition of All-Star pitcher Hank Borowy from the New York Yankees in a waiver deal at the end of July. No one knew how Borowy, one of the Yankees' top starters, cleared waivers in the American League, but Borowy won 11 games for the Cubs and helped them win the flag by two games.

Though the two major leagues agreed to cancel the 1945 All-Star Game (which was set to be held at Fenway Park in Boston on July 9), *The Sporting News* and the Associated Press made their own All-Star selections. Ernie, who led the National League in homers with 13 at the end of June, was named to both squads. Van Mungo was the only other Giant on either team.

The Giants were always looking for catching prospects, but in 1945 they missed out on a future star. In June the Giants played an exhibition game against a team from the Naval Submarine Base in Groton, Connecticut. The Naval team, managed by former Cincinnati outfielder Jim Gleeson and with another ex-Red, Junior Thompson, on the pitching staff, defeated the Giants by a score of 8 to 3. One player, a 20-year-old catcher named Lawrence Berra, caught Mel Ott's eye. Berra, whom everyone called Yogi, belted two hits and smashed a fly ball to deepest center field that traveled over 400 feet. After the game Ott asked Gleeson about the young catcher, but Gleeson informed him that Berra belonged to the Yankees.

That's when Horace Stoneham, usually an astute dealmaker, made a mistake. At Ott's urging, Stoneham called the new Yankee general manager Larry MacPhail (who had left the Dodgers three years before) and offered $50,000 for Berra. This hefty figure convinced MacPhail that the previously obscure minor league backstop must be worth keeping, so the Yankees promoted Berra to their top farm team in Newark. By 1946 Berra was a Yankee. He would go on to play for 14 pennant winners and 10 World Series champions.

The Giants finished in fifth place, 19 games behind the pennant-winning Cubs, but Horace Stoneham must have been pleased with his manager, because he gave Mel Ott a new five-year contract to lead the team into the 1950 season. Ott led the team with 21 homers, 79 runs batted in, and a .308 average, but Ernie Lombardi (19 HR, 70 RBI, .307 average) was right behind him. Despite his rash of injuries in August and September, Ernie bounced back nicely from his troubled 1944 campaign. If a Comeback Player of the Year award existed in 1945, Ernie may well have won it.

When Ernie returned to Oakland in October a reporter asked him about his future. "Sure, I'm going to keep playing ball," he said, "[for] two, maybe three more years. I haven't heard from the Giants about my 1946 contract, but I expect to be with them next season."[11] But for once, Ernie did not take the winter off. In November of 1945, after playing in his customary round of Bay Area charity games, he went to work in a sheet metal plant in West Oakland.

16

Backup

> In keeping with his plan to inject some speed into his club, Manager Mel Ott announced yesterday that a 60-yard dash will be staged later in the week. Ironically, the winner will receive the Ernie Lombardi trophy.
> —*Rochester* (NY) *Democrat*, March 5, 1947

The war was over, and baseball was about to change.

In November of 1945, Branch Rickey, general manager of the Dodgers, signed Negro Leagues star Jackie Robinson to play for the team's top farm club in Montreal. Robinson was the first African American to sign a professional contract in organized baseball in the 20th century. This signing was the first crack in the wall of baseball's long-standing whites-only policy, and should Robinson succeed, he stood to be the first of many talented Black players to, at long last, integrate the major leagues.

This movement was a long time coming and had been brewing for years by the time of Robinson's signing. In 1939 Wendell Smith, a reporter for the prominent Black newspaper, the *Pittsburgh Courier*, interviewed major league players and managers to gauge their level of acceptance for an integrated game. To his surprise, many players—at least those who agreed to talk to Smith—revealed themselves to be quite receptive to the idea.

On April 29, 1939, when the Reds came to Pittsburgh for a three-game series, Smith entered the Cincinnati dugout before the game to talk to manager Bill McKechnie and his players. McKechnie, though he allowed that "it is not up to me to decide upon that question," had no objection to integrating the Reds. "I have seen at least 25 colored players who could have made the grade," he said. "Yes, if given permission I would use a Negro player on my team." Several Reds praised the Black players they had seen and played against in exhibition contests. As Bucky Walters said, "I grew up in Philadelphia which at that time was the hotbed of colored baseball. I saw any number of Negroes who should have made the big leagues. They had some of the best players I have ever seen on those teams."[1]

Several other Reds made similar statements, while Johnny Vander

Meer went a step farther, questioning the color line itself. He recalled a game he pitched against the Philadelphia Stars of the Negro National League. "I am sure that there were at least four men on that team good enough for the majors," said Vander Meer, "[and] I certainly wouldn't object to a good Negro ball player on our team. I was born and reared in the North. I have a different viewpoint than some of the other boys. Although it's none of my business, I don't see why they are barred."[2]

Ernie Lombardi listed intently to the conversations, and when Smith turned to the big catcher, Ernie echoed his teammates' sentiments. "A few years ago," said Ernie, "we played an exhibition game in Oakland, California, against a Negro all-star team. Satchel Paige, the fast ball wizard, pitched against us, and I'm telling you he was great. I said right there that he was as good as Dizzy Dean. He's as fast as Dean, maybe faster. When he whipped that fast one in there you could hardly see it.... There are a number whom I have seen and are good enough to play in the majors."[3]

Smith surveyed the players on several other teams during the next few weeks and heard similar praise for the talent level of Black players. He published his findings in the *Courier* that summer, and though his articles received no attention outside of the Black community, perhaps he had planted a seed. Seven years after Smith's interviews, integration came to organized ball, with Jackie Robinson leading the way.

Ernie Lombardi's career as a regular ended on January 5, 1946, when New York Giants owner Horace Stoneham, who served as his own general manager, pulled off one of the biggest cash deals in baseball history up to that time. Stoneham bought Walker Cooper, the All-Star catcher of the St. Louis Cardinals, for $175,000.

Cooper, considered by most to be the best catcher in baseball, was the backbone of the Cardinal team that won three pennants and two World Series titles from 1942 to 1944. But Cooper was dissatisfied with his salary in St. Louis, and when the Cardinals came up with young catching prospects Del Rice and Joe Garagiola, Cooper was suddenly expendable. Cooper spent most of the 1945 season in the Navy and was still in the service when the Giants bought him, but the team expected the new catcher to be available soon, perhaps in April, but no later than early May.

Cooper's Cardinal teammates were shocked at the news of the deal. Said Enos Slaughter, "I honestly believe that with that tough raw-boned catcher behind the plate for us instead of for the Giants, we could have remained a dynasty for another five or six years."[4] But the top catcher in the game now belonged to the Giants, pushing Ernie Lombardi into a new role as Cooper's backup.

Mel Ott, optimistic as always, was not bothered by the idea that Cooper would not be available right away. "I expect to have Walker Cooper in action by the first week of May," he said, "and, previous to that, Ernie Lombardi can take care of things. Lom is always in shape in the spring and he's okay until he tires in the summer heat."[5] Actually, Ernie's holdouts sometimes kept him from being in shape at the start of a season, but Ott preferred to look at the bright side.

Ernie was not thrilled with the loss of his starting spot. After all, Lombardi had belted 19 homers in 1945, batted .307, and made the All-Star team. On the other hand, Ernie had accomplished all this against inferior wartime competition. With almost all the best players off to war, the level of play in 1944 and 1945 was probably the lowest in the 20th century, and teams were so strapped for talent that they put players in uniform that they would never have considered otherwise. The Cincinnati Reds put a fifteen-year-old boy on the mound, the St. Louis Browns employed a one-armed outfielder, and the Brooklyn Dodgers brought Babe Herman back after seven years away from the majors. The overall caliber of play was not very high.

But Ernie appeared to be a little miffed, and with spring training about to start, the Giants could not reach him. "He won't talk," said Mel Ott. "He even refuses to answer the telephone. We don't even know if he's dissatisfied or just doesn't want to begin training this early."[6] When a reporter from the *Oakland Tribune* saw Ernie around town, Ernie merely said, "Tell Ott I'll write him in a few days."

The veteran catcher left on February 17 for Miami, though the Giants did not know he was coming. When Ott called the Lombardi home on February 19, Berice Lombardi assured him that Ernie was on his way. He finally arrived at camp on February 22, and Ott immediately noticed that Ernie was heavier than usual. He ordered his catcher to get down to 235 pounds with a regimen of running. Ernie was not much interested in that. "There is no use doing much running," he said, "because I'll never learn to run anyway."[7]

With the war now over, hundreds of ballplayers streamed back into the game, and the sixteen major league clubs had to find places for them. The two major leagues decided to expand the team rosters to 48 from the usual 40, and to allow teams to carry 30 players during the season, up from the usual 25. The Giants had more than 50 players report to their spring camp in Miami and competition for jobs was fierce. But even with the trade for Walker Cooper, Ernie Lombardi's position with the Giants appeared safe. He had hit well in 1945 and seemed to be a perfect fit for a role as Cooper's backup.

But all was not well with the Giants. There were too many players in camp for Mel Ott to evaluate properly, and many of the wartime players grumbled when they were pushed aside by the men returning from the service. Dolf Luque, the popular pitching coach who served under both Bill Terry and Ott, quit the team in a contract dispute, and outfielder Danny Gardella was suspended after an altercation with the team secretary. Perhaps Ott and Stoneham did not realize it, but there were many unhappy men in camp.

The Giants had high hopes for 1946. With Johnny Mize returning from the military, the team's power core of Mize, Walker Cooper, and Mel Ott looked like one of the best in the National League. And the pitching looked good, with holdovers Bill Voiselle and Ace Adams joining Dave Koslo and Hal Schumacher, back from the service. Ott was also counting on Van Mungo, who stayed sober in 1945 and surprised the league by winning 14 games, and Sal Maglie, who won five games for the Giants in limited action.

There were some concerns, however. Cooper, the new catcher, was not released from the Navy until spring training was almost over, and he was not yet in shape. He hit a triple in an exhibition game against the Senators in Washington and remarked, "I ran it all uphill." He was happy to hit a triple, "but I wasn't so glad by the time I got to third."[8] Mel Ott was beaned by one of his young charges late in spring training, though he recovered enough to start the season, while Van Mungo fell off the wagon, caused trouble in camp, and drew his release.

The biggest threat to the Giants came from south of the border, when a wealthy businessman named Jorge Pasquel, president of the Mexican League, made big-money offers to American and National League stars like Bob Feller, Ted Williams, and Stan Musial. Pasquel dreamed of turning his Mexican League into a third major circuit, and believed that, with the postwar glut of returning players, he could skim a fair amount of talent from the existing majors. He reportedly offered Feller, Williams, and Musial blank contracts and invited them to fill in their own salaries. For a young player like Musial, who was earning $13,500 a year at the time, the temptation must have been great.

Pasquel also pursued mid-range players and found a ready audience with the many disgruntled Giants. Danny Gardella made only $5,000 in 1945, and when Pasquel offered to triple his salary, Gardella not only jumped to the Mexican League, but acted as Pasquel's agent in luring other players to follow his lead. Dolf Luque, who mentored many Giants pitchers, signed to manage the Mexican League club in Puebla and, like Gardella, made offers on Pasquel's behalf. Established stars like Ernie Lombardi were not interested—it is possible that he was never asked—but the younger, lower-salaried Giants listened to Gardella and Luque.

Pasquel failed to land any of the biggest American stars, but five New York Giants—Gardella, pitchers Adrien Zabala and Sal Maglie, and infielders George Hausmann and Nap Reyes—quit the team and headed for Mexico. So did Brooklyn catcher Mickey Owen, Cardinals pitcher Max Lanier, and about a dozen others. The new Commissioner of Baseball, A.B. (Happy) Chandler, threatened to suspend each player for life unless they returned to their American team within ten days, but in late April two more Giants, star reliever Ace Adams and starter Harry Feldman, made the jump. These defections left the Giants short-handed, especially on the mound.

Despite the Mexican League raids, the 1946 season started off well. On Opening Day, with Cooper not yet in playing condition, Ernie drew the starting assignment against the Phillies at the Polo Grounds. In the first inning, Mickey Witek walked and Mel Ott followed with a long home run to right, the 511th of his career. After Babe Young singled, Ernie belted a two-run homer of his own, also into the right field seats. Bill Voiselle pitched a solid game as the Giants won by a score of 8 to 4.

Unfortunately, from that point on, 1946 was one of those seasons in which everything went wrong for the Giants. Ott injured his knee the next day while diving for a fly ball, and afterward he could not get his bat untracked. After hitting .074 in 31 games, the manager benched himself. The homer he hit on Opening Day was the last of his career. Walker Cooper broke a finger on a foul tip on April 25 and missed five weeks, then battled more injuries for the rest of the year. Johnny Mize hit as well as ever, leading the league in homers in August when he suffered a broken finger and missed a month. In his first game back, he hurt his toe in a play at first base and was lost for the season.

All the while, Ernie made the most of his role as backup catcher and pinch-hitter. He belted three pinch homers in 1946, including a walk-off shot in the 11th inning on May 24 that gave the Giants a 2–1 win over the Braves. In September, Brooklyn's Kirby Higbe threw a one-hitter against the New Yorkers in which the only hit for the Giants was Ernie's home run in the second inning. A few days earlier, Lombardi's grand slam was one of three Giant homers in a 16–2 rout of the Phillies at the Polo Grounds.

Ernie also hit a homer against the second Lombardi to play major league baseball. Vic Lombardi, no relation to Ernie, was a left-handed pitcher who joined the Brooklyn team in 1945. Vic Lombardi was small in stature and wore glasses, but somehow became a Giant killer, defeating the New York team nine times without a loss in 1945 and 1946. On July 4, in the second game of a doubleheader at the Polo Grounds, with the Dodgers ahead by an 8–4 score, Ernie pinch-hit in the ninth with one out against Vic Lombardi. Ernie launched a home run into the second deck in left field, but Vic got the last two outs for an 8–5 win.

But Ernie had some bad days too. On April 18, in Brooklyn's home opener against the Giants, the Dodgers scored in the third inning on a triple by Billy Herman and a passed ball by Ernie. In the fifth, the Dodgers ran wild on the bases. Pete Reiser walked, stole second, and took third when Ernie's throw sailed into the outfield. With Gene Hermanski at bat, Reiser then stole home. Hermanski walked and promptly stole second, and rookie Carl Furillo singled him home. With Ernie on the ropes, Furillo then stole second, the fourth Dodger steal of the inning. The Dodgers wound up winning by a score of 8 to 1.

The Dodgers entered the fifth inning that day leading 6 to nothing, and most teams would not have gone on a base-stealing binge with a six-run lead. But the Dodgers, under manager Leo Durocher, were not like most teams. They were out to destroy the opposition, especially their crosstown rivals, the Giants. The Brooklyn and New York teams, and their fan bases, actively hated each other, and Durocher had no problem with embarrassing the Giants, even when the game was out of hand. In short, Durocher was the exact opposite of Giants manager Mel Ott. As Durocher said in his autobiography, "I come to play! I come to beat you! I come to kill you! That's the way Miller Huggins, my first manager, brought me up, and that's the way it has always been with me."[9]

Durocher made that point in mid-season in a conversation with announcer Red Barber and a group of reporters. The Dodger manager was fuming that the Giants had belted five homers, two by Ernie Lombardi, in a July 4 doubleheader split at the Polo Grounds. The Giants were in last place at the time, and when Barber said, "Ott's a nice guy," Durocher went on a rant. "Do you know a nicer guy in the world than Mel Ott?" he demanded. "He's a nice guy. In last place! Where am I? In first place. I'm in first place. The nice guys are over there in last place, not in this dugout."[10]

This speech by Durocher was eventually distilled into the memorable motto "Nice guys finish last," a phrase that became part of the American lexicon (and the title of Durocher's autobiography). But it also pointed out what many perceived to be the problem with the New York Giants. Mel Ott was, indeed, a nice guy and a close personal friend of owner Horace Stoneham. Perhaps he was too nice to be a manager. Ott's two predecessors at the helm of the Giants, John McGraw and Bill Terry, were tough, stern, demanding taskmasters who won 13 pennants and four World Series titles between them. Mel Ott was not cut from the same cloth.

If Durocher saw a lot of nice guys on the Giants bench, he could have found no nicer one, and no less worried one, than Ernie Lombardi. As Bobby Thomson, a rookie outfielder in 1946, said:

> Ernie used to sit on the bench with his catcher's glove just like a big pancake. He'd roll it up and he'd sit on the bench. He was just pinch-hitting then, and he'd just sit on the bench with that under his arm, and his shoes were always

untied, and sometimes he had them off, I guess. We used to watch Mel Ott, when he was looking for a pinch-hitter, come down on the bench, and all he would say was, "Hey Lom." That's all. He would just nod at him and say, "Hey Lom." He didn't have to say anything else. Lom knew he was a pinch-hitter, and he always was just very relaxed. He'd bend over and tie his shoelaces and go over to the bat rack and grab a bat and just drag it up to home plate. He wouldn't even swing it sometimes, you know, like a lot of guys want to do, to get loosened up. He was just a very nonchalant guy.[11]

Still, Ernie thought that the 1946 campaign might be his last. On September 1, in the second game of a doubleheader against the hated Dodgers, Ernie belted a homer in the fifth inning to give the Giants a 1–0 lead. But the Dodgers tied the score, and in the ninth, it all fell apart. Brooklyn's Pee Wee Reese singled, went all the way to third when Ernie was slow to retrieve a wild pitch, then scored on a passed ball by Lombardi. This run proved to be the difference in a 2–1 Dodger win, and after the game a dejected Ernie told a reporter, "I'm through after this season. My dogs have gone back on me."[12]

He could put on a burst of speed when he needed to. After a game at the Polo Grounds in September, a 12-year-old boy snatched Lombardi's cap off his head and made a dash for the exits. The kid had a head start, but Ernie chased him down and turned him over to park security, though the thief had passed the cap off to someone else.

In the end, the Giants finished last in 1946 for the second time in Mel Ott's five seasons as manager. Though the Giants led the league in home runs with 121, their pitching and defense dragged them down again, and the papers were filled with rumors about Ott's job security. One report stated that Stoneham offered the job to Lefty O'Doul, manager of the pennant-winning San Francisco Seals of the Pacific Coast League, but that O'Doul turned it down. Stoneham was also concerned about losing the popularity battle with the resurgent Brooklyn Dodgers, who finished the season tied with the Cardinals for the pennant before losing in a playoff.

On a positive note, the fans loved the Giants' home run display, enough to bring a record 1.2 million of them through the turnstiles at the Polo Grounds. The farm system, now overseen by Carl Hubbell, was beginning to produce talent that promised to lift the team back into contention in short order. Besides, Ott was a personal friend of Horace Stoneham, and his contract had four more years to run. So Stoneham assured the papers that Ott would, indeed, return to manage in 1947.

Both Ott and Stoneham wanted Ernie back for the 1947 campaign. The Giants had two catching prospects in their minor league chain, Wes Westrum and Sal Yvars, but both were a year or more from being ready for the big show. So despite his aging legs, the 39-year-old Ernie agreed to play one more year with the Giants.

16. Backup

In early 1947, the Giants and the Cleveland Indians set up their spring training camps in Arizona, with the Giants based in Phoenix and the Indians in Tucson. Team owners Horace Stoneham of the Giants and Bill Veeck of the Indians owned real estate and business interests in the state, so the two teams created their own Cactus League.

Spring training was an enjoyable time for Ernie and the Giants. They avoided the rainy season in Florida and were able to play every day in the Arizona sun. And in mid–March, Stoneham took his Giants and the San Francisco Seals of the Pacific Coast League to Hawaii to play a five-game series in Honolulu. The players loved Hawaii, and even the usually reticent Ernie didn't mind being photographed in his Giants uniform with leis around his neck and a coconut hat. For the Giants, it felt more like a vacation than a training camp.

But Ernie, struggling to get his weight down, could hardly run at all. In a spring training game, Ernie lined a shot off the left field wall, 331 feet away, but was only able to make it to first. "He stretched a double into a single," said one writer. One newspaper cartoonist drew a picture of players chasing a ball to the outfield wall. An infielder calls out, "Quick, guys! We can still get him at first! It's Ernie Lombardi!"

Despite their last place finish in 1946, the Giants liked their chances as the new season approached. Johnny Mize and Walker Cooper were healthy, and the infield appeared solid with Mize at first, Buddy Blattner at second, Buddy Kerr at short, and either Sid Gordon or Jack Lohrke at third. The outfield looked promising with Willard Marshall in left, Whitey Lockman in center and newcomers Bobby Thomson and Clint Hartung vying for positions.

Pitching was still a problem area, but Horace Stoneham made a splash when he bought Larry Jansen, who won 30 games for the San Francisco Seals in 1946, and several other minor leaguers to battle for positions with Bill Voiselle and others. Mel Ott also told the papers that he would manage from the bench. Ott said that he might grab a bat every now and then, but that Ernie Lombardi would be his main pinch-hitter.

When the season began, Walker Cooper was so healthy that Ernie barely saw any action. He did not appear in a game until April 30, the 11th game of the season, in a failed pinch-hitting assignment against the Cardinals. He pinch-hit the next day, and then stayed on the bench for the next two weeks. Cooper started 29 of the first 30 games and left little room for Ernie. The big catcher made the most of his first start on May 18, walloping two homers and driving in six runs in an 11–6 win at Pittsburgh, but then it was back to the bench for nine more days.

While Ernie played the role of spectator and cheerleader, the Giants gave the fans an incredible power surge. Johnny Mize belted 51 home runs,

Walker Cooper added 35, Willard Marshall 36, and Bobby Thomson 29. The Giants started slow, but a 17–7 record in May vaulted them into first place, one game ahead of the Cubs and two in front of the Braves and Dodgers. They were hitting home runs at a record pace, and their power kept them in the race.

The New York fans loved the home run display, and the Giants drew a record 1.6 million fans to the Polo Grounds that year. Team secretary Eddie Brannick, a fixture with the Giants since the days of John McGraw, called the team the "Windowbreakers," and the name stuck. On August 24 the Giants topped the existing National League record for homers in a season, and on September 1 they passed the major league record of 182, set by the 1927 Yankees of Babe Ruth and Lou Gehrig.

However, the team was still weak in other areas. Larry Jansen won 21 games as a rookie, but the Giants led the major leagues in errors, and though they scored more runs than any other team, they allowed more than every other club save the Pirates. Their sheer power kept them in first place for a while in May and June, but their poor pitching and defense caught up with them. An eight-game losing streak in August dropped the team to fourth place. There they remained at season's end, 13 games behind the pennant-winning Dodgers.

The Giants belted 221 home runs in 1947, obliterating the previous record, and Horace Stoneham was so proud of his Windowbreakers that he commissioned a ring for each player to commemorate the new record. Ernie contributed four homers, only two of them after his two-homer game in May. His last home run of the season, and the final one of his career, came on August 24 in a loss to the Cubs.

The 1947 season was Ernie's 17th in major league baseball, and the big catcher could see the end of his career fast approaching. Walker Cooper was healthy and started 130 games, while Ernie started only 21 contests and pinch-hit 25 times. Ernie spent most of the season on the bench, only occasionally starting the second games of doubleheaders. He was the oldest player on the Giants roster, and as the season progressed, it became clear that he was at the end of the road. In September, Lombardi made only six appearances on the field, five of them as a pinch hitter.

Lombardi played his final major league game on September 17, 1947, at Wrigley Field in Chicago, and he went out with a bang. The Giants trailed by a 10–4 score in the top of the ninth inning against the Cubs that day but erupted for three runs and drove Hank Borowy from the mound. Paul Ericksen came in to pitch for the Cubs with runners on first and second and two out. Mel Ott sent Ernie up to pinch-hit for second baseman Bobby Rhawn, and Lombardi delivered a line drive off the top of the fence in center field.

Ernie made it to second as the two runners scored, and umpires Lou Jorda and George Barr gave the home run signal, claiming that a fan had knocked the ball back onto the field. After a long dispute with all the umpires and both managers, chief umpire Jocko Conlon ruled the hit a double and sent Ernie back to second. The score was now 10–9, and Buddy Blattner came in to run for Ernie, who left the field to a round of applause. It was his last major league hit. The Giants tied the score at 10, but the Cubs scored two in the bottom of the inning on a homer by Bill Nicholson to win it.

Two days later, on the train from Chicago to New York, Mel Ott gave the big catcher his release. The Giants needed to make room for younger (and lower-salaried) catchers, and the 39-year-old Ernie no longer fit into their plans. Ott, nice guy that he was, felt badly about it. "I remember the last game Ernie Lombardi played for the Giants.... On the train back to New York, it was my duty to hand Lom his release," he said. "At the same time I took myself off the active list. I haven't played a game since."[13]

The papers were genuinely sorry to see Lombardi go. The *Daily News* called him "an amiable soul with a heart as big as a watermelon,"[14] while the *Brooklyn Eagle* called him "one of the greatest right-handed hitters of modern baseball."[15] The *Eagle* also reported a rumor that Horace Stoneham would hire Ernie to manage the Giants' farm club at Minneapolis in 1948.

Arthur Daley, the veteran baseball writer of *The New York Times*, gave Ernie a proper sendoff:

> When you look back on him and his 17 years in the majors, you almost come to the conclusion that he was the greatest hitter of all time. Every hit he made—with few exceptions—was an honest one. Where a Ty Cobb would scratch out hundreds of infield singles as a result of his flashing speed afoot, Lumbering Lom did all his running in the same spot. He ran on a treadmill and couldn't outrace a snail, even with a head start.[16]

So ended the major league career of Ernie Lombardi. He left the game with a .306 career batting average, 190 home runs and 990 runs batted in, all respectable figures for a catcher in that era. He also held two major league records, though both were negative ones. He grounded into 30 double plays in a single season (1938) and totaled 261 for his career,[17] putting him at the top of the leaderboard in both departments. (Both records have since been broken.) He was also the all-time home run leader for the Cincinnati Reds, hitting 120 round trippers during his ten years with the club. This record stood until Ted Kluszewski passed it in 1954.

Perhaps Ernie was most proud of his stolen bases. "I got eight or nine stolen bases in my 17 years in the big leagues," he recalled years later. "Averaging it out, I figure I stole a half a base a year."[18]

17

Back to the Minors

> "Schnozz is 40 years old now and the Giants have a couple of superb young prospects coming. Ottie had to make room for them, even though he hated to let Lom go. Here's hoping that the big fellow will be able to swing a profitable deal for himself."[1]
>
> —Arthur Daley, *The New York Times*

Ernie's major league career was over, but he was not done with baseball. After his release by the Giants, he returned to his home in Oakland and let it be known that he was interested in continuing his career in the Pacific Coast League.

The Pacific Coast League, which was tottering when Ernie left it after the 1930 season, was on much more solid footing by 1948, due to a boost in attendance and popularity after the end of the Second World War. The eight PCL teams—six in California and one each in Washington and Oregon—played to bigger and more enthusiastic crowds than ever before and represented the most popular and stable of the three AAA-level minor leagues (the others being the American Association and the International League). With league cities such as Los Angeles, San Francisco, and San Diego booming in population and size, club owners dreamed of turning the circuit into a third major league.

Ernie Lombardi set his sights on his old team, the Oakland Oaks, now managed by his former Boston Braves skipper Casey Stengel. Stengel had taken over the manager's post in Oakland in 1946 and found immediate success, finishing a strong second behind the perennial champions, the San Francisco Seals. In 1947 the Oaks ended the year in fourth position but won their first round of the post-season playoffs before dropping the final series to the Los Angeles Angels. Now, in early 1948, Ernie hoped that his old manager would invite him to join the Oaks. He could still hit, and his throwing arm remained as strong as ever. Besides, Ernie and his wife Berice lived in an apartment not far from the old Emeryville ballpark. It seemed like the perfect match.

However, Ernie, now nearing his 40th birthday, discovered once again that sentiment has no place in baseball. Stengel was satisfied with his catching situation and passed up the opportunity to be reunited with his old catcher. In early February, Ernie signed instead with the Sacramento Solons.

The Solons had ended the 1947 season in seventh place, and the franchise was not as stable as the PCL clubs in bigger cities. A new five-man ownership group, headed by local businessman Oscar Salenger, took over the club in early 1948 and went to work improving the Sacramento ballpark, which had fallen into disrepair. Salenger hired a new manager, Joe Orengo, a veteran infielder who played on the Giants with Ernie in 1943. He also signed a raft of veteran players, so many that the papers jokingly referred to the Solons as the Slowuns. Among the new Solons were Babe Dahlgren (the Yankees' first baseman who had replaced Lou Gehrig nine years before), Ernie's long-ago Cincinnati teammate Johnny Rizzo, and others long past their 30th birthdays. Ernie was the oldest man on the team, but just barely, as veteran pitcher Tony Freitas (another ex-Red) was only one month younger.

Ernie looked good at the Solons' spring training camp in Anaheim, and the papers reported that he regularly walloped long drives over the left field fence in batting practice. His presence, and the well-publicized makeover of the team, drew notice in Sacramento, and on March 31 the club drew an overflow crowd on 13,476 for its home opener against the San Francisco Seals. With hundreds of fans standing behind rope barriers in left field, the Seals defeated the Solons by a 7–4 score as Ernie went hitless in four times at bat.

The Solons stumbled out the gate, with four losses in their first five games, and a slew of rainouts canceled some potentially profitable dates, including a Sunday doubleheader. By mid–April the Solons had dropped into last place, while the members of the new ownership group bickered among themselves. The ballpark restoration program proved inadequate, as rival clubs complained about the poor field conditions and the cold, leaking visitors' locker room. The team, the oldest in the league, was slow and lacked enthusiasm. The fans stayed home, and as the Solons played to thousands of empty seats, the team teetered on the edge of insolvency.

Ernie Lombardi started the season slowly, as did almost all of his teammates. He did not hit his first home run until April 16 in a 3–1 win at Los Angeles and stumbled along with a batting average near the .200 mark in the early going. Baseball was no fun for Ernie in Sacramento, and perhaps he came to regret signing with the Solons. In late April Berice Lombardi fell ill with an unknown ailment, and Ernie left the team to take care of her. On April 28, Ernie announced his retirement and asked for his release.

A few days later Ernie changed his mind and returned to the club, and perhaps the short absence energized the 40-year-old ballplayer. Ernie's second home run of the season came on May 4 against Oakland, a monstrous shot that cleared a 60-foor light tower above the left field stands and landed in a parking lot. But such displays were rare for the veteran catcher, who soon reverted to form as the team floundered.

Oscar Salenger and his co-owners now realized that their policy of signing aging retreads had failed. "Our problems," said Salenger to the press, "are youth, speed, and pitching," none of which the Solons had. Salenger, with the season slipping away, decided to gut his roster. He sold or released several of the older Solons, while trading others for younger men. "I don't want to buy anybody over 27 or 28,"[2] he said. It came as no surprise to anyone that Ernie Lombardi, with a .219 average and only three homers and eight runs batted in in 73 times at bat, would be shown the door as well. On May 19 the Solons sold Ernie's contract to Casey Stengel and the Oakland Oaks.

This deal put Ernie back in the uniform of his hometown team, the one he had left 17 years before. The Oaks had had their ups and downs in that time, sending many players to the major leagues but failing to win a pennant since 1927, when Ernie, still a teenager, saw limited action. In recent years, the San Francisco Seals and the Los Angeles Angels had dominated the Pacific Coast League, but Casey Stengel had rejuvenated the Oakland club and was determined to win the pennant for the first time in 21 years.

Stengel and team president Brick Laws initially hesitated to sign a 40-year-old catcher with limited mobility, but they were impressed by the homer Ernie hit against them a few weeks before. The local papers claimed that Ernie's blast traveled 570 feet. It was certainly an exaggeration, but the Oaks wanted more power in their lineup, and if Ernie regained his hitting form, the signing would be worth it. "I'll tell you one thing," said Stengel to the press. "If we've got the winning run on base and I send in Lombardi as a pinch hitter and the other infield

Billy Raimondi failed a tryout with the Reds in 1936. Twelve years later, Ernie was his backup in Oakland (author's collection).

plays in to save the run, I'll delay the game until I can call an ambulance. Because the big fellow is apt to kill somebody with a line drive."[3]

Though Ernie now weighed nearly 250 pounds—the papers reported that the team trainer had difficulty in finding a uniform big enough to fit him—this move immediately gave Ernie a new lease on life. In his first game for the Oaks on May 21, he mashed a home run and a double, driving in six runs in a 13–2 win over San Francisco. He settled into his new role, catching once or twice a week and pinch hitting whenever needed. He backed up the starting catcher, Billy Raimondi, a minor league veteran who debuted with the Oaks in 1932 and had held down the starting position ever since. Raimondi hit with little power, but his defense and pitch calling skills were outstanding. Raimondi, Lombardi, and Ed Fernandes (a Coast League veteran who played briefly for the Pirates and White Sox) gave the Oaks a strong three-man catching unit.

Raimondi, whom the papers called "160 pounds of action and as dependable as the tide,"[4] was 35 years old and had attended the Cincinnati Reds spring training camp in 1936 but failed to make the team as a backup to Ernie. He had managed the Oaks for part of the 1945 season before Stengel took over in 1946. Raimondi was, as usual, expected to carry most of the catching load, with Fernandes as the main backup and Ernie available as a part-time catcher and frequent pinch-hitter.

The rest of the Oakland roster was populated by former major leaguers, mostly in their thirties, several of whom had played for Stengel in the past. Jim Tobin, Ernie's old Boston teammate and fishing partner, was there for part of the season, while Nick Etten, who led the American League in homers in 1944 with the Yankees, was Oakland's main power hitter. Maurice Van Robays had once driven in 116 runs for the Pirates, and Lou Tost won 10 games for Stengel's 1942 Braves.

Les Scarsella was also an Oak. Scarsella, a longtime friend of Ernie's from the Bay Area, played first base for the Reds during the middle 1930s. Scarsella was five years younger than Lombardi, but told the team publicity department that Ernie was his childhood hero. Harry (Cookie) Lavagetto, one of the stars of the 1947 World Series for Brooklyn, played third base, and Dario Lodigiani, once with the White Sox, played both second and third. Ernie Lombardi had never played with so many fellow Italians.

In Oakland, Ernie met a young man who gave him a run for his money as the "Schnozz." Billy Martin was a 20-year-old infielder, a tough, hyperactive Italian kid from the streets of Berkeley. Martin came from a rough background and was already ready to fight, on the field and off. At a try-out camp in 1946 his attitude and determination impressed Casey Stengel, who sent him to Phoenix of the Arizona-Texas League in 1947. There he batted .392 with 174 runs batted in, earning a promotion to the Oaks. Martin owned the biggest nose on the team aside from Ernie's, and the old catcher gruffly submitted to side-by-side photos of their huge proboscises for the newspapers, with Stengel holding a ruler. ("I came in third," said the manager.)

Young Martin, however, was very sensitive about his nose, and in May he had a minor nose job done by a local doctor. He played with a bandage on his face for the next few weeks. Still, the papers called him "Little Schnozz" with Lombardi as "Big Schnozz." Stengel enjoyed the nose debate. "Now you take Ernie Lombardi who's a big man with a big nose and you take Martin who's a little man with a bigger nose," he said. "How do you figger it?"[5]

Les Scarsella, Ernie's teammate on the Oakland Oaks, played for the Reds from 1935 to 1939 (author's collection).

Martin, who served the Oaks as a utility infielder and defensive replacement, soon became Casey Stengel's favorite player. "He's a fresh kid, ain't he?" the manager said, hiding a smile even when the 20-year-old talked back to him and needled his much older teammates. Martin brought a jolt of youthful energy to the Oaks, a collection of veteran players that the papers called the "Nine Old Men." When Martin saw more playing time as the season wore on, the Oaks became "Eight Old Men and the Kid." Still, Billy complained about batting eighth in the lineup. "The groundskeeper is probably hitting higher than me," he told the manager. "I hit .392 last year."

"That fresh punk," said Stengel. "I love him."[6]

Ernie loved playing for Oakland, and he found his batting stroke as the Oaks challenged for the pennant. When he joined the club, the Oaks held third place, six games behind the San Francisco Seals and two behind the Los Angeles Angels. Perhaps it was no coincidence that immediately after signing the popular catcher, the Oaks drew some of the biggest crowds in their history. On May 21, the day that Lombardi drove in six runs in his Oakland debut, more than 14,000 fans overflowed the Oakland ballpark, with more than 3,000 turned away. Another 13,000 saw the Oaks and Seals the next day, a Saturday, and on Sunday, in the second game of a doubleheader (the first contest was played in San Francisco), 13,000 more people came through the turnstiles.

Baseball was fun again in Oakland, largely because of Casey Stengel. One veteran player recalled, "If we won a doubleheader Casey would come into the clubhouse and say, 'You fellas did pretty well today and it's up to me to buy you each a three-dollar dinner.' Three dollars meant a pretty good meal then, but he'd come in the next day with a pocket full of bills and give each of us three bucks."[7] Stengel might also pay for a case of beer on ice in the clubhouse after a win.

On August 26, Oakland management held an "Ernie Lombardi Day" for the local hero. Before 9,918 fans, one of Oakland's biggest crowds of the season, Ernie received a television set worth $2,000, a pocket watch from his teammates, and a variety of other gifts, including cash. Ernie was so happy that he belted a double and two singles in an 8–3 win over Seattle. Not only that, but in the second inning he beat out a slow roller to shortstop, then delighted the crowd when he stole second base.

By this time, the pennant race had boiled down to two teams, the Oaks and the San Francisco Seals. The Seals held a three-game lead at the end of August, but Oakland chipped away, the Seals hit a losing streak, and in September the Oaks went ahead by two games. Stengel used his entire roster masterfully, leading Bill Kelly, the manager of the Los Angeles Angels, to complain, "You never know who he's going to use.... Every time we play the Oaks, I feel like walking over to his dugout and counting the players. It doesn't seem possible that the club is within the player limit."[8]

Disaster struck on September 17 in a game against the San Diego Padres in Oakland. The Oaks won that day by a score of 12 to 3 to maintain their two-game lead over the Seals, but Billy Raimondi was lost for the season when he broke a wrist in a collision at first base. That left the catching duties for the final 11 games of the season to Ed Fernandes and Ernie Lombardi during the most important part of the pennant race. Fernandes had been out with a split finger for about a week but wrapped the injured digit tightly and kept playing.

Fernandes and Lombardi alternated at catcher for the first few days after Raimondi's injury. Fernandez backstopped the Oaks to a win over the Padres, but with Ernie behind the plate, the Oaks lost the first game of a twin bill next day by a 9–0 score to snap their eight-game winning streak. They lost the nightcap as well to put their lead in jeopardy. Both Fernandes and Lombardi were banged up and (in Ernie's case) exhausted by the long season, so the Oaks promoted veteran catcher Gene Lillard from Phoenix of the Arizona-Texas League to help out.

Fortunately for the Oaks, the season-ending series at Sacramento was moved to Oakland (because Sacramento's stadium burned down that summer), and the Oaks rode that advantage to the league title. The Oaks lost their first game with Lillard behind the plate on September 23 against Sacramento, but three wins in a row clinched the pennant for the Oaks, their first Pacific Coast League flag since 1927. In the clincher, a 10–8 win, Ernie cracked two singles and drove in a run, while Jim Tobin, Lombardi's old Boston teammate, earned the save. Now it was on to the post-season playoff, the Governor's Cup.

The Oaks drew the Los Angeles Angels in the first round of the two-round tournament, and the Angels won two of the first three contests in Oakland with Fernandes behind the plate. Games Four and Five of the best-of-seven round were played in Los Angeles on October 3, and the Oaks evened the series with a 6–3 win in the first game. For the second contest, Stengel decided that Ernie, at age 40, had one good game left in him. He gave Ernie the starting assignment.

It was the wildest game of the season. The Angels stormed out to a 9–2 lead and stretched it to 14–6 after Johnny Ostrowski belted two grand slam homers. In the fifth, the Angels pulled off a triple play when Oakland's Merrill Combs hit a liner to the shortstop, who caught Ernie off second base and Lou Tost off first. It looked like a lost cause with the Angels ahead by eight runs, but the Oaks exploded in the seventh. Two Angel errors and six singles brought in five runs, and then two homers by Cookie Lavagetto and one by Les Scarsella produced seven more runs in the eighth and four in the ninth to give the Oaks a 23–15 win.

And what did Ernie contribute? He was one of the hitting stars for Oakland with two doubles, two singles, and two runs batted in. After the game, Stengel told his jubilant Oaks, "Every man here rates a ten-dollar dinner from the old man." The next day, the manager passed out ten-dollar bills to each player on the roster. "From his own pocket," said one veteran player. "No wonder we played our asses off for him."[9]

The Oaks dispatched Los Angeles the next day to clinch the series and advance to the finals against the Seattle Rainiers. Once again luck came into play; all seven games would be played in Oakland, as torrential rains in Seattle made it impossible to play there. The Rainiers took Game One, but in the second contest Ernie took over. He smacked a home run, two doubles, and a single, scoring four runs and driving in two in a 10–4 win that evened the series. Billy Martin's bases-loaded triple in the eighth inning was the game winner in Game Three, and on October 10, a double-header sweep by the Oaks, 11–1 and 4–1, brought the Governor's Cup to Oakland.

Ernie caught the Cup-clinching contest and contributed a single. It was his final hit in his last professional game. He ended the season with a .264 average, with 11 home runs in 102 games, counting the stats from both Sacramento and Oakland. The city of Oakland held a parade and a banquet in honor of the champions, and each Oakland player received a gold championship ring and a winner's share of $1,007.93.

Despite the satisfying conclusion to the 1948 season, Ernie Lombardi hit the end of the line. The papers reported that he was "close to exhaustion" in September, especially after the injury to Billy Raimondi, and the 40-year-old catcher's excess weight and slowing reflexes convinced the Oaks that Ernie's playing days were over. Casey Stengel might have kept Lom around for 1949, but the "Old Perfesser" was hired away by the New York Yankees on October 11, one day after the final playoff game. Nine days later, the Oaks gave Ernie his unconditional release. After 23 years in professional baseball, 17 of them on the major league level, Ernie Lombardi's career was finished.

He did, however, sign up for one more game in 1948. Satchel Paige, the premier Black pitcher and gate attraction of his time, had joined the Cleveland Indians at the age of 42 and posted a 6–1 record, helping the Indians win the pennant and the World Series. Now, Paige brought his barnstorming team to the Bay Area, as he had many times before. Ernie had faced the great Black pitcher several times with varying degrees of success, and he wanted to test himself once more against a living legend. So he joined the local all-star team that challenged Paige's crew in a game at the Emeryville ballpark. Paige pitched three shutout innings that day and allowed only two hits. One was an infield single. The other was a double on a line shot off the left field wall by Ernie Lombardi.

18

Aftermath

"I think that if I could have run just a bit faster I would have had a lot more hits. I'm not complaining, though. The game was good to me."[1]
—Ernie Lombardi, 1970

In 1949, for the first time in more than 20 years, Ernie Lombardi was out of baseball.

Except for a stint as a sheet metal worker in a factory during the war, Ernie had not been employed in any other profession save baseball since he left his father's grocery store in 1926. At age 41, with decades of his life still ahead of him, Ernie was cast adrift. Baseball was his entire world, and he missed the games, the camaraderie, the teasing and socializing with his teammates.

Ernie hoped to stay in the game in some capacity but found one avenue after another closed to him. Casey Stengel might have brought him back to Oakland, but Stengel was off to New York. The new Oakland manager was Charlie Dressen, Ernie's old Cincinnati skipper, but the Oaks were in the mood to cut salary, and Dressen never called. Besides, Ernie was finished as a player. He barely made it to the end of the 1948 season, and no one was eager to sign a catcher who could no longer run or play the field.

While Ernie's career wound down in New York and then in Oakland, his old team, the Cincinnati Reds, fell on hard times. The Reds sank in the standings after Ernie's departure in 1941, and during the 1946 campaign, Warren Giles fired Bill McKechnie as manager. Johnny Neun failed to lift the Reds out the second division in 1947, and in mid–1948 Giles named Ernie's longtime teammate, pitcher Bucky Walters, as manager.

Ernie would have jumped at the chance to return to Cincinnati as a coach, and Walters, according to reports, was interested in hiring his old catcher. But Warren Giles and his right-hand man, Gabe Paul, vetoed the selection. Giles and Paul well remembered the intense, bitter annual contract disputes and holdouts, and Giles, no doubt, never forgot the insulting comments that Ernie made at that post-season banquet in 1938.

18. Aftermath

So Ernie had to be satisfied with the occasional old-timers' game or charity exhibition in the Bay Area. He could still swat the baseball, and Brick Laws, owner of the Oaks, hesitated to bring Ernie on board for one exhibition contest. Laws told the papers that some of the old-timers last played in the 1910s or 1920s, and he feared that Ernie would kill an elderly ballplayer with a line drive. Otherwise, Ernie was always welcome.

But it wasn't the same as spending an entire baseball season with a ballclub. Ernie's teammates, especially those on the Reds, provided a protective cocoon in which the big catcher felt safe and valued. He really did not know how to make a life for himself outside of the only world he knew. When he left the game, the papers claimed that the big catcher had more than enough money to last for the rest of his life. Ernie, from all reports, was frugal with his money during his playing days, and he no doubt had a nest egg, but he was barely into his forties and had a lot of life ahead of him.

During the early 1950s, Ernie's name rarely appeared in the papers, not even in Oakland. When it did, it was often faintly insulting, referring to his weight, or his lack of speed, or his prominent nose. In 1952, *Parade* magazine—a Sunday newspaper insert distributed nationwide—printed an article by sportscaster Ernie Harwell that discussed the eating habits of major league players whose weight problems put their careers in jeopardy. The photo that accompanied the article showed Ernie Lombardi, smiling over a steaming pot of (presumably) Italian food with a ladle to his lips. The article was titled "Fat Men Don't Win Pennants." Harwell also claimed that Bill Essick, who scouted Ernie for the New York Yankees in 1928, turned the big catcher down because of Ernie's love of spaghetti.[2]

And every October, the subject of "Lombardi's Snooze" in the 1939 World Series came up again. It was as if no one remembered that Ernie was a two-time batting champ, a World Series winner, and a Most Valuable Player. Every year at World Series time, Ernie had to relive that disastrous inning that the nation's sportswriters would never let him forget.

The old catcher might even have taken a low-paying job as a coach for a minor league team, but the postwar boom in minor league baseball was over. During the early 1950s, television made its way into American homes, and people discovered that they did not have to go to the local ballpark to see a game. They could watch the major league Game of the Week at home or hear the national Game of the Day on radio. Some pointed to the rise of air conditioning as a factor; people used to go to the ballpark (or to the movies) to get out of their stuffy houses in the summer, but now they didn't have to. People were moving out of the decaying cities, where the ballparks were, and into the leafy suburbs, a trend that gained momentum during the 1950s.

The effects of demographic and cultural change on the baseball industry were devastating. Sixteen minor leagues closed up shop between 1952 and 1956, and many of those that remained played in rundown, old ballparks (like the decaying Oakland Oaks park in Emeryville). With a dwindling number of teams and leagues, there was no place for Ernie in baseball, not even at the minor league level.

In early 1953, Berice Lombardi was worried about her husband. Ernie, usually a happy and friendly type, was not himself. He had turned morose and listless, a feeling that had only deepened since his baseball career ended. For several years, Ernie was adrift, both physically and psychologically.

His opportunities in the baseball world had all dried up. Nothing came of the newspaper speculation that Horace Stoneham, owner of the New York Giants, wanted the old catcher to manage at Minneapolis in 1948, and rumors that had him managing at Stockton in 1949 and at Albuquerque in 1951 also never came to pass. Mel Ott, dismissed by the New York Giants midway through the 1948 season, managed the Oakland Oaks in 1951 and 1952, but the team was struggling financially, and Ott had no room for Lombardi either. Baseball was Ernie's entire life, and he had no place in it.

He and Berice no longer lived in West Oakland, though his sisters still lived in the family home on 13th Street. The couple had an apartment on Dante Avenue in the southern part of Oakland, away from his old neighborhood and old friends. For many years, his brother-in-law Vince Monzo was perhaps his closest friend, but that relationship most likely changed when Monzo and Ernie's sister Stella divorced.

Ernie tried to fill his days with activity, but he no longer played in the post-season All-Star charity games in Oakland and San Francisco; those were for younger men, still active in the baseball world. He spent a lot of time fishing in the Bay, and during the early 1950s, his name appeared nearly as often in the fishing column of the *Oakland Tribune* as it did on the sports page. The 1950 United States Census listed his occupation as "none," so perhaps he had indeed saved enough money from his baseball days to live somewhat comfortably. Still, by 1953 he had found employment running a liquor store in San Leandro, just south of Oakland.

In March of 1953, the Oakland paper ran a photo essay that featured the pennant-winning 1948 Oakland Oaks and explained what each man was doing. Casey Stengel was the most successful manager in baseball. Billy Martin was the starting second baseman for Stengel's Yankees, Cookie Lavagetto coached for the Brooklyn Dodgers, and Ernie's two fellow catchers, Ed Fernandes and Billy Raimondi, were minor league managers, as was Dario Lodigiani. A few of the 1948 Oaks were still active players, and several more of Ernie's old teammates held other positions in the baseball world. But, said the article, "Lombardi has left the game."

The title of the article was "Old Champions Fade Away."[3]

Berice sensed that Ernie was fading away and convinced him to see a doctor about his depression. The doctor recommended that Ernie seek psychiatric help for his melancholic state, and so Berice arranged for her husband to enter a treatment facility in Livermore, east of Oakland. Ernie asked to visit a friend of his, Art Van Ness, who lived in Castro Valley, which was on the way to Livermore, so the couple arranged to stay the night at the Van Ness house. On April 8, two days after Ernie's 45th birthday, he and Berice set out for Castro Valley.

At the Van Ness home, Ernie and Berice visited for a while, but as afternoon turned to evening Ernie told his hosts that he didn't feel well. He went to an upstairs bedroom to lie down, and after a while, Berice went upstairs to check on him.

The bed, and Ernie, were covered with blood.

In a replay of Willard Hershberger's suicide thirteen years before, Ernie had grabbed a razor from the bathroom and slashed his own throat from ear to ear. He was still alive, but losing blood quickly, and begged his wife not to interfere. "Let me die! Let me die!" he yelled.

Berice and the Van Nesses called for an ambulance. Two sheriff's deputies arrived, and Ernie fought them both with his steadily decreasing strength. "Let me die!" he repeated, but the deputies and the ambulance attendants gained control of the weakening man, stopped the bleeding, and packed him into the ambulance. They took him to a local hospital, but he needed immediate surgery, so they transferred him to Highland Hospital in Oakland.

At first, the hospital reported that Ernie was not expected to survive his self-inflicted wounds, but the razor had narrowly missed the jugular vein. After two blood transfusions, the doctors stabilized the patient. He remained on the critical list for a day, but the transfusions had saved his life. Upgraded to fair condition on April 10, Ernie had a long recovery ahead of him, but his life was no longer in danger. When his condition improved enough for him to be moved, he was transferred to his original destination, the Livermore inpatient facility.

Ernie's suicide attempt made national headlines, and was front page news in Cincinnati, Oakland, and many other cities. His plight drew a wave of sympathy, as summed up by Gayle Talbot of the Associated Press. "The huge man who lumbered mightily getting down to first," wrote Talbot, "but who hit the ball so hard it usually didn't matter, never made anything but friends in his long, quiet stay in the majors. He was the fellow who lent money to teammates just before payday and who caddied for them when they golfed."

Of course Talbot, like many other writers, mentioned the infamous play in the 1939 World Series, "when a thundering herd of New York Yankees ran over and trampled Lom at home plate. Not so well known is the fact that not one of the big man's Cincinnati teammates mentioned it to him in the clubhouse after the game (we were there) or ever afterward. He looked like a stricken water buffalo as he sat looking at the floor."[4]

Even Warren Giles, Ernie's former boss with the Cincinnati Reds and now the president of the National League, offered his condolences. "He was sort of an easygoing fellow and nothing seemed to bother him," said Giles. "I'm shocked and surprised."[5]

Many writers noted the unmistakable similarities between Ernie's failed suicide try and Willard Hershberger's successful attempt thirteen years before. Both men were catchers with the Reds, both were known to be despondent, and both cut their throats with a razor. But there the parallels end. Hershberger had a family history of suicide, while Ernie did not. Ernie was as easygoing as could be, while Hershberger was a troubled mass of insecurities who mostly kept to himself. The two men were totally different personality types, so why did both decide to end their lives in the same manner?

Bill James, the baseball historian and statistician, ruminated about that very issue in his *Historical Baseball Abstract*:

> Did Ernie invent guilt for himself over the tragic death of Hershberger? At the very minimum, he must have said to himself that if he had just been in there playing instead of Hershberger, this would never have happened; for him not to have done that would not be human....
>
> Lombardi always felt that he was supposed to be in the lineup, that he was letting the team down if he had to miss a few games with an injury. He was famous for being tough. He was out of the lineup, and the kid [Hershberger] had to play, and the kid couldn't handle it. How much of this did Lombardi bury in the dark corners of his mind, where he would find it fourteen years later in his own black hours?[6]

Ernie stayed in the Livermore sanitarium for several months, and in early 1954 some positive news began to emerge. A paper in Tracy, California, reported in January of that year that Ernie and Berice had visited the home of one of Ernie's childhood friends, who said that the old catcher "had been quite ill, but is getting along fine now."[7] Though Jimmy Powers of the *New York Daily News* referred to the catcher in print as "the late Ernie Lombardi" in January, Ernie seemed to be making progress.

And his Bay Area baseball friends rallied around him. In April a group of ex-players from the Ogden Gunners held a banquet for Ernie and presented him with $300 worth of fishing equipment. There were always plenty of sports banquets in the Bay Area, and Ernie was always welcome. These banquets allowed Ernie to reconnect with his old baseball buddies, especially the Italian American ones. Everyone wanted to see him, and the organizers always asked the still-popular former catcher to wave to the crowd and say a few words. It took some coaxing, but Ernie grew to like the attention. He had always hated public speaking, but he learned how to tell a brief story or two and then sit down to a round of applause.

Things were looking up for Ernie, and his family was thrilled with his apparent recovery. As his sister Rena's son Ernest McElderry, named after Ernie, put it years later, "He was sick for about six months [after the suicide attempt]. But when he did get well, he was a completely different person. He would go to the Italian Club and make speeches, something he would never do before."[8] During the summer of 1954 the old ballplayer, who always loved kids, helped coach a Little League team in Oakland. It wasn't the National League, but it was baseball, and to Ernie Lombardi, that was all that mattered. Ernie, it seems, could not live without baseball.

19

Later Years

"I sure hope Ernie Lombardi gets along all right. He was my roommate at Oakland, just a big, jolly kid breaking in. I couldn't believe it when I saw he'd tried to kill himself. Some of the fellows just never adjust after they quit playing, I guess."[1]

—Roy Carlyle, former Oakland Oaks teammate

On Ernie's birthday in 1954, a year after his suicide attempt, his attitude appeared to be more positive. In a letter to a friend in Brooklyn, Frank Herbert, the old catcher wrote, "Feeling pretty good now and hope to keep that way. Had a little offer from the Oakland club and Charley Dressing [sic] but it hasn't materialized yet." Ernie asked his friend to say hello to several old New York Giants teammates such as Buddy Kerr and Danny Gardella. He signed it and added in a postscript, "The wife says hello."

Charlie Dressen, his old manager in Cincinnati, had spent three years with the Brooklyn Dodgers from 1951 to 1953, winning two pennants, then quit in a contract dispute and returned to Oakland to manage the Oaks. Nothing came of Ernie's attempt to latch on as a coach with the Oaks, but at least his spirits seemed good.

A job with the local team would not have lasted very long anyway. Though Dressen led the Oaks to the league's postseason championship in 1954, the team was in severe financial trouble, as a rapidly deteriorating Emeryville ballpark and competition from television drove attendance down from the boom years of the late 1940s. The 1955 Oakland Oaks finished in seventh place with the worst attendance in the Pacific Coast League, after which the team owners moved the franchise to Vancouver, British Columbia. For the first time in Ernie's life, his hometown had no minor league baseball.

In 1958, major league baseball expanded to the West Coast. The Brooklyn Dodgers, highly successful on the field but a disappointment at the box office in the small, antiquated Ebbets Field, moved to Los Angeles, while the financially struggling New York Giants, who played in an even

19. Later Years

more ancient and rundown park, the Polo Grounds, claimed San Francisco as their new home. Ernie Lombardi, now recovered from his suicide attempt of five years before and looking for work, took the direct approach. He called his old Giants teammate Bill Rigney, now the manager of the team, and asked for a job.

Rigney relayed Ernie's request to Giants management. The relocated club needed some positive publicity in their new hometown and hired the still-popular ex-catcher as a press box attendant at Seals Stadium, their temporary home field. He held this post for more than a decade, even after the Giants moved to their new home, Candlestick Park, in 1960.

The writers were glad to see him. As Prescott Sullivan wrote in the *San Francisco Examiner*, "Old Schnoz is still a big, strong fella and with Johnny Antonelli, the Giant pitcher, feeling as he does about Bay Area baseball writers and press photographers, it's a comfort to have such a mass of muscle around." Antonelli had recently threatened to break a camera over a photographer's head.[2]

Ernie worked in the press box for Giants home games as a combination security guard and attendant. He fetched drinks and sandwiches for the writers, retrieved the ticker tape with out-of-town scores, distributed publicity sheets and statistics, and kept intruders at bay. It almost certainly did not pay much, but Ernie liked the job. He was part of a team again, and Horace Stoneham, who moved the Giants from New York to San Francisco, had always treated Ernie well.

As he aged, Ernie became more open with the sportswriters. During his playing days, the big catcher rarely said more than a few words at a time to the press corps, many of whom saw Ernie as surly and uncooperative. But Ernie was never comfortable with publicity and always hesitated to reveal much of himself. His pride, and his fear of public ridicule, led him to brush off the writers. But in San Francisco, he was able to open up. Sportswriters, then and now, are always on the hunt for items to fill their column inches, and Ernie, still popular in Cincinnati and in the Bay Area, was good for a column or two every now and then.

In 1965 he admitted to a Pittsburgh reporter that he saw the games differently as he aged. "When you're not playing anymore, some of the games seem real long," said Ernie. "I played 22 full years, including the Pacific Coast League. Now I don't always have the patience to watch nine full innings."[3]

During the summer of 1958, the Cincinnati Reds opened their own team Hall of Fame. The Reds conducted a fan vote to select the first five inductees, and, not surprisingly, all five men chosen played on the 1939–40 championship team. The five were Ernie Lombardi, Bucky Walters, Paul Derringer, Frank McCormick, and Johnny Vander Meer. Not only did

The first five inductees to the Cincinnati Reds Hall of Fame in 1958: (from left) Bucky Walters, Ernie Lombardi, Paul Derringer, Johnny Vander Meer, and Frank McCormick (Rhodes/Klumpe Reds Hall of Fame Collection).

Ernie top the vote, but also, when the five were honored between games of a doubleheader on July 18, the popular former catcher received the biggest ovation from the fans. Ernie, who had left the Reds 17 years before, was still a hero in Cincinnati.

His job with the Giants allowed Ernie to travel when the team was on the road. He enjoyed taking part in old-timers' games, events at which he was welcome due to his continuing popularity. In 1962 he went to New York to play in one such contest at Yankee Stadium, a reunion of the living participants in the 1937 All-Star game. Ernie had gained weight and wore glasses, but he banged out a double and drove in a run. Later that year, an old-timers' exhibition at Candlestick Park featured Ernie behind the plate and all three DiMaggio brothers—Joe, Dom, and Vince—in the outfield. Joe DiMaggio walloped a home run, but Ernie grounded into two double plays.

19. Later Years

The old catcher was good about answering autograph requests. During his playing days he dreaded signing for people, but the story goes that one day, after turning down a group of autograph-seeking kids, one of the youngsters piped up, "That's OK. He can't write anyway." After that he signed autographs, but he didn't enjoy it, as Ernie was one to shy away from attention. Sometimes he would stay in the clubhouse for hours after games, drinking beer and waiting for the kids with pens and baseballs to go away.

But now, a more comfortable Ernie responded to the requests in the mail. "I have small photographs of myself taken in lots of dozens, to keep my young fans happy," he told a reporter in 1966.

> I'd be less than human if I didn't admit it keeps me happy, too. I autograph each picture to the kid seeking it. Guess the word got around to the young collectors, because I've gotten requests from all over the country.
>
> Those young autograph seekers are pretty nice kids. They write friendly letters and almost always enclose stamped return envelopes. And the majority

Ernie (4) chats with Cincinnati players Roy McMillan (11) and Ed Bailey (6) at a Reds reunion in 1959 (Rhodes/Klumpe Reds Hall of Fame Collection).

say they'd heard favorable reports about my catching and hitting from their fathers. Wouldn't I be a heel if I turned any of them down?[4]

All the while, Ernie, the winner of two batting titles, a Most Valuable Player award, and a World Series championship, longed for one more recognition. His fondest wish was to be granted baseball's highest honor, a place in the Baseball Hall of Fame.

Several of the men he played with and against owned plaques on the wall in Cooperstown, New York. Joe DiMaggio, who slid past a stunned Lombardi and scored in the last game of the 1939 World Series, had a plaque, of course. So did Wilbert Robinson, Ernie's first major league manager, and Mel Ott, his last. Ernie played on All-Star teams with Frank Frisch, Bill Terry, Gabby Hartnett, and several other stars of the 1930s who gained the coveted honor. Dizzy Dean was in the Hall, and Ernie always hit well against the Cardinals star. So were Carl Hubbell, who once said that Ernie was the only batter he was afraid to face, and Dazzy Vance, a teammate in both Brooklyn and Cincinnati.

In 1962, the Hall of Fame inducted Jackie Robinson, Bob Feller, Edd Roush, and Bill McKechnie. Ernie played against Robinson, was managed by McKechnie, and was coached by Roush (the hero of Cincinnati's 1919 world championship season). The next year, Eppa Rixey, for whom Ernie served as catcher during the last two seasons of the ageless pitcher's career, gained the honor. Ernie firmly believed that he deserved to join them all in Cooperstown, and his desire for his sport's ultimate recognition burned brighter with each passing year.

Also, the old catcher's health was not good. He suffered a heart attack in early 1967, and a second one about a year later. Ernie turned 60 in 1968, and he wanted to gain entry to the Hall while he was alive to enjoy it. He recovered enough to resume his job at Candlestick Park each time, but from the late 1960s onward he no longer played in old-timers' games.

Unfortunately for Ernie, his popularity made little impression on the members of the Baseball Writers Association of America (BBWAA) who voted for the Baseball Hall of Fame. In 1950, Ernie's first year on the ballot, the big catcher received only three votes from the 168 participating writers. (Those same voters failed to elect anyone that year, passing on Mel Ott, Jimmie Foxx, Bill Terry, and other stars of the recent past.) Lom garnered three votes in 1951, and then none at all during the next four years. In 1956 the Hall of Fame decided to hold elections every two years instead of one, and Ernie's total increased to 8 votes, but remained in the single digits in 1958, 1960, and 1962. Ernie's dream of a Hall of Fame plaque, so dear to his heart, appeared to be farther away than ever.

In 1964, Ernie's vote total jumped to 33, but his burst of momentum quickly stalled out. In 1966, he received 34 votes, after which the BBWAA decided to resume voting annually. In 1967, Lom's last year on the ballot, he gained 43 votes from the 292 writers, which was 14.7 percent of the total, far short of the 75 percent necessary for election. Nineteen players received more votes than Ernie; among them were two pitchers he caught on the championship Cincinnati teams, Johnny Vander Meer (with 87 votes) and Bucky Walters (65 votes). Al Lopez, who beat out Lombardi for the starting catching job with the Dodgers in 1931, finished well ahead of Ernie with 114 votes. Now, Ernie's Hall of Fame hopes rested with the Veterans Committee.

The Veterans Committee was a panel of old players, writers, and broadcasters, charged with selecting deserving players, managers, and executives (and the occasional umpire) who had been passed over by the BBWAA. This committee represented a second door of entry into the Hall of Fame, and while it was created with good intentions, it had made some head-scratching choices over the years. In 1945 and 1946 the panel, then called the Permanent Committee, concerned about the slow pace of selections from the writers, unilaterally inducted 21 men from the late 19th and early 20th centuries. Many of the new honorees were long dead, and few modern fans had ever heard of most of them. Some of the 21 were no doubt deserving, but others look like poor selections in retrospect. In the words of columnist Dan Daniel, the Permanent Committee "announced the baseball beatification of a vast number of worthies" and "decided to load up the Cooperstown pantheon by the wholesale."[5]

After this, the Permanent Committee played a much smaller role in the selection process, and in 1953 the panel was reformed as the Veterans Committee. It was this committee that voted each year on Ernie's candidacy beginning in 1970.

Ernie had his supporters. In early 1973, the Society for American Baseball Research (SABR), which was founded in Cooperstown, New York, less than two years before, polled its 125 members and asked which ten players deserved to be enshrined in the Hall of Fame. SABR instructed its members to choose one deserving player at each position, including a right-handed pitcher and a left-handed pitcher. SABR released the list under the title "The 10 Greatest Players NOT in the Baseball Hall of Fame," and it appeared in *The Sporting News* on June 9, 1973. The leader at catcher, and the top vote-getter of all players at all positions, was Ernie Lombardi with 70 percent of the vote.

Even the President of the United States gave a shout-out to Ernie. In 1972, President Richard Nixon, a lifelong baseball fan, selected his all-time All-Star teams for the Associated Press. With the help of his son-in-law David Eisenhower, the President made two teams, one for each league, for the 1925–1945 period, and another pair of teams for the years 1945 to

1970. He selected two catchers for the 1925–1945 National League team. Ernie Lombardi was the first, and Gabby Hartnett was the second. Nixon probably never met Ernie, but the future President had attended Fullerton Union High School in California, where he played (briefly) on the baseball team with Ernie's Cincinnati teammate Willard Hershberger.

For all the support Ernie enjoyed in the popular press, his Hall of Fame candidacy appeared to be stalled in the Veterans Committee. Anonymous sources claimed that, with 12 votes from the 16 committee members needed for election, Ernie gained as many as nine votes at some point during the early 1970s but fell back to five or six votes in subsequent years.

It's not like the Committee was idle. Between 1970 and 1973, the Veterans Committee selected 12 players, three executives, and one umpire, some of which are now recognized as the weakest choices ever made by the Committee. Bill James, in his book *The Politics of Glory*, explained how the Committee chose such apparently undeserving candidates. Two of the committee members were Frank Frisch, playing manager of the St. Louis Cardinals during the 1930s, and Bill Terry, who held the same position with the New York Giants. "Beginning in 1970, the Veterans Committee made a series of simply appalling selections," charged James, "littering the Hall of Fame with Frisch and Terry's old cronies."[6] Some of the honorees from the period, such as George Kelly, Jim Bottomley, Chick Hafey, and Jesse Haines were good ballplayers, but hardly all-time greats. They benefited from their relationships with Frisch and Terry, and with sportswriters from New York and St. Louis on the committee.

All the while, Ernie Lombardi remained on the outside. Some say, apparently with some foundation, that one man personally blocked Ernie Lombardi's path to the Hall of Fame. That man was Ernie's old Cincinnati general manager Warren Giles.

Giles had remained with the Reds as general manager and club president for ten years after selling Ernie to the Braves. During this time, the Reds faded after their 1940 World Series win, falling once again to the second division and posting losing records nine seasons in a row beginning in 1945. Nonetheless, Giles was a leading candidate for the post of Commissioner of Baseball after A.B. (Happy) Chandler was forced out in 1951. He lost to Ford Frick, but succeeded Frick as president of the National League. He held that post until 1969. Giles joined the Veterans Committee during its reorganization in 1953 and remained until 1978, passing judgement on all candidates for 25 years.

Giles no doubt remembered the big catcher's annual holdouts and the insulting comments Ernie made at that post-season banquet in 1938. The relationship between the outspoken catcher and the powerful baseball executive grew progressively worse during Ernie's tenure in Cincinnati, and as Ernie had predicted, Giles sent Lombardi packing after his first sub-par season. Now, decades later, Warren Giles stood in the way of Ernie's fondest dream. It appeared that Lombardi would never make the Hall as long as Giles had a voice on the committee.

To be fair, Giles always denied that he was the one blocking Ernie. Lombardi "certainly had the tools and credentials," said Giles to the *Cincinnati Enquirer* in 1976. But "nobody seemed to know him well."[7] Two years earlier, Giles told a reporter, "We had Lombardi's name on the ballot several times, but he received only a few votes."[8]

Lombardi did, however, have his advocates. Bob Broeg, a sportswriter from the *St. Louis Post-Dispatch* who joined the committee in 1972, was a Lombardi fan and talked up the old catcher's qualifications for the Hall. Longtime Detroit Tiger star (and committee member since 1953) Charlie Gehringer cited Ernie, along with Arky Vaughan, Joe Medwick, and others, as men he always voted for. Ken Smith, then the director of the Hall of Fame, necessarily refrained from endorsing Lombardi or any other candidate, but still complimented the old catcher's defense. "Pie Traynor once told me," said Smith in 1974, "during a training camp game at Fort Myers [that] he didn't think that Paul Derringer and Bucky Walters, the Reds' pitching aces back in 1939, were charged with a wild pitch while Ernie was catching them. Ernie really covered the plate."[9]

But some committee members focused their attention on the infamous "snooze" in the World Series of 1939, and that memory, while grossly unfair to the old catcher, helped to keep Ernie out of the Hall. It was as if some panelists remembered only three things about Ernie—his huge nose, his legendary lack of speed, and his World Series embarrassment.

Year after year, Ernie saw other players—men he had played with and against—enter the Hall of Fame while he remained on the outside, and he could not help but be resentful. The Hall was the one honor that he desired more than any other, but the Veterans Committee kept passing the old catcher by. He had played the publicity game during his time as a press box attendant at Candlestick Park, making himself available for interviews and keeping his name in the papers, but those same writers now rejected his candidacy for the Hall of Fame. It angered him, and it embittered him.

His job at Candlestick Park had ended after more than a decade. The story goes that a much younger sportswriter, one who did not know Ernie's history and had never seen him play, insulted Lombardi one day during the late 1960s, and the proud old catcher quit in embarrassment. Oakland gained a major league team of its own in 1968 when the Kansas City Athletics moved there, and Oakland-Alameda County Stadium was only a couple of miles from Ernie's apartment. But when Ernie inquired about employment, the Athletics turned him down. He was finished with baseball, and baseball appeared to be finished with him.

This rejection was the final straw for Ernie Lombardi. In 1970, while watching his old team, the Cincinnati Reds, play the Baltimore Orioles in the World Series, Ernie told reporter Joe Sargis of UPI that "the game was good to me."[10] But by July of 1972, when Tom Callahan of the *Cincinnati Enquirer* caught up with him, Ernie had turned his back on the game and the Hall of Fame as well. "There are guys who didn't belong in the big leagues who got more votes than I used to get when I was getting them," he complained. And what was he doing now? "Now I don't do nothing. Stay home is all," he said. "Oh, I take rides, go over to a gas station a friend of mine owns. Sometimes I ride his pickup and haul some parts. I have had a couple heart attacks and so I don't do no real labor. My wife Berice and I live quiet."[11]

Berice Lombardi died in Oakland on July 1, 1973, leaving Ernie a widower after 29 years of marriage. The 65-year-old former ballplayer was no longer spry enough to play in old-timers' games and had, by this time, severed all connections to the game. After his wife's death, Ernie became ever more reclusive as his health slowly deteriorated with age.

One day in April of 1974, reporter Ed Levitt of the *Oakland Tribune* stopped at Lou's Arco Station on MacArthur Boulevard and thought that one of the employees looked familiar.

The employee was the 66-year-old Ernie Lombardi.

"No, I'm not the new gas attendant," said Ernie. "I just run errands, pick up parts and drive people home. It's a nice way to kill a few hours with my friends."[12]

The widowed former catcher was living on Social Security and a pension of $300 a month from major league baseball. His hair was solid white, but Ernie was still an imposing presence at 240 pounds. He lived alone with a dog in an apartment around the block from the gas station, and on most days ate dinner at his sister Rose's place a short distance away.

When Levitt asked Ernie about the Hall of Fame, the old catcher did not bother to hide his resentment.

> I wouldn't accept. The way they treated me, I wouldn't have anything to do with it. You know what I'd do if they voted me in? I wouldn't show up for the ceremony.
>
> They can stuff it. I don't want any part of it. They didn't do right by me. For years they've been voting guys into the Hall who couldn't carry my bat. I should have made it ages ago. I've been disappointed too many times. Now I'm no longer interested. As far as I'm concerned, the Hall of Fame is the Hall of Shame.[13]

He was not happy with baseball's pension plan either. "Frankie Crosetti [the longtime Yankee shortstop and coach] once got 115 of us old ballplayers to put up $100 each to hire an attorney and sue the people handling the major league pension plan," he said. "But then some baseball people warned us that if we pushed it, we'd lose everything. They wouldn't even give us a dollar in pension money. That ended it. They scared us from fighting back."[14]

His gig at Candlestick Park, which lasted for about a decade, also ended badly, in what Levitt described as a "misunderstanding" which resulted in Lombardi quitting the job. "I got a bad deal. I'm still sort of bitter. I haven't seen the Giants play in years. I'm not even going to Los Angeles to play in the Giants-Dodgers Old Timers' Game." He had recently been invited to an Oakland A's game for a ceremony to honor his old Boston and Oakland manager Casey Stengel, but Ernie simply checked the "no" box on the reply form and sent it back without explanation.

Year after year, the Veterans Committee selected Ernie's contemporaries, but bypassed the big catcher. In 1977, the Committee chose three men—Yankee third baseman Joe Sewell; nineteenth-century pitcher Amos Rusie; and Al Lopez, who followed his playing career with a successful run as a pennant-winning manager of the Cleveland Indians and Chicago White Sox. When asked about Lombardi, one unidentified committee member said tersely, "We considered him. Maybe next time."[15] Perhaps Ernie knew that he was running out of time. "They're putting fellas in there who can't even carry my bat,"[16] he complained.

His old teammates were firmly in Lombardi's corner. "Lombardi belongs in the Hall of Fame," said Bucky Walters. "He did everything but run good. And he was a hell of a guy on the club. Everybody loved him." Johnny Vander Meer added, "How he's not in the Hall of Fame, I don't know. If you took a survey of every big league pitcher, they'd tell you Lombardi was the last guy they ever wanted to face in a clutch situation."[17]

Fred Lieb, appointed to the committee in 1966, was still on the panel in 1977. Lieb, the dean of New York sportswriters, was 88 years old and had watched, and written about, major league baseball for nearly 70 years, since his first job writing short biographies for *Baseball* magazine in 1909. He was not impressed with Lombardi and, as the big catcher's public support grew, Lieb explained his negative vote.

"The Lombardi case came up again," said Lieb. "He did win two National League batting championships. But he wouldn't have won those under present scoring rules. Also, he caught only 112–115 games a year, so he didn't work as much as some catchers. Al Lopez worked 150 games. Muddy Ruel caught 151 games. Lombardi was a good catcher, but probably the slowest man to play major league baseball."[18] Lieb also said that Ernie received "four or five" votes from the eleven panelists, with eight needed for election. Several of the nation's sporting columnists were quick to correct Lieb; Ernie's 1938 batting title would have been legitimate under any application of the rules, past or present.

Ed Levitt, the writer who interviewed Ernie at the gas station in Oakland three years before, reported that Lombardi was "fantastically bitter" and was now a recluse who wanted to avoid people. Levitt reported that Ernie enjoyed his job in the Candlestick Park press box, "until some punk kid sportswriter embarrassed him. It was a crushing blow and he quit. It was his last link to baseball."[19]

Ernie was not totally forgotten. A few honors came his way late in life, including a plaque in the Ohio Baseball Hall of Fame as a charter member in 1976. And his name appeared in the lyrics of the song "Van Lingle Mungo," which was written in 1969 by jazz pianist Dave Frishberg. Frishberg composed a melody and struggled to write lyrics for it; only when he perused a baseball encyclopedia one day and found the name of the former Dodgers and Giants pitcher did he decide to fill his creation with the names of ballplayers from the 1930s and 1940s. (Johnny Vander Meer, Eddie Joost, and a few more of Ernie's old teammates appear in the lyrics too.) Ernie's reaction to the song was not recorded, but Mungo, long retired from baseball and running a movie house in his native South Carolina, reportedly enjoyed it.

But the big prize eluded Ernie, and the days were running short.

According to his family, Ernie was financially stable during his last years. He worked at Candlestick Park because he loved baseball, and he ran odd jobs at a gas station to keep himself busy and connect with friends. His father Dominic was good at saving money, they said, and so was Ernie. In 1975 Ernie, now 67 years old, moved into a duplex on 17th Avenue in Santa Cruz with two of his sisters, Rose and Stella. Said his oldest sister Rena, "He bought our other two sisters and himself a home in Santa Cruz, a beautiful home. He paid cash for that home. He always had enough money."[20]

There Ernie spent his last two years, far from public attention as his health slowly declined. His illnesses included heart failure and blood clots, and hospital stays of a few days or a few weeks were a regular feature of his final years. In early September of 1977 he completed a 10-day stay in the local hospital. But he would not live to see the Hall of Fame. As he told his sister Stella Monzo, "They better not put me in when I'm dead."[21] On September 26, 1977, Ernie Lombardi died of heart failure in Santa Cruz at the age of 69. He was survived by all three of his sisters and was buried at Mountain View Cemetery in Oakland.

Ernie's hometown newspaper, the *Oakland Tribune*, had followed his career since the 1920s, when he starred for the Oaks as a teenager. Now, upon his death, the paper eulogized the local hero on its editorial page:

Although one of the greatest catchers ever to don a mask and chest protector, Mr. Lombardi was never voted into the Hall of Fame. His lifetime batting average of .306 in 17 years of big league play surely made him as qualified for that great honor as many others who have been inducted into the hall....

As a final tribute to Mr. Lombardi, he should be posthumously awarded a coveted spot in the Hall. It is long overdue.[22]

20

The Hall of Fame

> "The only thing Ernie couldn't do was run. And that's not enough to keep a guy out of the Hall of Fame."[1]
> —Bucky Walters, 1977

Ernie Lombardi was gone, but his Hall of Fame candidacy remained alive.

The Veterans Committee underwent major personnel changes during the 1970s. St. Louis sportswriter Bob Broeg, who joined the committee in 1972, was a Lombardi enthusiast who did his best to convince his fellow panelists of Ernie's fitness for the Hall. Another supporter, Stan Musial, joined in 1973. The longtime Cardinal star played against Lombardi while the big catcher's career wound down with the Braves and Giants, and Musial was always impressed by Ernie's hitting skill. "The shortstop would play him back on the outfield grass," Musial said to *The New York Times*, "because he hit the ball so hard so often and he was too big and bulky to run out infield hits. You have to be awfully good to hit .300 when you can't run."[2]

The always outspoken Red Sox legend Ted Williams was not yet on the Committee but took up Lombardi's cause. Williams knew Lombardi well from spring training games, and in 1942, when Lombardi played for the Braves, both men brought batting titles home to Boston. "I played against Lombardi many times in spring training," said Williams, "and I'd always watch him and say 'This guy can hit.' He was a natural hitter, a huge man who couldn't run but who swung a really heavy bat, made great contact all the time and hit line drives."[3]

A positive development in Ernie's case came in 1978, when Warren Giles left the committee due to poor health. Giles, by many accounts, had personally blocked Lombardi's path to the Hall of Fame. Unfortunately, Giles' replacement was every bit as hostile to Lombardi's candidacy as Giles had been. This new committee member was Gabe Paul, Giles' right-hand man in Cincinnati. Paul had built a successful career with several teams and served as president of the New York Yankees during the late

1970s. He, like Giles, remembered Ernie in an unflattering light, and he, too, rebelled against the very idea of giving the late catcher a plaque on the wall in Cooperstown, New York.

Birdie Tebbetts was an American League catcher, mostly with the Detroit Tigers and Boston Red Sox, during the 1930s and 1940s. He played against Ernie and the Reds in the 1940 World Series and knew Ernie well from spring training games in Florida. After a long post-playing career as a manager of the Reds, Braves, and Indians, Tebbetts joined the Veterans Committee in 1979 with the intention of backing Ernie's quest for enshrinement. "You don't have a Hall of Fame without Ernie Lombardi in it," Tebbetts told his fellow panelists at the first meeting he attended. "It's not fair."

That's when he ran into an immovable object in the person of Gabe Paul. In fact, as Tebbetts stated in his autobiography, three committee members, including Paul, stood firmly in Ernie's path.

After one voting session, Tebbetts and Paul met privately and discussed the day's events. "After it was over, Gabe Paul and I had coffee," Tebbetts wrote. "Gabe and I always had coffee before and after the meetings. I said, 'How did you vote?' And he said, 'Out of respect for you I did not vote. I could not vote for that man.' I said, 'You did not vote for him because of your dislike for him in your days as the Reds' traveling secretary. It has nothing to do with his ability as a baseball player.'"[4] Paul's attitude frustrated Tebbetts. "Ernie would get within three votes of getting elected," he wrote, "and these guys would block it."[5]

Still, Ernie had his supporters, and one of them was his old Cincinnati teammate Johnny Vander Meer, the man who pitched two consecutive no-hitters. Vander Meer, interviewed in 1981 during that year's meeting of the Veterans Committee, dismissed his own chances for election. "As far as I'm concerned," he said, "there'll never be a Hall of Fame until Ernie Lombardi is in it. There's a guy who ought to be in there. One of the best all-around catchers who ever lived."[6]

Another was also a long-ago teammate on the Reds. Bill Werber left baseball in 1942 to concentrate on his insurance business, which he built into a profitable enterprise. In 1977, a few months before Ernie died, Werber made his support public.

> I've written to Warren Giles, chairman of the old-timers committee and with statistics, showed him that there's no comparison at all between Lombardi and [Roy] Campanella [who was elected in 1969]. In 17 years, Lombardi had a lifetime batting average of .306 and in 10 of those 17, he hit over .300.
>
> [Johnny] Bench can't compare with the fella. He'll never reach the status this fella reached. It's been a very bad injustice.[7]

As the years passed, the movement to give Lombardi a spot in the Hall of Fame gathered momentum. Johnny Vander Meer lobbied the committee members with letters and phone calls. The Italian American Sports Hall of Fame in Chicago, into which Ernie was inducted in 1979, collected 20,000 signatures on a petition and delivered it to the committee. Don Monzo, Ernie's nephew, launched a letter-writing campaign from his home in the Bay Area.

But the committee continued to elect Ernie's contemporaries while skipping over the big catcher. In 1981 the panel selected Johnny Mize, the power-hitting first baseman and Ernie's teammate on the New York Giants, and Black baseball pitching star and promoter Andrew (Rube) Foster. The 1982 vote saw the election of Travis Jackson, Bill Terry's old shortstop on the Giants, while George Kell, an American League third baseman whose career average of .306 was a match for Ernie's, got the call in 1983.

In 1984 the Veterans Committee passed over Lombardi once again but selected a catcher from the 1930s and 1940s. The newest Hall of Famer was Rick Ferrell, who played in the American League for 18 seasons, mostly for sad-sack teams like the Washington Senators and St. Louis Browns. Ferrell posted a lifetime batting average of .281 and made six All-Star teams but hit only 28 home runs during his career. He was a very good catcher, outstanding on defense, but hardly a great one. Some believed that Ferrell, who enjoyed a long post-playing career as a highly regarded team executive, was selected for his popularity in baseball circles and not for his playing skill. Also, Ferrell was still living, and perhaps the Committee wanted to honor him for that reason.

As a fan named Jerry Gregory from Annandale, Virginia, wrote in a letter to *The Sporting News*, "I couldn't believe it when I learned that Rick Ferrell had been elected to the Baseball Hall of Fame. No disrespect to Mr. Ferrell, but how in good conscience could the Veterans Committee select Ferrell over Ernie Lombardi?" He continued that Lombardi "had more hits, more homers, more runs batted in than Ferrell and his career batting average was 25 points higher than Ferrell's.... I guess the Veterans Committee wanted Rick to smell the roses."[8]

Gregory's opinion was shared by many fans and observers both inside and outside the game, and perhaps Ferrell's election gave Ernie's candidacy a boost. It was difficult to explain why Ferrell owned a plaque in Cooperstown while Ernie remained on the outside of the baseball shrine.

In 1985 the Committee chose two longtime National League stars, outfielder Enos Slaughter of the Cardinals and shortstop Arky Vaughan of the Pirates, but Ernie's public support continued to grow. The final boost to Ernie's cause came in 1986, when Ted Williams joined the committee. Williams had long been an outspoken advocate of Lombardi's. Now, with Williams, Birdie Tebbetts, and Bob Broeg working on Ernie's behalf, his eventual election now seemed inevitable.

On March 10, 1986, 17 of the 18 committee members (all except the longtime Dodgers general manager Emil [Buzzie] Bavasi, who was ill) met in Tampa, Florida, to vote for the Hall of Fame. A candidate needed 75 percent of the vote, or 13 votes from the 17 members present, for election. When they emerged from the meeting, the panelists revealed their selections. The two newest members of the Hall of Fame were Bobby Doerr, second baseman of the Boston Red Sox (and longtime teammate of Ted Williams), and Ernie Lombardi.

The Veterans Committee never revealed how its members voted, but we do know that Ernie received at least 14 of the 17 possible votes. Three candidates—Doerr, Lombardi, and Vic Willis (a right-handed pitcher who performed in the National League from 1898 to 1910)—reached the 13-vote threshold, but the committee was limited to two selections. So, the top two vote-getters were enshrined, while Willis, who died in 1947, waited for several more years. (He was finally elected in 1995.)

Because Ernie was a widower with no children and had lived out of the spotlight during the last years of his life, the Hall of Fame had trouble contacting his family. As one Hall staffer said, "We don't have a clue about any of his relatives. We're burning up phone lines all over the country, particularly in Oakland and Santa Cruz, California, but all we're doing is giving a lot of operators a workout."[9] But the Hall soon found the Lombardi family in the Bay Area, and the *Oakland Tribune* interviewed Ernie's sister Stella Monzo. "I think Ernie is looking down on us and he knows about it," she said. "He's smiling. Absolutely."[10]

His old teammates and opponents were happy to see him in the Hall.

Buddy Kerr: "When I played with Lom he was going downhill, but darn if he wasn't still a great hitter. You could see what kind of hitter he had been. When you see the guys they put in the Hall of Fame over him, it's just shameful because, believe me, Lom was a Hall of Famer. It was tragic that he didn't get the award while he was still alive."[11]

Stan Musial: "Lombardi was in consideration the last four or five years, always very close in the voting. This year he went in very easily."[12]

Johnny Vander Meer: "The people who say Lom wasn't a good defensive catcher must all have been fans, not ballplayers. The ballplayers I knew all thought he was a fine defensive catcher. His arm rated right up there with guys like Dickey, Hartnett, and Cochrane, and he should have been voted in 20 years ago."[13]

Cookie Lavagetto: "Now that he's gone, what good is it? He should have been voted in a long time ago, while he was still living."[14]

Fellow inductee Bobby Doerr: "I remember Ernie Lombardi well. One of the great hitters. Once he hit the ball so hard at me that it tore the glove off my hand, and I was playing deep. I thought my thumb was broken."[15]

Ernie's Hall of Fame plaque (author's collection).

Bucky Walters: "He should have been there long ago, I thought, but I'm glad to hear it. I wish he were here so I could tell him so."[16]

Ernie's sister Rose had passed away in 1980, and Stella Monzo was too ill to make the trip to Cooperstown. But on August 3, 1986, Rena (Lombardi)

Lenhardt, at age 80, led a contingent of friends and family members to see her brother's induction. Rena told the press that she had never traveled outside the Bay Area since her parents brought her there as an infant in 1906, but that she would never have missed this important ceremony. "We're just so proud and elated about this. Ernie would have said, 'It's about time.'"[17]

Rena was not used to public attention, and the national spotlight may have seemed overwhelming to her at times. But as the senior member of the Lombardi family, it fell to her to speak to the press, and also to give the induction speech for her late brother. Though Ernie had expressed bitterness about the Hall of Fame and vowed that he would reject the honor had it been offered to him, Rena believed that Ernie would have made the trip anyway. "He would have been very proud," she said. "He was very proud of his records."[18]

In an eerie coincidence, the date of the Hall of Fame induction ceremony was the 46th anniversary of Willard Hershberger's suicide. Though Ernie never talked about the tragedy in public, he apparently discussed it with his family. "Ernie knew what was bothering Hershberger, and he would instruct teammates to go easy on him," said Rena. "Some didn't listen to Ernie when they should have."[19]

The day of the ceremony was overcast, and a light drizzle fell while Bobby Doerr, selected by the Veterans Committee, gave his speech and Willie McCovey, elected by the writers, awaited his turn at the podium. Rena Lombardi spoke after Doerr, and when she looked out at the crowd of 5,000, she let out a breath and said, "Oh, boy." But she spoke, quietly at first, gaining volume as she went on. Her speech was brief but heartfelt, and she closed with gratitude for the honor "on behalf of my loving brother, Ernie 'Schnozz' Lombardi."[20]

The Commissioner of Baseball, Peter Ueberroth, presented the three inductees with copies of their Hall of Fame plaques. Ernie's plaque reads:

ERNEST NATALI LOMBARDI
BROOKLYN, N.L., 1931
CINCINNATI, N.L., 1932–1941
BOSTON , N.L., 1942
NEW YORK, N.L., 1943–1947
HIT .306 OVER 17 SEASONS DESPITE SLOWNESS AFOOT-TEN TIMES BATTING OVER .300. WON N.L. BATTING TITLE WITH .342 IN 1938 AND AGAIN IN 1942 WITH .330. HELD HANDS LOW, WITH INTERLOCKING GOLF GRIP AND QUICK STROKE. N.L. MVP IN 1938. SKILLED RECEIVER AND HANDLER OF PITCHERS. OUTSTANDING ARM FROM CROUCH POSITION, RIFLING THROWS WITH SIDE-ARM RELEASE.

So Ernie Lombardi, nine years after his death, finally took his place in the Baseball Hall of Fame.

He is not forgotten in Cincinnati. The trophy given to the Cincinnati Reds' most valuable player each year is called the Ernie Lombardi Award. (And the honor for the top pitcher is called the Johnny Vander Meer Award.) He occupies a prominent place in the Cincinnati Reds Hall of Fame as a charter member. Best of all, in 2004 the Reds unveiled a statue of Ernie outside the entrance to their new stadium, Great American Ball Park. The bronze statue, one of a group of four sculpted by Tom Tsuchiya, depicts Ernie in a crouch, preparing to receive a pitch from Joe Nuxhall while Frank Robinson bats and Ted Kluszewski waits on deck.

In the end, Ernie Lombardi was one of baseball's most memorable characters. With his unorthodox grip, he swung the heaviest bat in the game and hit the hardest line drives in baseball. Despite his almost comical lack of speed—as John Thorn and Pete Palmer once wrote, "He was the slowest of all the Hall of Famers, including the exhibits"[21]—he won

In 2003, sculptor Tom Tsuchiya created a statue of Ernie that stands outside Great American Ballpark in Cincinnati. Ernie is pictured in a crouch while Frank Robinson bats. This photograph was taken by Carol M. Highsmith (Carol M. Highsmith Archive, Library of Congress, Prints and Photographs Division).

two batting titles and a Most Valuable Player award. His cannon arm, the strongest in baseball, kept the running game in check, and he saved many a wild pitch by sticking his bare hand out to catch an errant delivery. His huge nose, ungainly body, and smiling nature—and even his legendary snoring—gave him a humanity that made him the most popular player in Cincinnati Reds history until Pete Rose came along.

But he also had his faults as a player, mostly due to his slowness, and some modern observers question his qualifications for the Hall of Fame. They point out that Ernie never scored more than 60 runs in a season, hit into double plays at a higher rate than any other player in history, and though he rarely struck out, he hardly ever walked either. They say, correctly, that Ernie would not have qualified for his second batting title under modern rules. As a catcher, he threw from a crouch because he was too big to rise out of it. His range factor each year was usually below the league average, and he led the National League in passed balls nine times, including seven years in a row.

Bill James was not a Lombardi man. The baseball historian had labeled Ernie "a reasonably good Hall of Fame selection"[22] in 1994, but by 2015 he had changed his mind. "Ernie Lombardi was a tremendously unique, colorful and interesting player," wrote James in an article on his website, "but was not a player deserving of Hall of Fame selection.... Ernie Lombardi finally got into the Hall of Fame, in part, because Bob Broeg had a selective memory about Lombardi's defense. Broeg outlived most everybody else who had seen Lombardi play, and Broeg ignored Lombardi's defensive liabilities and exaggerated his strengths, eventually convincing people that Lombardi was an outstanding defensive player, which he was not."[23]

Certainly, Ernie was no Johnny Bench behind the plate, and he was no Joe Morgan on the basepaths. But he was one of the greatest players in Cincinnati Reds history. His exceptional skills with his bat and his throwing arm kept him in the major leagues for 17 seasons and made him an eight-time All-Star. He was a World Series champion, a distinction that such all-time greats as Ty Cobb, Ted Williams, and Barry Bonds, among others, cannot claim. Ernie was a great player, he was fun to watch, and he was one of the most famous players of his time.

It is the Hall of Fame, after all.

Appendix: Ernie Lombardi's Statistics

Regular Season

	G	AB	R	H	2B	3B	HR	RBI	BB	SO	GDP	SB	CS	AVG	SLG
1931 BRO N	73	182	20	54	7	1	4	23	12	12	6	1	0	.297	.412
1932 CIN N	118	413	43	125	22	9	11	68	41	19	16	0	0	.303	.479
1933 CIN N	107	350	30	99	21	1	4	47	16	17	**26**	2	1	.283	.383
1934 CIN N	132	417	42	127	19	4	9	62	16	22	**24**	0	1	.305	.434
1935 CIN N	120	332	36	114	23	3	12	64	16	6	11	0	2	.343	.539
1936 CIN N	121	387	42	129	23	2	12	68	19	16	15	1	1	.333	.496
1937 CIN N	120	368	41	123	22	1	9	59	14	17	12	1	0	.334	.473
1938 CIN N	129	489	60	167	30	1	19	95	40	14	**30**	0	0	**.342**	.524
1939 CIN N	130	450	43	129	26	2	20	85	35	19	24	0	0	.287	.487
1940 CIN N	109	376	50	120	22	0	14	74	31	14	18	0	0	.319	.489
1941 CIN N	117	398	33	105	12	1	10	60	36	14	19	1	0	.264	.374
1942 BOS N	105	309	32	102	14	0	11	46	37	12	17	1	1	**.330**	.482
1943 NY N	104	295	19	90	7	0	10	51	16	11	18	1	2	.305	.431
1944 NY N	117	373	37	95	13	0	10	58	33	25	**23**	0	0	.255	.370
1945 NY N	115	368	46	113	7	1	19	70	43	11	12	0	1	.307	.486
1946 NY N	88	238	19	9	4	1	12	39	18	24	8	0	0	.290	.466
1947 NY N	48	110	8	31	5	0	4	21	7	9	4	0	0	.282	.436
	1853	5855	601	1792	277	27	190	990	430	262	283	8	9	.306	.460

World Series

	G	AB	R	H	2B	3B	HR	RBI	BB	SO	GDP	SB	CS	AVG	SLG
1939 CIN N	4	14	0	3	0	0	0	2	0	1	1	0	0	.214	.214
1940 CIN N	2	3	0	1	1	0	0	0	1	0	0	0	0	.333	.667

The information used here was obtained free of charge from and is copyrighted by Retrosheet. Interested parties may contact Retrosheet at www.retrosheet.org.

Chapter Notes

Chapter 1

1. *Santa Cruz Sentinel*, July 30, 1986, page 15.
2. Bay View Park is now called Ernie Raimondi Park, named for a local ballplayer who was killed in World War II.
3. Lazzeri, another Italian American from the Bay Area, was the first professional player to hit 60 home runs in a season. Babe Ruth was the second.
4. Arlett hit 432 home runs in the minor leagues. On August 3, 2015, Mike Hessman of the Toledo Mud Hens hit his 433rd home run to break Arlett's mark.
5. *Ogden Standard-Examiner*, May 16, 1927, page 8.
6. *Ibid.*, June 12, 1927, page 10.
7. Brian Mulligan, "Ernie Lombardi's Bittersweet Road to the Hall of Fame," *Elysian Fields Quarterly*, Fall 2003.
8. *Oakland Tribune*, June 11, 1928, page 12.
9. Reference books say that the Portland club was called the Beavers, but the newspapers of the period used the name Ducks.
10. *Oakland Tribune*, September 30, 1929, page 16.
11. *Ibid.*, July 28, 1930, page 13.
12. United Press report in *Long Beach Sun*, March 9, 1930, page 15.

Chapter 2

1. *Brooklyn Standard Union*, February 6, 1931, page 10.
2. Bill James, *The Bill James Historical Baseball Abstract* (New York: Villard, 1987), page 319.
3. *Brooklyn Eagle*, March 14, 1931, page 14.
4. *Ibid.*, February 8, 1931, page 44.
5. *Ibid.*, April 26, 1931, page 36.
6. *Ibid.*, March 14, 1931, page 14.
7. *Brooklyn Times-Union*, January 28, 1931, page 42.
8. *San Francisco Examiner*, January 21, 1931, page 25.
9. *Brooklyn Times-Union*, March 17, 1931, page 13.
10. *Ibid.*
11. *Brooklyn Citizen*, May 1, 1931, page 7.
12. *Ibid.*
13. Donald Honig, *The Man in the Dugout: Fifteen Big League Managers Speak Their Minds* (Chicago: Follett, 1977), page 132.
14. *Washington Evening Star*, May 7, 1958, page C-3. Actually, Haines only hit Ernie once in his career, and that came on July 30, 1935. Ernie recalled it as happening in his first year.
15. Honig, pages 132–133.
16. *Brooklyn Eagle*, June 2, 1931, page 22.
17. *Ibid.*
18. *Ibid.*, April 21, 1931, page 26.
19. *Brooklyn Standard Union*, September 17, 1931, page 8.
20. *Ibid.*
21. *Ibid.*

Chapter 3

1. William Braucher, *Miami News*, March 31, 1932, page 8.
2. *Brooklyn Times-Union*, March 15, 1932, page 13.
3. *Ibid.*, March 15, 1932, page 57.
4. Leo Durocher and Ed Linn, *Nice Guys Finish Last* (New York: Simon & Schuster, 1975), page 55.

5. Rickey's official title was "business manager," but he discharged the same responsibilities as a general manager of today. This book will use the two titles interchangeably.
6. *Cincinnati Enquirer*, March 25, 1932, page 11.
7. *Cincinnati Times-Star*, May 9, 1932, page 18.
8. *Brooklyn Daily Eagle*, June 10, 1032, page 24.
9. *Ibid.*
10. The first batter to do so was Pat Duncan of the Reds in 1921.
11. *The Sporting News*, June 2, 1932, page 3.
12. Jack Zanger, *Great Catchers of the Major Leagues* (New York: Random House, 1970), page 125.
13. Bill James, *The Bill James Historical Baseball Abstract* (New York: Villard, 1987), page 383.
14. *Cincinnati Enquirer*, June 24, 1932, page 12.

Chapter 4

1. *Brooklyn Eagle*, January 8, 1933, page 24.
2. *Lewiston* (ME) *Sun*, November 18, 1932, page 15.
3. *Cincinnati Post*, March 25, 1933, page 12.
4. *Knoxville Journal*, March 22, 1933, page 7.
5. *Brooklyn Eagle*, April 11, 1933, page 20.
6. *Cincinnati Post*, May 1, 1933, page 11.
7. *The Sporting News*, July 6, 1933, page 1.
8. *Brooklyn Eagle*, July 23, 1933, page 30.
9. *Ibid.*, October 27, 1933, page 19.
10. *Cincinnati Post*, July 13, 1933, page 10.

Chapter 5

1. *Boston Globe*, August 28, 1933, page 10.
2. *Cincinnati Post*, June 26, 1934, page 11.
3. Marshall Smelser's book, *The Life That Ruth Built* (Lincoln: Bison Books, 1993), states that this was exactly what happened. The Dodgers had dropped Max Carey as manager, and had MacPhail been able to acquire Ruth, he would immediately deal the slugger to the Dodgers. Sensing this, Ruppert decided to keep Ruth for one more year. The Dodgers hired Casey Stengel instead.
4. Radio transmitters in the United States are now limited to 50,000 watts.
5. *Cincinnati Enquirer*, February 6, 1934, page 12.
6. Associated Press release, *Venice* (CA) *Evening Vanguard*, March 19, 1934, page 8.
7. Ray Robinson, *The Home Run Heard 'Round the World: The Dramatic Story of the 1951 Giants-Dodgers Pennant Race* (New York: HarperCollins, 1991), page 57.
8. *Ibid.*, page 57.

Chapter 6

1. Norman L. Macht and Dick Bartell, *Rowdy Richard* (Berkeley, California: North Atlantic Books, 1987), page 320.
2. Elden Auker with Tom Keegan, *Sleeper Cars and Flannel Uniforms: A Lifetime of Memories from Striking Out the Babe to Teeing It Up with the President* (Chicago: Triumph, 2001), no page numbers.
3. Greg Erion, "Chick Hafey," biography on the Society for American Baseball Research (SABR) Bioproject web site, https://sabr.org/bioproj.
4. Joe Hoppel, editor, *Cooperstown: Where the Legends Live Forever* (New York: Crescent Books, 1997), page 177.
5. Macht and Bartell, page 95.
6. *Cincinnati Post*, April 11, 1935, page 16.
7. *Ibid.*
8. *Memphis* (TN) *Commercial Appeal*, February 22, 1947, page 10. Actually, Lombardi's bunt single was the third hit off Passeau, not the first.

Chapter 7

1. *San Francisco Examiner*, June 5, 1967, page 54.
2. *The Sporting News*, April 2, 1936, page 6.
3. Greg Rhodes and John Snyder, *Redleg Journal: Year by Year and Day by Day*

with the Cincinnati Reds Since 1866 (Cincinnati: Road West Publishing Company, 2001), page 269.
4. Associated Press report in the Zanesville (OH) Times-Reader, February 21, 1936, page 12.
5. The Sporting News, February 6, 1936, page 6.
6. New York Daily News, August 19, 1965, page 66.
7. Oakland Tribune, March 16, 1965, page 46.
8. Boston Globe, February 14, 1965, page 54.
9. Cincinnati Enquirer, April 7, 1936, page 14.
10. The two previous ultimate grand slams were hit by Roger Connor in 1881 and by Babe Ruth in 1925.
11. Cincinnati Post, July 27, 1936, page 10.
12. Cincinnati Enquirer, May 4, 1936, page 3.
13. Portland (ME) Press-Herald, October 17, 1970, page 8.

Chapter 8

1. 1991 interview by John Ring on the Redleg Nation website, https://www.redlegnation.com.
2. Baltimore Sun, November 9, 2012.
3. Red Barber, "Once a Catcher Was Hired to Just Use His Fists," Tallahassee (FL) Democrat, March 10, 1974.
4. Richmond (VA) Times-Dispatch, January 10, 1937, page 16.
5. Massillon (OH) Evening Independent, February 13, 1937, page 6.
6. Decatur Herald and Review, March 16, 1937, page 12.
7. Cincinnati Enquirer, February 10, 1937, page 14.
8. James W. Johnson, Double No-Hit: Johnny Vander Meer's Historic Night under the Lights (Lincoln: University of Nebraska Press, 2012), page 57.
9. Cincinnati Post, May 1, 1937, page 11.
10. The Sporting News, March 18, 1937.
11. Decatur (IL) Daily Review, July 8, 1937, page 6.
12. Cincinnati Enquirer, August 14, 1937, page 10.
13. Arizona Republic, February 2, 1954, page 22.

14. Decatur (IL) Daily Review, September 14, 1937, page 16. Dressen was born and raised in Decatur, and his hometown paper always followed his career with interest.
15. Cincinnati Post, April 20, 1937, page 17.
16. Indianapolis News, November 2, 1937, page 15.

Chapter 9

1. Ogden Standard-Examiner, June 14, 1939, page 12.
2. Look, April 4, 1944, page 42.
3. Baseball Magazine, June 1950, page 247.
4. Lee Allen, The Cincinnati Reds (New York: G.P. Putnam's Sons, 1948), page 271.
5. Ed Rumill, "McKechnie Knew Plays, When to Use Them," Christian Science Monitor, November 4, 1972, page 11.
6. Jack Zanger, Great Catchers of the Major Leagues (New York: Random House, 1970), page 129.
7. The Sporting News, December 3, 1938, page 5.
8. William Nack and David Fischer, "The Razor's Edge," Sports Illustrated, May 6, 1991.
9. Gary Licavan, "The Tragic Story of Baseball's Unfortunate Hall of Famer, Ernie Lombardi," Baseball History Comes Alive web site, https://www.baseballhistorycomesalive.com.
10. Saturday Evening Post, August 17, 1938, page 44.
11. Boston's National League team used the name Bees from 1936 to 1940, then resumed the name Braves in 1941.
12. That previous no-hitter was pitched by Hod Eller against the Cardinals on May 11, 1919.
13. James W. Johnson, "Johnny Vander Meer," Society for American Baseball Research (SABR) Bioproject web site, https://sabr.org/bioproj.
14. Allen, page 258.
15. Brooklyn Eagle, June 16, 1938, page 16.
16. Ibid.
17. Ibid.
18. James W. Johnson, Double No-Hit: Johnny Vander Meer's Historic Night under the Lights (Lincoln: University of Nebraska Press, 2012), page 88.

19. Maury Allen, *Sports Illustrated*, June 13, 1960.
20. *Syracuse (NY) Post-Standard*, December 9, 1975, page 14.
21. Undated clipping, Ernie Lombardi file at the Baseball Hall of Fame, Cooperstown, New York.
22. The National League started counting double plays by batter in 1933, and the American League did not do so until 1939. It is possible that some player grounded into more than 30 double plays before 1933, but no such instance has yet been found.

Chapter 10

1. *Cincinnati Enquirer*, December 22, 1938, page 16.
2. *Wilmington (OH) News-Journal*, February 1, 1943, page 6.
3. *Ibid*.
4. John B. Foster, editor, *Spalding's Official Base Ball Guide, 1939* (New York: American Sports Publishing Company, 1939), pages 77–78.
5. James W. Johnson, *Double No-Hit: Johnny Vander Meer's Historic Night under the Lights* (Lincoln: University of Nebraska Press, 2012), page 118. Actually, five National League teams left more runners on base than the Reds in 1938.
6. *Miami Herald*, August 28, 1967, page 32.
7. *Cincinnati Enquirer*, July 1, 1939, page 12.
8. *The Sporting News*, September 7, 1939, page 1.
9. Lawrence Ritter, *The Glory of Their Times*, enlarged edition (New York: William Morrow, 1984), page 222. Privately, Roush, according to a SABR acquaintance of the author who knew the ballplayer, expressed himself more forcefully: "We would have kicked their asses!"
10. *Wilkes-Barre Record*, October 6, 1939, page 27, from AP report.
11. *The New York Times*, October 9, 1939, page 1.
12. *Ibid*., page 23.
13. *Cincinnati Post*, October 9, 1939, page 10.
14. Gabriel Schechter, "Lombardi's Snooze: Not-So-Instant Replay," National Pastime Museum web site, https://www.thenationalpastimemuseum.com.
15. Dave Kindred, "Ernie Lombardi a Bitter Recluse Because of 'Snooze,'" *Louisville Courier-Journal*, February 8, 1977.
16. Art Rosenbaum, "One Out From Hall of Fame," *San Francisco Chronicle*, September 28, 1977.
17. Kindred.
18. Schechter.
19. Bill James, *The Bill James Historical Baseball Abstract* (New York: Villard, 1987), page 323.
20. *Cincinnati Post*, October 9, 1939, page 11.

Chapter 11

1. United Press report in *Greenville (OH) Daily Advocate*, January 30, 1940, page 5.
2. *Saturday Evening Post*, September 14, 1940, page 39.
3. *The New York Times*, October 9, 1939, page 26.
4. *The Sporting News*, October 26, 1939, page 9.
5. Gabriel Schechter, "Lombardi's Snooze: Not-So-Instant Replay," National Pastime Museum web site, https://www.thenationalpastimemuseum.com.
6. *Eugene (OR) Guard*, January 11, 1940, page 12.
7. Associated Press story in *Wilkes-Barre Record*, January 12, 1940, page 25.
8. United Press report in *Greenville (OH) Daily Advocate*, January 30, 1940, page 5.
9. *Cincinnati Enquirer*, February 27, 1940, page 12.
10. *Ibid*., March 20, 1940, page 18.
11. *Ibid*.
12. *Ibid*., July 26, 1940, page 14.
13. *The New York Times*, August 1, 1940, page S27.
14. *Cincinnati Enquirer*, August 4, 1940, page 27.
15. *Ibid*., August 3, 1940, page 13.
16. *The Sporting News*, August 8, 1940, page 5.
17. "Willard Hershberger and the Legacy of Suicide," *The National Pastime: A Review of Baseball History* (Cleveland: Society for American Baseball Research, 2000), page 76.
18. William Nack, "The Razor's Edge," *Sports Illustrated*, May 6, 1991.
19. *Cincinnati Enquirer*, August 5, 1940, page 14.

20. *Cincinnati Post*, October 1, 1940, page 11.
21. Lee Allen, *The Cincinnati Reds* (New York: G.P. Putnam's Sons, 1948), pages 286–287.
22. *The New York Times*, October 5, 1940, page 9.
23. Kirk C. Jenkins, "October 7, 1940: Reds' Bucky Walters Hurls World Series Shutout to Force Deciding Game 7," SABR Games Project web site.
24. Dick Bartell and Norman Macht, *Rowdy Richard* (Berkeley: North Atlantic Books, 1987), page 304.
25. Daniel Daniel, *Baseball Magazine*, October 1940.
26. *Cincinnati Enquirer*, October 9, 1940, page 3.

Chapter 12

1. *Cincinnati Post*, January 17, 1941, page 18.
2. "25 Facts about Ernie Lombardi," Red Reporter web site, https://www.redreporter.com/.
3. *Oakland Tribune*, October 7, 1942, page 24.
4. Ibid.
5. Ibid.
6. *Cincinnati Post*, January 17, 1941, page 1.
7. *Oakland Tribune*, March 6, 1941, page 27.
8. *Cincinnati Post*, March 12, 1941, page 1.
9. *Oakland Tribune*, March 23, 1941, page 13.
10. *Cincinnati Post*, April 23, 1941, page 14.
11. Ibid.
12. Nancy Snell Griffith, "Elmer Riddle," Society for American Baseball Research (SABR) Bioproject web site, https://sabr.org/bioproj.
13. *Cincinnati Enquirer*, July 6, 1941, page 25.
14. Ibid., July 14, 1941, page 13.
15. *Buffalo Evening News*, November 18, 1941, page 5.

Chapter 13

1. Tommy Holmes' column, *Brooklyn Eagle*, November 8, 1941, page 9.
2. *Cincinnati Post*, December 17, 1941, page 21. By all accounts, Hemsley, who died in 1972 at age 65, kept his abstinence pledge to the end of his life.
3. *Cincinnati Post*, December 17, 1941, page 21.
4. *Oakland Tribune*, January 21, 1942, page 16.
5. *Cincinnati Enquirer*, February 8, 1942, page 25.
6. *Boston Globe*, March 3, 1942, page 10.
7. Jim Kaplan, "Warren Spahn," Society for American Baseball Research (SABR) Bioproject web site, https://sabr.org/bioproj.
8. *The New York Times*, July 3, 1984, Section B, Page 10.
9. *Boston Globe*, March 30, 1942, page 10.
10. Ibid.
11. Marty Appel, *Casey Stengel: Baseball's Greatest Character* (New York: Doubleday, 2017), page 126.
12. Ibid., page 127.
13. *Boston Globe*, May 14, 1942, page 24.
14. Robert Creamer, *Stengel: His Life and Times* (New York: Simon & Schuster, 1984), pages 193–194.
15. Bill James, *The Bill James Historical Baseball Abstract* (New York: Villard, 1987), page 318.
16. Gene Fehler, *More Tales from Baseball's Golden Age* (Champaign: Sports Publishing, 2002), page 203.
17. Donald Honig, *Baseball Between the Lines: Baseball in the Forties and Fifties as Told by the Men who Played It* (Lincoln: University of Nebraska Press, 1993), page 209.
18. Jack Zanger, *Great Catchers of the Major Leagues* (New York: Random House, 1970), page 134.
19. *The Sporting News*, December 24, 1942, page 7.
20. George Vass, "Baseball Records: Fact or Fiction?" *Baseball Digest*, June 2005.
21. *The Sporting News*, December 24, 1942, page 7.
22. *Boston Globe*, December 4, 1942, page 36.

Chapter 14

1. Wide World Features report in *Rushville (IN) Republican*, October 3, 1942, page 2.

2. *The Sporting News*, May 6, 1943, page 10.
3. *The New York Times*, April 4, 1943.
4. John McMurray, "Connie Ryan," Society for American Baseball Research (SABR) Bioproject web site, https://sabr.org/bioproj.
5. Joseph Wancho, "Ernie Lombardi," Society for American Baseball Research (SABR) Bioproject web site, https://sabr.org/bioproj.
6. Warren Corbett, "Gus Mancuso," Society for American Baseball Research (SABR) Bioproject web site, https://sabr.org/bioproj.
7. Dick Young in *New York Daily News*, July 12, 1943, page 41.
8. *Long Beach Press-Telegram*, March 10, 1948, page 14. Durocher played in two games at second base at the start of the 1945 season but never appeared again at short.
9. *Tacoma* (WA) *News Tribune*, July 21, 1943, page 13.
10. Ace Adams interview by Brent Kelley, September 27, 1991, SABR Oral History Committee collection.
11. Bob Cairns, *Pen Men* (New York: St. Martin's, 1992), page 51.

Chapter 15

1. *Few and Chosen Giants: Defining Giants Greatness Across the Eras* (Chicago: Triumph, 2007), page not numbered.
2. *New York Daily News*, March 25, 1944, page 82.
3. *Ibid.*, March 30, 1944, page 56.
4. Ralph Berger, "Phil Weintraub," Society for American Baseball Research (SABR) Bioproject web site, https://sabr.org/bioproj.
5. *Palm Beach Post*, May 27, 1944, page 16.
6. *Brooklyn Eagle*, September 2, 1944, page 6.
7. Bill James, *The Bill James Historical Baseball Abstract* (New York: Villard, 1987), page 325.
8. *New York Daily News*, April 28, 1945, page 110.
9. *Burlington* (VT) *Daily News*, May 17, 1945, page 9.
10. *Ibid.*
11. *San Francisco Examiner*, November 11, 1945, page 17.

Chapter 16

1. *Pittsburgh Courier*, July 15, 1939, page 16.
2. *Ibid.*
3. *Ibid.*
4. Enos Slaughter with Kevin Reid, *Country Hardball—The Autobiography of Enos "Country" Slaughter* (Greensboro: Tudor, 1991), page 81.
5. *New York Daily News*, January 22, 1946, page 19.
6. Associated Press report in *Johnson City* (TN) *Press*, February 19, 1946, page 6.
7. *Dayton Daily News*, February 24, 1946, page 19.
8. Bill Gilbert, *They Also Served: Baseball and the Home Front, 1941–45* (New York: Crown, 1992), page 265.
9. Leo Durocher with Ed Linn, *Nice Guys Finish Last* (New York: Simon & Schuster, 1975), page 15.
10. Steven Treder, *Forty Years a Giant: The Life of Horace Stoneham* (Lincoln: University of Nebraska Press, 2021), page 113. The New York papers all gave different accounts of the conversation, but they all agreed on the gist of it.
11. Tom Harris, "But the Polo Grounds Belonged to the Giants: An Interview with Bobby Thomson," *The National Pastime* 28 (2008), pages 74–75.
12. *Moline* (IL) *Dispatch*, September 7, 1946, page 11.
13. *Oakland Tribune*, June 24, 1952, page 28.
14. *New York Daily News*, September 24, 1947, page 508.
15. *Brooklyn Eagle*, September 22, 1947, page 11.
16. *The New York Times*, September 24, 1947, page 32.
17. The National League started counting GIDP (grounded into double plays) in 1933, Ernie's third year in the majors. The Retrosheet.org web site credits Ernie with 22 GIDP in 1931–32, giving him a career total of 283.
18. *Oakland Tribune*, April 25, 1974, page 38. Actually, Ernie stole eight bases and was caught stealing nine times.

Chapter 17

1. *The New York Times*, September 24, 1947, page 32.

2. *The Sporting News*, June 2, 1948, page 24.
3. *Oakland Tribune*, May 20, 1948, page 29.
4. *Valley Times* (North Hollywood, CA), March 16, 1948, page 6.
5. Jonathan Fraser Light, *The Cultural Encyclopedia of Baseball* (Jefferson: McFarland, 1995), page 474.
6. Bill Pennington, *Billy Martin: Baseball's Flawed Genius* (New York: Houghton Mifflin Harcourt, 2015), page 50.
7. Robert Creamer, *Stengel: His Life and Times* (New York: Simon & Schuster, 1984), page 208.
8. *The Sporting News*, September 8, 1948, page 20.
9. Creamer, page 208.

Chapter 18

1. UPI report in *Terre Haute* (IN) *Tribune-Star*, October 18, 1970, page 46.
2. *Oakland Tribune*, July 13, 1952, Sunday supplement.
3. *Oakland Tribune*, March 15, 1953, page T-3.
4. *Ogden* (UT) *Standard-Examiner*, April 10, 1953, page 18.
5. *Cincinnati Post*, April 9, 1953, page 1.
6. Bill James, *The Bill James Historical Baseball Abstract* (New York: Villard, 1987), page 328. Actually, it was 13 years later, not 14.
7. *Tracy* (CA) *Press*, January 21, 1954, page 12.
8. *Newsday*, August 3, 1986, sports section, page 5.

Chapter 19

1. *Atlanta Constitution*, April 22, 1953, page 9.
2. *San Francisco Examiner*, April 28, 1958, page 33.
3. *Pittsburgh Press*, October 10, 1965, page 70.
4. *Oakland Tribune*, July 29, 1966, page 30.
5. Bill James, *The Politics of Glory: How Baseball's Hall of Fame Really Works* (New York: Macmillan, 1994), page 44.
6. *Ibid.*, page 163.
7. *Cincinnati Enquirer*, October 3, 1976, page 31.
8. *Hamilton* (OH) *Journal News*, October 6, 1974, page 19.
9. *Syracuse* (NY) *Post-Standard*, August 27, 1974, page 11.
10. UPI report in *Terre Haute* (IN) *Tribune-Star*, October 18, 1970, page 46.
11. *Cincinnati Enquirer*, July 8, 1972, page 25.
12. *Oakland Tribune*, April 25, 1974, page 38.
13. *Ibid.*
14. *Ibid.*
15. Associated Press report in *Camden* (AR) *News*, Feb 1, 1977, page 6.
16. *Santa Cruz* (CA) *Sentinel*, July 30, 1986, page B1.
17. Article by Dave Kindred in *Louisville Courier-Journal*; printed in *Richmond* (CA) *Independent*, February 8, 1977, page 18.
18. *Richmond* (CA) *Independent*, February 8, 1977, page 19.
19. *Ibid.*
20. *Record* (Hackensack, NJ), August 4, 1986, page 46.
21. *Cincinnati Post*, July 30, 1986, page 33.
22. *Oakland Tribune*, September 28, 1977, page 29.

Chapter 20

1. *The Sporting News*, October 15, 1977, page 51.
2. *The New York Times*, March 11, 1986, sec B, page 7.
3. *Ibid.*
4. Birdie Tebbetts with James Morrison, *Birdie: Confessions of a Baseball Nomad* (Chicago: Triumph, 2002), page 191.
5. Tebbetts and Morrison, page 190.
6. *Santa Cruz* (CA) *Sentinel*, March 12, 1981, page 42.
7. *Naples* (FL) *Daily News*, May 22, 1977, page 25.
8. *The Sporting News*, March 19, 1984, page 6.
9. *Cincinnati Post*, March 11, 1986, page 21.
10. *Oakland Tribune*, March 21, 1986, page 59.
11. *New York Daily News*, August 3, 1986, page 65.
12. *Cincinnati Enquirer*, March 11, 1986, page 21.

13. *Cincinnati Post*, March 11, 1986, page 19.
14. *Oakland Tribune*, March 11, 1986, page 35.
15. *The New York Times*, March 11, 198,6 section B, page 7.
16. *Cincinnati Enquirer*, March 11, 1986, page 21.
17. *San Francisco Examiner*, August 4, 1986, page 58.
18. *Baltimore Sun*, August 4, 1986, page 18.
19. *Newsday*, August 3, 1986, sports section, page 5.
20. *San Francisco Examiner*, August 4, 1986, page 58.
21. Dennis Corcoran, *Induction Day at Cooperstown: A History of the Baseball Hall of Fame Ceremony* (Jefferson: McFarland, 2010), pages 150–151.
22. Bill James, *The Politics of Glory: How Baseball's Hall of Fame Really Works* (New York: Macmillan, 1994), page 303.
23. "The Fielding Jones, Parts XXXI–XXXV," Bill James Online, January 27, 2015.

Bibliography

Books

Allen, Lee. *The Cincinnati Reds*. New York: G.P. Putnam's Sons, 1948.
Appel, Marty. *Casey Stengel: Baseball's Greatest Character*. New York: Doubleday, 2017.
Auker, Elden, with Tom Keegan. *Sleeper Cars and Flannel Uniforms: A Lifetime of Memories from Striking Out the Babe to Teeing It Up with the President*. Chicago: Triumph, 2001.
Cairns, Bob. *Pen Men*. New York: St. Martin's, 1992.
Corcoran, Dennis. *Induction Day at Cooperstown: A History of the Baseball Hall of Fame Ceremony*. Jefferson: McFarland, 2010.
Creamer, Robert. *Stengel: His Life and Times*. New York: Simon & Schuster, 1984.
Durocher, Leo, and Ed Linn. *Nice Guys Finish Last*. New York: Simon & Schuster, 1975.
Fehler, Gene. *More Tales from Baseball's Golden Age*. Champaign: Sports Publishing, 2002.
Foster, John B., editor. *Spalding's Official Base Ball Guide, 1939*. New York: American Sports, 1939.
Freedman, Lew. *Lightning Strikes Twice: Johnny Vander Meer and the Cincinnati Reds*. Jefferson: McFarland, 2021.
Gilbert, Bill. *They Also Served: Baseball and the Home Front, 1941–45*. New York: Crown, 1992.
Honig, Donald. *Baseball Between the Lines: Baseball in the Forties and Fifties as Told by the Men Who Played It*. Lincoln: University of Nebraska Press, 1993.
_____. *The Man in the Dugout: Fifteen Big League Managers Speak Their Minds*. Chicago: Follett, 1977.
Hoppel, Joe, editor. *Cooperstown: Where the Legends Live Forever*. New York: Crescent, 1997.
James, Bill. *The Bill James Historical Baseball Abstract*. New York: Villard, 1987.
_____. *The Politics of Glory: How Baseball's Hall of Fame Really Works*. New York: Macmillan, 1994.
Johnson, Harold (Speed). *Who's Who in Major League Baseball*. Chicago: Buxton, 1933.
Johnson, James W. *Double No-Hit: Johnny Vander Meer's Historic Night Under the Lights*. Lincoln: University of Nebraska Press, 2012.
Johnson, Lloyd, editor. *The Encyclopedia of Minor League Baseball: The Official Record of Minor League Baseball*. Durham: Baseball America, 1997.
Light, Jonathan Fraser. *The Cultural Encyclopedia of Baseball*. Jefferson: McFarland, 1995.
Macht, Norman, and Dick Bartell. *Rowdy Richard*. Berkeley: North Atlantic, 1987.
Pennington, Bill. *Billy Martin: Baseball's Flawed Genius*. New York: Houghton Mifflin Harcourt, 2015.
Ritter, Lawrence. *The Glory of Their Times*. Enlarged edition. New York: William Morrow, 1984.
Robinson, Ray. *The Home Run Heard 'Round the World: The Dramatic Story of the 1951 Giants-Dodgers Pennant Race*. New York: HarperCollins, 1991.

Slaughter, Enos, with Kevin Reid. *Country Hardball: The Autobiography of Enos "Country" Slaughter.* Greensboro: Tudor, 1991.
Tebbetts, Birdie, with James Morrison. *Birdie: Confessions of a Baseball Nomad.* Chicago: Triumph, 2002.
Thomson, Bobby, and Phil Pepe. *Few and Chosen Giants: Defining Giants Greatness Across the Eras.* Chicago: Triumph, 2007.
Treder, Steven. *Forty Years a Giant: The Life of Horace Stoneham.* Lincoln: University of Nebraska Press, 2021.
Werber, Bill, and C. Paul Rogers III. *Memories of a Ballplayer: Bill Werber and Baseball in the 1930s.* Cleveland: Society for American Baseball Research, 2001.
Zanger, Jack. *Great Catchers of the Major Leagues.* New York: Random House, 1970.

Newspapers

Boston Globe
Brooklyn Eagle
Brooklyn Standard Union
Brooklyn Times-Union
Chicago Tribune
Cincinnati Enquirer
Cincinnati Post
Cincinnati Times-Star
Knoxville Journal
Lewiston (ME) Sun

Memphis (TN) *Commercial Appeal*
Miami News
New York Daily News
New York Post
New York Times
Oakland Tribune
Portland (ME) *Press-Herald*
San Francisco Examiner
Washington Evening Star
Zanesville (OH) *Times-Reader*

Magazines

Baseball Digest
Baseball Magazine
Baseball Research Journal
The National Pastime

Sport
The Sporting News
Sports Illustrated

Internet Sites

Baseball History Daily (https://baseballhistorydaily.com)
Baseball Reference (http://www.baseball-reference.com)
Bill James Online (http://www.billjamesonline.com)
Library of Congress (http://www.loc.gov)
National Baseball Hall of Fame and Museum (http://www.baseballhalloffame.org)
Project Retrosheet (http://www.retrosheet.org)
SABR Baseball Biography Project (http://sabr.org/bioproject)
Society for American Baseball Research (SABR) (http://www.sabr.org)

Index

Abbaticchio, Ed 13
Adams, Ace 141, 155–156
Akers, Bill 27
Aleno, Chuck 122
Allen, Johnny 143
Allen, Lee 78, 83
Antonelli, Johnny 177
Arlett, Russell (Buzz) 7, 9, 11–12
Asbjornson, Bob 26
Averill, Earl 113

Baker, Bill 106–107, 112, 117
Baker, Del 7–8
Ballanfant, Lee 74
Barber, Red 157
Barlick, Al 128
Barr, George 161
Barrett, Red 68
Bartell, Dick 49, 93, 111, 113, 121
Baseball Hall of Fame 180–195
baseball integration 152–153
Bauers, Russ 72
Bavasi, Emil (Buzzie) 191
Becker, Joe 18
Bench, Johnny 189, 195
Benton, Larry 27, 43
Berger, Wally 8, 79, 82, 84, 96
Berra, Lawrence (Yogi) 150
Berres, Ray 137, 143
Bissonette, Del 20
Bithorn, Hiram 129
Blades, Ray 94
Blanton, Cy 61
Blattner, Buddy 159
Bodie, Ping (Francesco Pezzolo) 13–14
Bolton, Cliff 47
Bonds, Barry 195
Bool, Al 8
Bordagaray, Frenchy 96
Borowy, Hank 150, 161
Bottomley, Jim 34–35, 45, 54, 57, 182
Brack, Gibby 72
Brannick, Eddie 160
Breadon, Sam 41, 77
Brennan, Don 45, 61, 63

Bressler, Rube 19
Brewer, Chet 51
Bridges, Tommy 111
Brittain, Gus 67–68
Broeg, Bob 183, 188, 190, 195
Buckner, Bill 99–100
Burnett, Johnny 57
Burr, Harold C. 147
Bush, Guy 26
Bush, Owen (Donie) 33–37, 43, 45
Butcher, Max 84
Byrd, Sammy 51–52, 54, 61, 70

Callahan, Tom 183
Camilli, Dolph 8, 80, 85, 122
Campanella, Roy 189
Campbell, Bruce 112
Campbell, Gilly 51–53, 55–56, 58, 60–61, 63–64
Carey, Max 22–24, 127
Carlyle, Roy 176
Carpenter, Bob 137
Carter, Bob 6
Carter, Walter 22
Chandler, A.B. (Happy) 156, 182
Chapman, Calvin 61, 63
Chapman, Charles 43
Christie, Walter 59
Cicotte, Eddie 95
Cincinnati Reds Hall of Fame 177–178
Clark, Watty 20
Clifford, Neil 117
Cobb, Ty 33, 137, 195
Cohen, Dan 107
Cohn, Art 116
Collins, Eddie 95
Combs, Merrill 168
Comorosky, Adam 44
Conlon, Jocko 161
Considine, Bob 103, 121
Cooney, Johnny 82, 128
Cooper, Mort 93, 149
Cooper, Walker 131, 139, 149, 153–156, 159–160
Crabtree, Estel 26–27

Craft, Harry 68, 73, 79, 81, 84–86, 91, 93–94, 96, 121–122
Cronin, Joe 33
Crosetti, Frank 98, 184
Crosley, Powel 42, 48, 51, 66, 76, 83
Cuccinello, Tony 23–24, 38, 50, 82, 128
Cuyler, Hazen (Kiki) 33, 54, 63, 71, 73, 75

Dahlgren, Babe 114, 163
Daley, Arthur 161–162
Daniel, Dan 113
Danning, Harry 106, 121, 136–137
Daubert, Jake 43
Davis, Curt 94
Davis, Ray (Peaches) 59, 71–72
Davis, Virgil (Spud) 67, 71, 74, 80–81, 83
Dean, Jay (Dizzy) 36, 45, 48, 63, 66–67, 71, 73, 76, 116, 180
Dean, Paul 48
DeBerry, Hank 12
Derringer, Paul 1, 36, 43, 45, 54–55, 58, 62–65, 68, 75, 82, 90–91, 94, 96–98, 101, 104, 107, 111–113, 119, 121, 123, 139, 177–178, 183
Dickey, Bill 80, 96–98
DiMaggio, Dominic 5, 114, 178
DiMaggio, Giuseppe 5
DiMaggio, Joe 5, 13–14, 96–101, 103, 114, 116, 178, 180
DiMaggio, Vince 5, 178
Doerr, Bobby 118, 191, 193
Douthit, Taylor 26–27, 35
Drebinger, John 99, 138
Dressen, Charlie 45, 47–48, 51–52, 55–57, 60–61, 65, 67–68, 71, 73–75, 77, 170, 176
Durante, Jimmy 50
Durocher, Leo 24–26, 31, 35–36, 38–39, 85–86, 103, 116, 139–140, 147, 157

Ebbets, Charles 15, 22
Eckhardt, Oscar (Ox) 14
Eisenhower, David 181
Ens, Jewel 34–36, 121
Ericksen, Paul 160
Erickson, Hank 51–53, 55
Essick, Bill 12, 171
Etten, Nick 165

Feathers, Beattie 43
Feldman, Harry 156
Feller, Bob 124, 128, 155, 180
Fernandes, Ed 165, 167–168, 172
Ferrell, Rick 190
Fischer, Rube 140
Fitzsimmons, Fred 20
Foster, John B. 90
Foster, Rube 190
Foxx, Jimmie 132–133, 180
Frankhouse, Fred 91
Freitas, Tony 45, 163
French, Larry 71

Frey, Benny 25, 76
Frey, Lonny 81, 91, 93, 96, 110, 122
Frick, Ford 117, 132, 139, 182
Frisch, Frank 149, 180, 182
Frishberg, Dave 186
Fuchs, Emil 54
Furillo, Carl 157

Galan, Augie 92
Gallagher, Joe 109
Garagiola, Joe 153
Gardella, Danny 155, 176
Garms, Debs 117, 133
Gehrig, Lou 26, 57, 97, 116
Gehringer, Charlie 111–113, 183
Gelbert, Charlie 36, 66, 73
Gilbert, Wally 20, 23–24, 31
Giles, Warren 66–67, 70–71, 75–77, 79, 81, 83, 87, 89–90, 101–02, 109–110, 117, 122–124, 170, 174, 182–183, 188
Gleeson, Jim 118–119, 151
Gomez, Vernon (Lefty) 97
Goodman, Ival 51, 54, 56, 58, 81, 84, 104–111
Gordon, Joe 80, 93
Goslin, Leon (Goose) 49–50
Gowdy, Hank 82, 99, 108
Graham, Frank 140
Grantham, George 25–26, 28, 37, 39, 41
Grayson, Frank 115
Greenberg, Hank 109, 111, 113, 128
Griffith, Clark 33
Grimes, Burleigh 84
Grimm, Charlie 79
Grissom, Lee 55, 73, 75, 82, 92–93, 97
Grove, Lefty 91

Hack, Stan 93
Hadley, Bump 97
Hafey, Chick 25, 28, 30, 45, 50, 52–54, 57, 73, 75, 182
Haines, Jesse 19, 64, 182
Hamlin, Luke 85
Handley, Lee 61
Harridge, Will 132–133
Hartnett, Charles (Gabby) 59, 74, 76, 79, 86, 89, 91, 180
Hartung, Clint 159
Harwell, Ernie 171
Hassett, Buddy 85
Hausmann, George 143
Heath, Mickey 26–27
Heathcote, Cliff 27
Heilmann, Harry 25, 27, 81
Hemsley, Rollie 34, 36–37, 124–125, 128, 130–131
Herman, Billy 92, 157
Herman, Floyd (Babe) 16, 23–25, 28, 31, 34, 53–55, 58, 60, 63, 71, 154
Hermanski, Gene 157
Herring, Art 147

Index

Hershberger, Willard 80–81, 84, 90, 92–93, 103–109, 117, 125, 173–174, 182, 193
Higbe, Kirby 156
Higgins, Mike 111–112
High, Andy 27
Hogan, Shanty 20
Hollingsworth, Al 72, 83
Holmes, Tommy (ballplayer) 130
Holmes, Tommy (writer) 16, 85
Hornsby, Rogers 41, 77
Howard, Del 10
Howard, Ivan 7, 17–18
Howley, Dan 24, 26, 28, 33–34, 45
Hubbell, Carl 57, 63, 133, 137, 142, 158, 180
Huggins, Miller 157
Hunter, Eddie 38
Hyland, Robert 52

Italian immigration 3–4

Jackson, Joe (Shoeless Joe) 95
Jackson, Travis 190
James, Bill 7, 30–31, 100, 130, 174, 182, 195
Jansen, Larry 159–160
Johnson, Si 25, 37, 43–45, 66
Joost, Eddie 64, 68, 73, 110, 113–114, 118, 121–123, 186
Jorda, Lou 161
Jurges, Billy 64

Kahle, Bob 82
Kampouris, Alex 64, 72
Kell, George 190
Keller, Charlie 80, 96–103
Kelly, Bill 167
Kelly, George 182
Kemp, Abe 17–18
Kerr, Buddy 141, 159, 176, 191
Kieran, John 99
Kluszewski, Ted 161, 194
Kluttz, Clyde 133, 150
Koslo, Dave 155
Koy, Ernie 85
Krause, Harry 7, 91

Lackey, Mike 101
Lammano, Ray 131
Landis, Kenesaw M. 83, 95, 127
Lanier, Max 156
Lardner, John 149
Lary, Lyn 12
Lavagetto, Harry (Cookie) 85, 165, 168, 172, 191
Laws, Brick 164, 171
Lazzeri, Tony 7, 13–14
Leiber, Hank 63, 67
Lenhardt (Lombardi), Rena 4–5, 115, 186, 192–193
Leonard, Lank 18–19
Levitt, Ed 184–186

Lieb, Fred 185
Lillard, Gene 167–168
Lodigiani, Dario 165, 172
Lohrke, Jack 159
Lombardi, Berice Marie (Ayers) 146, 154, 163, 172–173, 184
Lombardi, Domenico (Dominic) 4–6, 115, 123, 136, 139
Lombardi, Ernesto Natali (Ernie): All-Star 64, 73, 87, 92, 104, 131, 137, 150; birth 4; death 186; election to Baseball Hall of Fame 191; family 3–6, 115, 136, 139, 186, 192–193; golf grip on bat 10–11, 16, 138; Italian heritage 3–4, 13–14; marriage 146; nicknames 6, 13–14, 30, 50, 116; Selective Service 128, 139, 141; snooze in World Series 98–100, 171, 174, 183; snoring 50; speed 59, 140, 147–149, 159; suicide attempt 173–174; trade to Boston 124; trade to Brooklyn 12; trade to Cincinnati 23; trade to New York 136–137
Lombardi, Marianna (Maria) 4–5
Lombardi, Rose 4, 115, 136, 186, 192
Lombardi, Vic 156–157
Lopez, Al 16, 18–20, 23–24, 121, 181, 185
Lucas, Red 25–26, 37, 41
Luque, Dolf 155

Mack, Connie 91
MacPhail, Andy 66
MacPhail, Larry 40–45, 47–48, 51–53, 55, 57–59, 64, 66–67, 80, 84, 103, 123, 150
Magerkurth, George 75
Maggert, Hal 82
Maglie, Sal 155
Mancuso, Gus 74, 79, 137–138, 140, 142–143, 147–148
Manion, Clyde 26, 28, 36–37
Maranville, Walter (Rabbit) 27
Marshall, Willard 159–160
Martin, Billy 165–166, 168, 172
Mattick, Bobby 118, 122
McCarthy, Joe 41, 96
McCormick, Frank 1, 68, 73, 81, 84, 87, 90–91, 96–98, 104, 111, 113, 119, 141, 177–178
McCovey, Willie 193
McCullough, William 18
McElderry, Ernest 175
McGee, Bill 93
McGraw, John 20, 126, 157
McKechnie, Bill 1, 40, 54, 67, 74, 77–85, 87, 90–91, 93, 95, 97, 101–102, 106–108, 110–113, 119–122, 124–127, 152, 170, 180
McKeever, Steve 15
McLean, Larry 18–19
McLemore, Harvey 110
McQuinn, George 53, 61
Medwick, Joe 45, 87, 94, 140, 144, 183
Melton, Cliff 140
Merkle, Fred 99

Miksis, Eddie 148
Miller, Eddie 135
Mize, Johnny 52, 87, 93–94, 126, 135, 137, 143, 155–156, 159, 190
Monzo, Don 190
Monzo (Lombardi), Stella 4, 115, 172, 186, 191–192
Monzo, Vince 114–115, 172
Moore, Dee 79
Moore, Eddie 12
Moore, Gene 82
Moore, Jo-Jo 63
Moore, Johnny 34
Moore, Lloyd (Whitey) 68, 72, 92, 97, 111, 119
Moore, Terry 94
Moran, Pat 94
Morgan, Joe 195
Morrissey, Joe 26–27, 37
Mueller, Ray 82
Mungo, Van 140, 149–150, 155, 186
Murphy, Art 8
Musial, Stan 133, 148–149, 155, 188, 191
Myers, Billy 63, 81, 91, 93, 98, 110, 118

Neun, Johnny 170
Newsom, Lewis (Bobo) 111–112
Nixon, Richard 181–182
Nugent, Gerry 83
Nuxhall, Joe 194

Oakland Oaks 6–12, 162–169, 176
Oakland Winter League 6
O'Doul, Lefty 158
O'Farrell, Bob 41–45, 77
Ogden Gunners 8, 174
Orengo, Joe 140, 163
Ostrowski, Johnny 168
Ott, Mel 19, 87, 106, 136–138, 140–144, 148–149, 151, 153–161, 172, 180
Owen, Mickey 121, 155

Pacific Coast League 6–12, 163
Paige, Satchel 153, 169
Palmer, Pete 194
Parmalee, Roy 63
Pasquel, Jorge 155
Passeau, Claude 55, 83
Paul, Gabe 79, 107–108, 170, 188–189
Pearson, Monte 96, 118–119
Phelps, Babe 73, 80, 85
Phelps, Ray 19
Picinich, Val 16, 18, 24
Piet, Tony 45
Pinelli, Ralph (Babe) 6, 61, 101
Poland, Hugh 136–137
Polli, Lou 144
Pressnell, Forest (Tot) 84–85
Pruett, Hubert (Hub) 7

Quinn, Bob 125, 127, 135–136
Quinn, Jack 20–21, 38, 43

Raimondi, Billy 58, 60, 164–165, 167, 169, 172
Read, Addison (Pete) 9
Reardon, Beans 74
Reese, Harold (Pee Wee) 1, 47, 129, 140
Reese, Jimmy 12
Reiser, Pete 131–132, 157–158
Reyes, Nap 155
Reynolds, Quentin 15
Rhawn, Bobby 160
Rice, Del 153
Richards, Paul 16, 19
Richbourg, Lance 34
Rickey, Branch 25, 34, 36, 40, 51, 66–67, 152
Riddle, Elmer 119–120
Riggs, Lew 51, 63–64, 81, 84–85
Rigney, Bill 177
Ripple, Jimmy 111–113
Ritter, Larry 95
Rixey, Eppa 25, 37, 43, 180
Rizzo, Johnny 163
Robinson, Frank 194
Robinson, Jackie 152, 180
Robinson, Wilbert 15–17, 19–22, 23, 63, 126, 180
Roettger, Wally 35
Rohde, Richard 118
Rolfe, Red 98
Root, Charlie 26
Rose, Pete 2
Rosen, Goody 86
Roush, Edd 24–25, 94–95, 133, 180
Rowe, Lynwood (Schoolboy) 59
Rowland, Clarence (Pants) 79
Ruel, Harold (Muddy) 185
Ruffing, Red 96
Ruppert, Jacob 41
Rusie, Amos 185
Russell, Jim 146
Russell, Rip 92
Ruth, Babe 26, 41, 52, 54, 57–59, 86, 146
Ryan, Connie 136–138

Sain, Johnny 134
Salenger, Oscar 163–164
Sargis, Joe 184
Scarsella, Les 61, 63, 165–166, 168
Schechter, Gabriel 100
Schott, Gene 73
Schumacher, Hal 137, 155
Sears, Ziggy 92–93
Seeds, Bob 106
Selkirk, George 98
Severeid, Hank 9
Sewell, Joe 185
Shaute, Joe 20
Shotton, Burt 39
Simmons, Al 98

Index

Sisler, Dick 148
Sisti, Sibby 130
Slade, Gordon 45
Slaughter, Enos 94, 131–133, 153, 190
Smith, Bob 34, 38
Smith, Ken 183
Smith, Wendell 152–153
Society for American Baseball Research (SABR) 181
Southworth, Billy 77, 139
Spahn, Warren 127, 129, 133–134
Speaker, Tris 137
Stengel, Casey 82, 125–131, 163–170, 172, 185
Stewart, Bill 86, 147–148
Stoneham, Horace 136, 140, 142–144, 146, 150–151, 153, 157–161, 172, 177
Stripp, Joe 23–24
Sukeforth, Clyde 23–24
Sullivan, Billy 112–113
Sullivan, Prescott 177
Swift, Bill 61
Swope, Tom 125

Talbot, Gayle 174
Tebbetts, Birdie 189–190
Terry, Bill 47, 67, 73, 79, 136–137, 180, 182
Thompson, Gene (Junior) 81, 92–93, 97, 104, 112, 119, 150
Thomson, Bobby 143, 157–160
Thorn, John 194
Tobin, Jim 129, 131, 165, 168
Todd, Al 73
Toncoff, Johnny 149
Tost, Lou 165, 168
Traynor, Harold (Pie) 61, 183
Tsuchiya, Tom 194
Turkin, Hy 149
Turner, Jim 104, 111

Ueberroth, Peter 193
Utah-Idaho League 8–9

Vance, Charles (Dazzy) 43–44, 180
Vander Meer, Johnny 2, 68–69, 71–72, 82–87, 92–93, 99, 104, 119–120, 131, 153, 177–178, 181, 185–186, 189, 191, 194

Van Ness, Art 173
Van Robays, Maurice 165
Vass, George 133
Vaughan, Arky 87, 183, 190
Veeck, Bill 159
Vergez, Johnny 12, 20
Veterans Commitee 181
Voiselle, Bill 146, 149, 155

Walker, Dixie 141
Walker, Hub 63, 65
Wallace, Bobby 75
Walters, William (Bucky) 1, 83–84, 90–91, 94, 96, 98–99, 104, 106, 111–112, 120, 131, 152, 170, 177–178, 181, 183, 185, 192
Waner, Lloyd 119
Waner, Paul 7, 14, 78, 128, 131
Warneke, Lon 44, 64, 122
Weil, Sidney J. 24–25, 31, 33–36, 38–39, 42
Weintraub, Phil 143–146, 149
Werber, Bill 90–91, 96–98, 111, 119, 123, 137, 189
West, Dick 109, 117, 121–122
West, Max 106, 131
Westrum, Wes 158
Wettig, Johnny 140
Whitehead, Burgess 106
Williams, Joe (pitcher) 51
Williams, Ted 121, 155, 188, 190, 195
Willis, Vic 191
Wilson, Jimmie 41, 61, 109–110, 112–113, 117, 119
Witek, Mickey 156
Wright, Taft 132
Wrigley, Phillip K. 79
Wysong, Biff 27

York, Rudy 109, 111, 113
Young, Babe 156
Young, Dick 139, 148
Yvars, Sal 158

Zabala, Adrien 155
Zachary, Tom 27
Zamloch, Carl 11

www.ingramcontent.com/pod-product-compliance
Ingram Content Group UK Ltd.
Pitfield, Milton Keynes, MK11 3LW, UK
UKHW041958140426
5217IPUK00015B/869